Finding
Meaning,
Purpose,
and
Fulfillment

MAKING SENSE OF GOD,
LIFE, AND SUCCESS

ART GIRARD

To my precious wife, Crystal, and my amazing family,
May you know that my life's journey is made full
by your presence and involvement.

To my friends, mentors, and fellow seekers
who inspire, teach, and encourage me,
May you know how much I appreciate, respect, and
value the influence you have had in my life.

To all who are searching, waiting, wandering, or doubting,
May these words help you realize that God sees you, loves you, fully
accepts you, and has a unique and magnificent purpose for your life.

And to God, whose purpose is to transform every search for truth
and meaning into a deeper journey of faith and trust in Him.

Contents

Preface

For as long as I can remember, I have been driven to understand how things work. For example, when I was about five or six years old and watched one of my younger siblings playing with a jack-in-the-box toy, my attention was captured in a surprising way. I began wondering how turning the crank created the song that played. Why did the sounds change even though you keep making the same motion with the crank? And how does the box "know" when it's time to pop open and release the clown, at the same point in the melody? Eventually, I was so motivated to find answers to these questions that I disassembled the toy in a determined search for answers to the questions that hounded me. However, much to my mother's dismay, I was unable to return the toy to its original, fully working condition. So, discovering how things work has always been a *driving force* in my life.

In my early elementary school years, my inquisitive nature was similarly demonstrated, and I experienced great success as I discovered the secrets to academic achievement. But somewhere around fourth grade, the focus of my questioning began to broaden; I started to wonder about how *life* works. Until this point in my school life, I was content finding answers to my teachers' questions. But now, the questions I found most interesting were the ones that began popping up in my mind rather than the questions presented in my textbooks and by my teachers. I started asking many "why" questions in school, but my teachers seemed only interested in helping us learn the answers to the who, what, where, and when textbook questions. For example, I recall being taught as a young boy in the mid-1950s that Christopher Columbus "discovered America" in 1492 – that was what my teacher wanted me to know. But I wondered, "What would motivate someone to embark on such a perilous adventure, having no assurance there was even anything other than just more ocean 'out there' to discover?" My teacher didn't seem to think that was a question worth investigating. This is when I began to lose interest in school.

Similarly, I struggled to find satisfactory answers to my questions regarding faith. I was raised in a Catholic family, attending church every Sunday and attending the church's elementary school with my five other siblings. As a young child, I took my faith seriously, and this motivated me to begin taking steps to become an altar boy. However, just before I was old enough to enter that position, I started asking those difficult questions in my religion class at school. Once again, my questions were not given the attention I believed they deserved – at least not the attention I needed for my faith to be nurtured.

For example, I recall being taught that if a person commits a mortal sin (like murder) and does not receive forgiveness by going to Confession before they die, then that person would end up going to Hell. This led me to ask the following question: "So, if my mother (who was a saint!) somehow "snapped" and happened to commit a mortal sin, but then, as she is running to church to make

Confession, she is hit by a car and killed, would my mom go to Hell?" The answer I received was "Yes"! It seemed stupid to me that an all-knowing, all-loving God would act that way! As additional questions became matched with seemingly stupid answers – or my questions were not even acknowledged as valid – I began to lose interest in church.

Since my young mind equated church with God, I also lost interest in God. I think it's important to note here that these are recollections from my childhood and may not accurately represent the tenets of Catholicism. My point is that past "religious" experiences or encounters with religious adherents often hinder our spiritual journey. In Chapter 3, "Eliminating Blockages", I address this and other related issues.

As I reflect on the early years of my life, I can see that beginning around the age of 11 or 12, I honestly didn't have confidence that there even was a God due to the lack of satisfactory answers to my many questions. But if there was, He was just "out there somewhere" and not connected to the life I was living in any meaningful way. And from what I understood from my teachers' (and other adults') answers to my "why" questions about God and faith, He wasn't someone I wanted to know or follow.

From that point in my life, I began trying to figure out how life works entirely on my own, without any reference to faith or God. Until I was about 23 years old, I was my own source of truth – my own god! I decided what was good, right, and true about life, and sought happiness and success in any way that made sense to me. I would not have been able to put it into words at the time, but I was searching for meaning, purpose, and fulfillment in my life.

During my second year of teaching, one of my students requested my assistance in completing an assignment for her Health class. She was tasked with taking a stand on marijuana legalization (yeah, it was even a political issue in the 1970s!) and composing a written argument. As I attempted to help her develop an argument against legalization, which was the position we both held, I began by considering what premises one must accept as "true" to frame a logical argument. When I started thinking about what makes any statement true or false, it became clear that it was intellectually hypocritical to make any such declaration unless there was some absolute authority upon which a judgment could be based. I thought: "If I can be my own god deciding what is right and wrong, then everyone else has that same right!" That realization, which I now believe was divinely inspired, prompted me to revisit the question of whether there is a God.

It took me about six years to complete this segment of my spiritual journey of exploration, but at age 29, I arrived at the point where I firmly believed that God is real and the Bible is the inspired Word of God. [I provide more details of my journey to this point in Appendix A, "The God Thing," – including a series of steps that might be beneficial for you to navigate your own journey of discovery.] Using those two beliefs as a foundation, I began to re-examine all my beliefs about life – about what is right, true, and good. At the time of this writing, I have continued that journey for 40+ years – experiencing an ever-growing sense of meaning, purpose, and fulfillment. The journey hasn't always been easy, but it has been very rewarding, enjoyable, and fruitful.

Because I am a teacher at heart, I feel compelled to share my discoveries with others. That is why I have undertaken the task of writing this book. Since I have experienced such profound levels of meaning, purpose, and fulfillment in my life, I long for you to experience the same amazing outcomes in your life. But that "full life" is also something God desires for you. I believe He has empowered me to create a series of lessons that will assist you in your own journey of discovery. Each discovery will enhance your understanding of who God is, how He created life to be lived, who you are, and what God is calling you to be and do. As your knowledge and understanding deepen in these areas, and you direct your life accordingly, you will discover the meaning, purpose, and fulfillment you have always longed to experience. That's not just my promise; it's God's promise to you.

"For I know the plans I have for you," declares the LORD,
"plans to prosper you and not to harm you, plans to give you
hope and a future." (Jeremiah 29:11)

The journey you will take will result in discoveries that will set you free from false beliefs and insecurities that have been hindering you. Some discoveries will be surprising, and others will cause you to say, "I always wondered if that was true!" But all the discoveries will be your own – in fact, they must be your own. And the discoveries you find most rewarding will empower you in surprising and life-changing ways. This is not a book that contains a large amount of dogma calling for blind obedience. Instead, I will present ideas – supported by Scripture – and challenge you to consider their truthfulness and how God might challenge you to respond. I will present an outline for you to follow, but the journey will – and must – be your own.

The final thing I'll share before you begin your journey is this: while many of the learnings will be amazing, it's not the learnings that matter most. The learnings will empower you to connect with God – in deep and meaningful ways. And, as you will discover later, the most significant part of your journey will be the journey itself!

[NOTE: My thinking and writing throughout the book are based on a biblical worldview – at least to the degree of my own understanding. If you are NOT a Christian who believes that God is real and that the Bible is the inspired Word of God, I suggest you stop reading here and read "The God Thing" in Appendix A. Then come back and continue reading. Even if you cannot *fully* commit to the idea that God is real or accept the Bible as the source for discovering foundational truths about life, I believe you will at least discover the "rationality" of a biblical worldview.]

The Great Adventure

My favorite vacations have been cruises. Our first cruise experience was a family vacation when all three of my daughters were teenagers. The idea of enjoying a morning cup of coffee on a balcony overlooking the ocean, visiting exotic locations (or lounging by the pool) during the day, enjoying fine dining in the evening, and returning to a clean, well-organized, comfortable room and finding our bed adorned with an animal creatively formed from towels by our cabin steward and a chocolate mint on my pillow is just the ideal vacation for me! There is also something delightful about visiting multiple locations without the repeated need to unpack and repack my suitcase! Since I understand God's design for life to be a journey of discovery – The Great Adventure – I have organized the parts of this book around the idea of taking a cruise vacation.

In Part I, I will walk you through several considerations, understandings, and commitments related to God's design for life. Before booking a cruise, you must decide where, when, and by which carrier you will travel. Making these decisions requires a significant amount of reflection and research. Similarly, in Part I of this book, I will examine several key issues that must be considered and addressed before embarking on a meaningful journey with God. Many people have several beliefs or questions that prevent them from approaching God and wondering what it even means to "follow God." In the book's first section, I will establish a rational foundation for following God and help you identify and resolve issues that may interfere with your ability to navigate this journey.

In Part 2, I will prepare you for departure. When taking a cruise, it is advisable to carefully consider what to pack and conduct some initial research and planning regarding the places you will visit on your trip. Failure in either of these two issues will cause unnecessary frustrations and disappointments. Similarly, in Part 2, I will present a conceptual framework for your journey with God. Many Christians feel that the idea of following God is overwhelming: "What am I supposed to do?" "Who am I supposed to become?" "What does God want from me?". Questions like these often go unanswered, causing unnecessary confusion and procrastination. The ideas presented in Part 2 will serve as a conceptual framework for processing the many questions that will challenge you. This framework will also enable you to synthesize and organize the learnings you will discover throughout your faith journey.

In Part 3, I will help you plan daily activities and excursions. On a cruise, you can explore and enjoy many exciting adventures on the ship and at each port you visit. One of the best ways to enjoy the ship and each port visit on your journey is to explore the possibilities and make preliminary plans before you begin each day. Similarly, one of the best things about life is that God allows us to begin an entirely new set of adventures each day! The past is gone, incapable of being re-lived, but containing a treasure of experiences from which we can extract essential life lessons. However, we are best served by having a "plan" to follow each day. In Part 3, I will review the main ideas from Parts 1 and 2, provide some thoughts about how to plan your way, and then challenge you to consider how you will launch your spiritual journey from this point forward. Now it's time to get started!

Our Dichotomy

A struggle exists within the human heart, simultaneously pulling us in opposite directions. On the one hand, we search inward to find joy and meaning in the activities and relationships that currently fill our lives. On the other hand, we look outward for new opportunities, relationships, and understandings that may lead to a more profound sense of meaning and purpose. The first force draws us inward in the search for stability and predictability. The second force draws us outward, or upward, away from our current life circumstances in the search for something better, something more. The second force exists because of feelings and thoughts that something might be lacking in our present circumstances, and a fear that we might be missing something vital. Our situation is complicated by our uncertainty about whether what we are missing might be an experience, a more profound understanding, a relationship, or some combination of all three.

These two opposing inward and outward forces are fueled by the belief that our lives are supposed to be characterized by a deep sense of meaning, purpose, and fulfillment, coupled with the recognition that we have not yet *arrived* at that point in our lives – at least not sufficiently enough to squelch the search for something "better." This internal turmoil is a condition that all humans share to varying degrees. The proper response to this inner turmoil is to accept the challenge and embark on a quest to find greater meaning, purpose, and fulfillment. To accept this challenge properly, one must recognize that life is designed to be a Great Adventure!

Most people attempt to find their way in life on their own,

tending to rely on their ingenuity, wisdom, and power to make sense of life and chart a course of action they hope will result in the greatest amount of happiness and success they think is possible given their background and current circumstances. And why not? Who else can I count on besides myself? Who understands me and my circumstances better than I do? Who else would be fully committed to helping me find my way? Even those fortunate enough to grow up in stable families and societies recognize how much their lives depend on their own abilities and efforts.

Some people, however, do not believe they are alone. Some people believe God is real and enthusiastically available for guidance and support. But even many people who believe in God wrestle with these same issues. If you wrestle with these opposing forces in the search for meaning, purpose, and fulfillment, and if you're open to the possibility that God might hold some of the essential answers to life, I would like to take you on a journey of discovery. That journey – The Great Adventure – is God's plan, not mine.

God designed life to be an adventure of discovery that unfolds in unique and challenging ways for each of us, but always – **when lived according to God's design** – in exciting, rewarding, and fulfilling ways. For many of us, however, a thrilling, rewarding adventure might not be how we would describe our life experience. Some people feel that their life is stagnant and unfulfilling, feeling trapped or stuck in a rut. I want to change that. In writing this book, I have four primary goals: 1) to ignite the deep passions within your heart that are necessary for living courageously; 2) to assist you in identifying the obstructions that may be preventing you from moving forward in a productive, planful way; 3) to assist you in developing a **mental framework** that can help you identify and remain focused on the goals that will lead to optimal achievement and success; and 4) to help you develop a personally designed pathway that will continually guide and empower you to experience the extraordinary life God desires for you. I want to serve as a travel agent on one of the most important journeys of your life – perhaps even THE most important journey of your life. And I'd like to begin this journey by challenging you to temporarily suspend judgment and be willing to reconsider everything you believe to be true about life. As you process the ideas presented within these pages, I believe life will begin to make greater sense, and you will develop a stronger faith and confidence in God – and in your ability to connect with Him in ever-deepening and productive ways. I invite you to embark on an exhilarating journey of discovery – The Great Adventure – that will forever change how you live.

My prayer and hope is that you will discover life *can* make sense, you *can* find meaning, purpose, and fulfillment, and you *can* embrace the idea that the "full" life you have always desired – and Jesus came to make possible for you – *can* be found as you purpose to know and follow Him.

John 10: [10] *The thief comes only to steal and kill and destroy*; I have come that they may have life, and have it to the full. (NIV)

What I have written is designed to assist you in removing "hindrances" that prevent you from discovering all God has intended for you. He will be your provider and strength, guiding and sustaining you throughout your journey. God designed life so that in Him we live, move, and breathe; on our own, we stagger and often fall.

Isaiah 41: [10] So do not fear, for I am with you; do not be dismayed, for I am your God. I will strengthen you and help you; I will uphold you with my righteous right hand.

Part One

Initial Considerations

Before you can enjoy a fantastic cruise vacation, you must determine which cruise you will take. However, making that choice requires many smaller decisions. What part of the world would you like to visit? Which cruise lines visit that part of the world? How much money can you afford to spend? How long do you want the cruise to last? What amenities are offered on each of the ships? What ports will the ship visit, and what opportunities does each port offer visitors? These, and many other factors, must be contemplated before selecting a cruise. Similarly, one must ponder many things before launching out on The Great Adventure of Life.

We all begin life with a mental blank slate – zero experiences or understanding about how life is supposed to work – and we are all challenged to find our way in life. Little by little, we collect, analyze, and organize our experiences and learnings to make sense of our life journey. Pursuing life's meaning gains momentum and focus as we progress through adolescence into adulthood.

Few of us, however, ever reach a point where we feel like we truly "have it all together." Many people find some level of satisfaction and meaning that sustains them, but sadly, many do not. Most of us are on a seemingly endless journey to experience a more profound sense of meaning, purpose, and fulfillment. We continually search for something better, something more. Our problem is that we have a faulty *mental framework* – a system of definitions, beliefs, and understandings – that fails to guide us toward optimal success in our most important life endeavors. I hope to assist you in examining, evaluating, and reprogramming many aspects of your mental framework to better align with God's design for life.

In Part I, I will present several ideas that I believe are instrumental in making it possible to establish a profoundly intimate and personal relationship with God. Within our relationship with God, we are empowered to create a mental framework of truth – replacing or modifying our current definitions, understandings, and beliefs – to form an optimal foundation for a truly successful and meaningful life. To fully benefit from these readings, you will need to suspend judgment and be willing to re-examine long-held beliefs temporarily. You need to create a "space" within which you can consider the validity of the ideas I will be presenting. This "space" will enable you to assess whether or not some of your foundational beliefs about life may need to be modified in some way or maybe even abandoned altogether and replaced with ideas that will serve you better.

> Proverbs 4: [7] The beginning of wisdom is this: Get wisdom. Though it costs all you have, get understanding. [8] Cherish her, and she will exalt you; embrace her, and she will honor you.

Before you begin this journey of exploration, I challenge you to commit to pursuing and embracing truth – whatever the truth might be – and to have the courage to follow the truths you discover. For you to benefit most from these writings, **the desire to know and follow the truth must become your highest priority.**

Chapter 1
Introduction

God has placed a dream in your heart that your life is meant to have meaning and purpose, and should be characterized by a deep sense of personal fulfillment. This is not a self-constructed delusion but a God-given inner motivation to drive you forward. Many places in scripture affirm this truth, but the most direct passage is Jesus's statement about His purpose for coming to earth.

> **John 10:** [10] "The enemy comes only to steal and kill and destroy; I have come that [you] may have life, and have it to the full."

The pursuit of experiencing a "full" life is not a passive endeavor, but an active, ongoing process that drives most of our critical choices and plans. You have the power to shape your life's journey toward fulfillment.

As we journey through life, we often find ourselves actively seeking experiences that bring us pleasure. Yet, as the satisfaction fades, we are left searching for another activity or experience to fill the vacuum. This pattern of pleasure-seeking continues, to some extent, throughout the entirety of our lives. However, as we mature, our focus broadens. As we navigate through adolescence, we begin to recognize that a singular orientation toward pleasure-seeking is inadequate, and we start searching for a way to find deeper meaning and purpose in our lives. As we enter adulthood, our focus matures, and we embark on an ardent search for a system of definitions, understandings, and beliefs – *a mental framework* – that we can use for making decisions and directing our lives in ways that will enable us to experience a truly meaningful, purposeful, and fulfilling life. However, most of us create this mental framework primarily, if not exclusively, on our own understanding and abilities rather than seeking God and relying on Him to lead us in our pursuit of truth.

As we experience happiness and success in our life journey, we solidify the beliefs in our mental framework that led to those positive outcomes. And when we experience less-than-desirable results, we modify or discard the beliefs that brought us to that point. If the outcomes we experience are extremely disappointing or even traumatic, we create entirely new beliefs (or propositions) that we hope will bring more desirable outcomes. Since most of us experience confusion and insecurity along the way, we often mimic the lives of others who seem to display great confidence or whose lives appear to be better in some way.

For example, I recall when I was about 14 years old and working in a restaurant. A young man in his mid-20s would regularly come into the restaurant, and all the waitresses were drawn to him. He was just unbelievably cool! Not surprisingly, I looked for ways to be like him – how he walked and talked, and his mannerisms as he interacted with the waitresses. I wanted to be cool like him! There were frequent instances like that throughout my adolescence and early adulthood, when I saw something in another person's life that I wanted to incorporate into my own and sought to emulate. Sometimes, those aspects of the other person's life "worked" for me and became a part of my life, and sometimes, I chose to discard them or apply them in a modified way.

Whether it's due to a change in our understanding or the influence of other people, again and again, we reorient our lives both in large and small ways in our attempt to experience the "full" life that we believe is possible – indeed, even to which we feel somewhat entitled. Unfortunately, this process leaves many, if not most, of us with a quality of life that falls short of the "full" life we had hoped to experience. Some give up chasing the dream entirely and lower their expectations to match the life they are currently experiencing, or seek ways to escape the emptiness they feel within their hearts. Others continue to seek new experiences that they hope will create a more profound sense of meaning, purpose, and fulfillment. Most people, however, never really experience the fullness of life that they truly desire – and that God desires for them.

Henry David Thoreau observed, "Most men lead lives of quiet desperation and go to the grave with the song still in them." Why do so many of us find ourselves in this position? Why are we failing to experience the "full" life that Jesus came to make possible? *I believe it's because we have many of the most essential foundational beliefs about life, either partially or entirely wrong!* These flawed beliefs undermine our significant relationships, interfere with our personal transformation, and cloud our understanding of God's will and other essential life issues. What are we to do?

When God created the heavens, the earth, and all it contains, He didn't just create the "stuff" of life (like planets, oceans, trees, animals, and people). At the time of creation, God also established the *principles* that govern every aspect of how all the "stuff" He created works! For example, when God created people, He also established the principle that people need air, food, and water to survive. On a more personal level, God established the principle that people need healthy relationships to find happiness and

fulfillment. However, there is much more that we need to understand about the principles God established for life! *The premise of
this book is that God fully desires to bring to fruition the dream for the
"full" life that He has implanted deep within your heart, and that
"full" life unfolds as you learn to follow His leadership in your life.*

> Isaiah 48: [17] This is what the Lord says – your Redeemer,
> the Holy One of Israel: "I am the Lord your God, who
> teaches you what is best for you, who directs you in the
> way you should go."

Following God

Following God is the surest way of experiencing a fantastic life.
The idea of following God is the central and most fundamental
theme that runs throughout all of Scripture. If you follow the
history of the people captured in the Bible, especially the Nation
of Israel, you will discover that they prospered whenever they
genuinely followed God. And each time they strayed from
following God, they experienced suffering and loss. The books of
the Old Testament – especially the prophets – are filled with
examples of God calling His people to follow Him and warning
them of the unfortunate consequences they will experience if they
fail to do so. When Jesus comes on the scene, He explicitly calls
people to follow Him. The epistles that follow the "gospel books"
(Matthew, Mark, Luke, and John) repeat that clarion call to follow
Jesus and articulate many ways to respond to that call.
Throughout the Bible, you will find hundreds of promises of
blessings that accompany those who seek to follow God. **By God's
design, the primary focus of life is for us to know and
follow Him.**

So, what does it mean to follow God? How can I direct my life
in that way? Questions like these should haunt you. We should

make it the highest priority of our lives to find meaningful answers to what it means to follow God. Our futures depend on the way we answer that question! A simple dictionary definition of what it means to follow is to "go or come after (a person or thing proceeding ahead); move or travel behind."

Following God has two components. First, one must be aware of what they are called to follow. That is, you need to understand what God wants you to do. Second, following requires a willingness to do what is asked of you. To follow God, you must take the time to understand what He wants you to do. Then, you must humble yourself and do your best to comply. That simple process is the surest – and only – way to experience the "full" life God desires for you. Everything that follows in this book is designed to help you better understand what God is asking you to do and how you can grow in your capacity to both understand and obey God's will for your life.

If you reflect on your own life, you will discover that most of your plans and goals have been related to the underlying motivation of experiencing the "full" life. However, most of us seek to fulfill this dream in ways that fail to give lasting and deeply satisfying results. Our problem is that we fail to understand many of the principles God put into place at the time of creation, designed to fully realize that underlying dream. *In short, we have a faulty mental framework that needs to be modified.*

God designed life to be a journey of discovery, a pilgrimage to find meaning, purpose, and fulfillment. However, life is not about conforming to a fixed life plan designed for everyone to follow, but for you to discover your unique life plan. *God desires you to take responsibility for your own life, seek to understand Him and His ways, and direct your life in those ways, leading you to experience a deep sense of meaning, purpose, and fulfillment!*

Deep down, I believe you have always known that there is something exceptional that you are called to do with your life. You were not created to conform to other people's expectations and plans. You have been called to discover and pursue your unique life purpose. Indeed, we will find many similarities to other people, but many aspects of our lives will be unique to us. How, then, are we supposed to find our way? How do we discover the "right" and "wrong" ways of living? Is there a trustworthy source of assistance? Yes, there is! You can connect with that Divine Source – and find *your way* – as you work through the ideas and processes outlined in this book.

Sometimes, complicated ideas are better understood by the use of an analogy. While no analogy is perfect, I believe our understanding of computers can enhance our understanding of how God designed life to function. Each of us is like a uniquely designed personal computer. God is the designer of our "architecture," the programmer of the "operating system" upon which we are designed to run, and the power source necessary for us to live. Our soul (mind, will, and emotions) is the operating system by which our lives are driven, and each of our operating systems has been seriously infected by many viruses – some big, some small.

God acts like a software company in that He desires to regularly send "updates" (fixes) to our operating systems to help us function more effectively. While sin is the virus that is the source of all our problems, each of our operating systems (souls) has been infected in different ways and requires personally designed updates. The number of "fixes" we need is significant, and God typically sends them little by little (although sometimes a great "fix" can occur instantaneously). The Holy Spirit is the conduit through which we receive our regular updates, and our spirit (which comes to life when we are born again) is the part of our inner architecture through which we receive our needed updates. Each update that God so mercifully sends our way is designed to modify our operating system (soul) in ways that will help us function more effectively. *The process functions optimally only if we are*

Introduction

regularly and adequately "connected" with God. The purpose of this book is to assist you in understanding your responsibilities in the process of connecting with God in meaningful and productive ways.

I trust you are reading this book because you genuinely desire greater meaning, purpose, and fulfillment. That is not to say these attributes are totally absent; you just sense that you might be missing some vital piece(s) of the puzzle. That's why I wrote this book. There is nothing extraordinary about me except that God has "programmed" me to analyze life experiences, extract the underlying principles, and communicate them in understandable and practical ways. In short, I'm a teacher. And I'd like to walk you through a series of lessons that will inform and empower you to discover what you're really looking for in life. But I want you to understand that the process of change and growth is a *journey*. There is no "silver bullet" that automatically produces the "full" life all at once; your "dream life" will develop over time. But it would be best if you recognized that this is a journey you must take individually, and as you proceed, an ever-deepening sense of meaning, purpose, and fulfillment will unfold. Throughout this journey, you will discover many new truths, understandings, and practices – *a divinely inspired mental framework* – that will redefine and redirect your life in new and exciting ways! I want to assure you that you **can** make the changes that will help you experience the "full" life Jesus desires for you. One important **"key"** to the process is revealed in Romans 12:2a (NASB): *"Do not conform to the pattern of this world but be transformed by the renewing of your mind."*

It is difficult for us to realize how much our life experiences ("pattern of this world") have contributed to our mental frame-work – the ways we think and many of our beliefs about life. We need to understand that there is a direct connection between our thinking and actions, including the goals and plans we set. The simple truth is that we each hold fast to many beliefs that are not *entirely* true. We must allow God to modify – and sometimes radically change – our understandings about Him and life. That's what "the renewing of your mind" is all about. God desires to "update" our minds to the principles and truths He established at the beginning of time. As our thinking changes, our lives change. *As our lives align more fully with God's ways, we experience a burgeoning sense of meaning, purpose, and fulfillment.*

As you work through this book, I will challenge you to focus on what I believe to be the four most Essential Questions in life: 1) Who is God? 2) How has God designed life to be lived? 3) Who am I? and 4) What is God calling me to do? Throughout the journey, I will guide you through several processes that will help you find *divinely inspired* answers to each question. *Your answers to these four questions will serve as the foundation of your mental framework.*

The most crucial point is that *you must engage in the inquiry process, finding your own answers* to each question. While no one can ever fully answer any of these questions, you will find that as you discover new and more profound answers – and allow God to direct your life accordingly – you will experience an ever-deepening sense of meaning, purpose, and fulfillment. *The "full" life you desire will unfold automatically from your diligent engagement in finding correct answers to these four Essential Questions.* That is what I have discovered and seen lived out in many people's lives.

It's really that simple, although following that process is not always easy! The journey will challenge you in many significant ways. You *can* fully achieve your dreams, but it will require you to be courageous in examining yourself, letting go of false beliefs, and adopting new ways of thinking and acting. Your eventual "dream life" will likely look much different from what you initially imagined, but it *will* produce the deep sense of meaning, purpose, and fulfillment you long to experience. The only question is: How badly do you want to find fulfillment of the dreams that dwell in the core of your being? Since you've taken the step to begin reading this book, I trust that your desire to fulfill your dreams is strong enough to meet the demands that will be required of you!

Because this journey is God-centric, you might wonder if God will accept you, if you are "good enough" to qualify to have God direct you into the "full" life you desire. Scripture answers that question in the affirmative in many different passages, but the Apostle Peter's comment in Acts 10:34 directly addresses that concern: "I most certainly understand now that God is not one to show partiality." *No one is __worthy__ of God's blessings, but He invites __everyone__ into a relationship with Him – __even you__!* God is not angry with you and is not disappointed in you. Nothing in your past is an obstacle! His only desire is that you seek Him and surrender to His leadership as He reveals Himself to you and helps you discover and understand the truths He put into place at the very beginning of time. Your calling – everyone's calling – is to seek after truth. And all truth is found in Him. In John 14:6, Jesus said, "I am the way and the truth and the life. No one comes to the Father except through me."

The Importance of the Bible

The entirety of this book is built on two premises. The first premise is that God is real and that He "created the heavens and the earth" (Genesis 1:1). The second premise is that the Bible is the "inspired" word of God and must be used as the foundational instrument upon which all truths are to be evaluated.

2 Timothy 3: [16] All Scripture is God-breathed and is useful for teaching, rebuking, correcting, and training in righteousness, [17] so that the servant of God may be thoroughly equipped for every good work.

These are huge assumptions! In Appendix A: "The God Thing," I explain some aspects of the journey that led to my acceptance of these two assumptions. If either of these two assumptions is difficult for you to accept, I suggest you stop here, read through "The God Thing," and then pursue whatever journey God might lead you through as you seek assurance that these two assumptions are valid. If you do not wholeheartedly accept these two assumptions, the argument for everything that follows is weakened and, therefore, of less value to you. Because confidence in the reliability and validity of Scripture is vitally important, I'd like to address the issue here, albeit in much less space than the topic deserves.

Two significant reasons exist for accepting the Bible as the basis for establishing truth. The first is the need for an objective source of truth from which the validity of arguments and reasoning can be evaluated; the second is the incredible power of scripture. I'll argue the first point from an intellectual standpoint and the second from an experiential perspective.

It should be clear to every reasonable adult that we are all capable of error. The simple fact that our thinking changes over time (hopefully for the better) is evidence that old thinking is regularly replaced with new thinking, thereby exposing our old thinking as having been considered faulty or wrong in some way. Therefore, we cannot fully trust our thinking and analysis, even of our own life experiences, simply because we are capable of error. We are all likely to misunderstand or misdiagnose a comment or experience at times. We are each limited in many ways. Therefore, we need an objective, external source to use as a basis for analyzing and evaluating our thoughts, feelings, and experiences. When you add other people to the mix, because all of us are capable of being wrong, the need for an objective source of truth becomes even more apparent. How can we ever expect to agree on anything of significance without an objective standard for truth?

The question then becomes, *what* can be used as the source of truth? Because the Bible is unchanging, tested, and has served as the source of truth for countless millions of people over many centuries, it meets the criteria for acceptance as a source of objective truth.

While the above intellectual argument for accepting the Bible as the singular arbiter of truth might be inadequate, I will also present an argument based on my experiences and the experiences of untold millions of others. But regardless of my argument, you will need to personally deal with the question of the Bible's reliability and validity. *Just remember, we each need some objective source of truth to protect ourselves from the mistakes we are surely capable of making.* The identification of such an objective and reliable source is your responsibility.

The Bible claims to be God's inspired Word and possesses the *power* to effect change in people's lives.

2 Timothy 3: [16] All Scripture is inspired by God and profitable for teaching, for reproof, for correction, for training in righteousness.

Hebrews 4: [12] For the word of God is alive and active. Sharper than any double-edged sword, it penetrates even to dividing soul and spirit, joints and marrow; it judges the thoughts and attitudes of the heart.

The first verse speaks to the Bible's validity and integrity as an objective source of truth, and the second speaks to the Bible's incredible power and reliability in bringing about significant changes in people's lives. I have experienced both.

Because I tend to be highly rational, I have mostly experienced the transformative power of Scripture to change my thinking. As I have read and reflected on Scripture, the typical outcome has been to challenge my thinking and understanding of truth. Ongoing reflection regularly results in a modification of thinking, which, in turn, results in a change in attitudes and behaviors. However, as I am not an *entirely* rational creature, I also have emotions that influence my thoughts and actions. Reflection on scriptural truths has also often led to changes in my feelings and how I respond to events that trigger emotions within me. I cannot say that I have experienced direct physical changes as a result of Scripture. However, recognizing the relationship between mental and physical health, it would certainly follow that applying biblical truths can have physiological consequences. Spend any time interacting with or reading about the experiences of Christians, and you will see that my experiences are like those of literally tens, if not hundreds, of millions of others.

Consider this one brief example. When I became a Christian, one of my major objections to the idea of religion was the seemingly idiotic statements and behaviors of religious leaders with whom I had interacted in my childhood. One of the first things I encountered in reading Scripture was Jesus calling out the stupidity of the spiritual leaders of His time (see Matthew 23:13-36). Wow! Jesus thought some of them were jerks, too! This one revelation opened up the possibility that God's intent for religion, the Church, and the whole idea of Christianity might differ entirely from what I had previously thought and been taught.

This one encounter with Scripture was cathartic and significantly altered my entire mental framework! Many things I had believed to be problematic with religion were validated, and I was free to pursue truth with a new hope that there might be a body of truth within Christianity that I could wholeheartedly embrace. Simultaneously, a whole set of feelings about the Church and my previous religious experiences were validated, and I was now free to pursue truth with my whole heart and mind!

I have experienced countless similar changes in both my

thinking and feelings throughout the past 40+ years of my spiritual journey. From both an experiential and intellectual standpoint, I fully embrace both the validity and the reliability of Scripture. Therefore, I readily accept the Bible as the foundational source upon which all truth must be evaluated. However, that doesn't mean that I have no problems with Scripture. I can't say that it all makes sense to me. There have been – and still are – passages that I don't fully understand, as well as some "truths" that appear to be at least somewhat contradictory. However, since I recognize that I cannot rely on myself as the ultimate arbiter of truth, I must suspend judgment on those issues, hoping to gain a more profound understanding at some point in the future. In many instances, the development of that deeper understanding has occurred, bringing needed clarity; yet, I still find some biblical passages perplexing.

As one reads through the Bible, a clear message emerges: God desires to reveal Himself to us. However, God places the responsibility on us to seek Him. He calls us, but we must respond to that call. Consider the following verses, just a few of the many places in Scripture where God calls us to seek Him.

Deuteronomy 4: [29] "But if from there you seek the LORD your God, you will find him if you seek him with all your heart and with all your soul."

Proverbs 8: [17] "I love those who love me, and those who seek me find me."

Jeremiah 29: [13] "You will seek me and find me when you seek me with all your heart."

Matthew 7: [7] "Ask and it will be given to you; seek and you will find; knock and the door will be opened to you."

Acts 17: [24] "The God who made the world and everything in it is the Lord of heaven and earth and does not live in temples built by human hands. [25] And he is not served by human hands, as if he needed anything. Rather, he himself gives everyone life and breath and everything else. [26] From one man he made all the nations, that they should inhabit the whole earth; and he marked out their appointed times in history and the boundaries of their lands. [27] God did this so that they would seek him and perhaps reach out for him and find him, though he is not far from any one of us. [28] 'For in him we live and move and have our being'."

Let those verses "speak" to you. Allow them to give you the hope and the courage to begin your search to know and follow God because He is reaching out to you. The journey ahead will be arduous at times, but your willingness to seek to know and follow Jesus will lead to fulfilling the deep-seated dreams within your heart. Embrace and enjoy the journey. As you'll discover later, the journey is what life is all about!

Chapter 2
Understanding Meaning, Purpose, and Fulfillment

Deep in your heart, you know that your life is meant to have meaning and purpose and that pursuing and achieving your life goals and ambitions should result in a profound sense of personal fulfillment. This God-given dream for the "full" life (that Jesus came to make possible – John 10:10) drives you to pursue many goals. Getting married, raising a family, pursuing a career, and buying a home are all examples of the goals most of us pursue because we believe attaining such goals will contribute to realizing the dream that resides within us. Most people, however, never arrive at a point where they feel they have fully accomplished the dream in their hearts. Most people feel like they are missing something. Some continue searching, while others merely settle for whatever they have already accomplished. The problem we all face is this: *the only way we can fully realize the dream within our hearts is by following God's Plan for our lives, not the plans we make for ourselves.* Before going into detail about how we can understand and follow God's Plan for our lives, we need a deeper understanding of the kinds of experiences and practices from which meaning, purpose, and fulfillment are derived.

Finding Meaning, Purpose, and Fulfillment

To have *meaning* is to have value, to be significant. Meaning is the interpretation, significance, or value we associate with a word, object, or experience. We say that something is "meaningful" to us when (and to the extent that) it contributes to our understanding of our present circumstances and how we might direct our lives toward experiencing more significant levels of satisfaction. Your life has meaning to the degree that you can *ascribe value or significance to the activities and experiences of your life.* The greater your value on some experience, the more significant the meaning it will have for you.

Meaning can be derived from many different types of experiences. The most obvious ways are experiences like parenting, where you recognize how your interactions with your children can positively contribute to the development of their character and personalities. You can also find meaning in the *challenges you face* throughout your day. For example, suppose you recognize that God is using difficult circumstances at your workplace to develop your character or to help you develop a deeper understanding of a significant life truth (e.g., how to appeal to a person in a position of authority). In that case, each day contains many opportunities for creating meaning. In general, the more directly you recognize the connection between an event and how it can lead to accomplishing your dream, the more meaning you will ascribe to that event.

The critical point is that, as you believe God has a specific goal for your daily experiences, you will experience more significant meaning in your life. *Meaning in life blossoms as you grow in your ability to see how God is working to accomplish important, identifiable goals through your daily activities.* This is also true of the meaning we can discover from reflecting on past experiences. One biblical passage that affirms this truth is Philippians 2:13, "For it is God who is at work in you, both to will and to work for *His* good pleasure." God's "good pleasure" involves moving you towards experiencing the "full" life He has planned for you. Our need, then, is to become more aware of how God is "at work in you" – guiding your life to accomplish His good purposes for you.

To have **purpose** means that one's **planned activities** are intentionally **directed** in ways that advance essential life goals. Regardless of your life goals, you will feel that your life has purpose to the degree that you see a connection between your planned activities and life goals. For example, if you desire to become a teacher, then your years of preparation in college will provide a sense of purpose for all the challenges you experience along the way. The more your life goals align with God's plan (which depends on your awareness of His plan), the more you will feel that your life has a purpose. The "connection" between your life goals and God's plan for your life is affirmed in Jeremiah 29:11,

> "'For I know the plans that I have for you,' declares the
> Lord, 'plans for welfare and not for calamity to give you a
> future and a hope.'"

If you recognize that God is using your daily challenges and activities to advance His plans *for* you and *in* you, you will sense both meaning and purpose in your daily plans and activities! Discovering God's plans and goals and maintaining an awareness of His workings are crucial to sensing that your life has meaning and purpose. Without understanding God's direction and involvement in your life, you will continue to experience low levels of meaning and purpose, and your satisfaction from reaching goals will quickly fade.

Since it is the **awareness of God's plans** for your life that will lead to finding purpose, you will need to develop the capacity to connect with God in ways that enable you to understand what God is presently working on in your life, as well as His long-range plans for you. When you know God's plans for your life, each goal you set and every plan you put into motion will be rich with meaning and purpose. It might be worth pointing out here that God's purposes are first directed toward growing your character and second to using you in ways that advance His Kingdom *purposes*. God must do a more profound work **in** us before He can do a significant work **through** us. If we fail to develop Christ-like character, the works we accomplish are more likely to lead to pride and personal character failures rather than fulfillment. You will discover that as you appropriately respond to God's challenges to develop your character (finding the true meaning and purpose in your daily activities and experiences), He will direct your life in ways that will produce greater fulfillment.

Fulfillment is a feeling of completion, happiness, and satisfaction. In its simplest form, fulfillment results from completing a task, like finishing your laundry or washing your car. There is always some level of satisfaction and fulfillment that comes from completing a task – checking something off your "to-do list." But most people are searching for something much more profound. Many people mistakenly believe that fulfillment can only be experienced through some noteworthy achievement or receiving acclaim from someone of high status. This belief, however, is a prime example of a faulty mental framework. In reality, the "magnitude" of the fulfillment we experience from completing tasks is related more to the correlation between the task and God's Plan for our lives than the "magnitude" of the accomplishment itself.

For example, many of us are inclined to believe that fulfillment in life grows as we achieve a significant income level or a greater professional or social status. However, we all discover there is never "enough" of any personal achievement to fully satisfy our deepest longings for the "full" life. We tend to search for something "more" or "different" to satisfy that inner hunger. One of the truths we need to discover is that *pursuing life fulfillment in our own power and wisdom will always fall short of fulfilling the dream that resides deep within our hearts.* King Solomon expresses his understanding of this truth in his writing in the Book of Ecclesiastes. In Chapter 2, he says,

> [10] "All that my eyes desired I did not refuse them. I did not withhold my heart from any pleasure, for my heart was pleased because of all my labor, and this was my reward for all my labor. [11] Thus I considered all my activities which my hands had done and the labor which I had exerted and behold all was vanity and striving after wind and there was no profit under the sun."

Likewise, everything we pursue based solely on our own understanding will lead to futility instead of fulfillment. But *each time we engage in a God-ordained task – a task that is part of God's plan for our lives – we will experience a sense of fulfillment!* That is why it is essential to understand what God is calling you to do!

Because of the way God created us, experiencing a deep sense of fulfillment in one's life results optimally from engaging in actions that express the person God created us to be. If God created you to be an artist, you will experience fulfillment as you create art. If God created you to be a teacher, you will experience fulfillment as you teach. If God created you to be a craftsman, you will experience fulfillment as you perform your craft. However, if God created you to be an artist and you work as an accountant, you will not find much fulfillment in completing daily tasks. Instead, you will just be relieved when the day is finished!

The more your daily activities are consistent with who God created you to be **and** how those activities advance God's purposes in the lives of others, the more fulfillment you will experience. Your spiritual gifts, for example, influence how you will find fulfillment in life. (In a later chapter, we will examine spiritual gifts and other factors in discovering who God created you to be in greater detail.) However, if you are *self-directed* – as opposed to being *God-directed* – using your spiritual gifts will bring a measure of fulfillment. On the other hand, *if your activities are a direct outgrowth of obeying a directive from God, the fulfillment you experience will be much more profound.* A personal example might be helpful.

One of my spiritual gifts is teaching. I was a high school and college math teacher for most of my adult life. Becoming a teacher was a self-directed goal; I never felt God called me to be a math teacher. In fact, I wasn't even a Christian when I decided to become a teacher. However, because teaching was a spiritual gift – part of who God made me to be – I found a measure of fulfillment throughout my professional teaching career. But honestly, much of the time I was teaching, it just felt like work! My personal "calling" (which we will examine in greater depth later), however, is to use my teaching gift to help others understand how God is at work in their lives and identify what might be blocking their spiritual growth. So, later in my career, after I became a Christian and had a one-on-one conversation with one of my students that focused on a personal aspect of their life, I experienced a much deeper sense of fulfillment. And when I could help them understand a life principle that God was trying to show them – when I could be God's instrument for assisting them to grow closer to Him – the fulfillment I experienced was immense! *You will experience meaning, purpose, and fulfillment – to an ever-deepening degree – as you increasingly see God is at work in how you plan and live out your daily life and the long-range plans you set.*

To summarize the three main ideas in this chapter, your life has meaning to the extent that you can connect your daily (or past) experiences to significant, personally held values and goals. Your life has purpose to the extent that you can connect your planned activities to goals you deeply value. You experience fulfillment to the extent that the accomplishment of your daily activities and your short- and long-term goals are aligned with who God created you to be and what He is calling you to do. Therefore, your life will have increasing levels of meaning, purpose, and fulfillment as your daily activities become more closely aligned with both short- and long-term goals that you value now and will continue to value in the future – God's Plan for your life.

Since no person can know what they will value in the future, the only way we can choose wisely now is to follow Someone who knows the future. This synthesis between daily experiences and short- and long-term goals is what makes following God so vitally important. Since He knows "the end from the beginning" (Isaiah 46:10), we have the assurance that *the activities God directs us to accomplish each day will result in an ever-deepening sense of meaning, purpose, and fulfillment.* Not only today but also in the future.

I hope you can see from this brief discussion that the most significant amount of meaning, purpose, and fulfillment comes from understanding how God is at work in your life and following through with His plans for you. For us to know God's plans, however, we need to be able to connect and interact with Him in profound ways. Before we can connect with God in ways that will enable us to clearly understand what He is calling us to do, we need to remove obstacles that prevent our faith from growing and develop some basic understanding of how God designed a relationship with Him to develop and flourish. The following two chapters are intended to accomplish these two outcomes.

Chapter 3
Eliminating Blockages

In the Introduction, I noted how our *mental framework* (our deep-seated *beliefs* about how life works) directly influences how we live, whether we are aware of it or not. I also discussed how, without God's influence, our interpretations of life experiences feed our mental framework in ways that often lead to faulty conclusions. Consequently, we need to maintain an openness to having our beliefs challenged. Maintaining an open mind enables our mental framework to be flexible and adaptable. A lack of openness makes it impossible to discover errors in our thinking and understanding. If you accept that you do not possess perfect knowledge of everything about life, then it follows that at least some of your beliefs need to change. This means we must be cautious about how we interpret our life experiences. Sometimes, we will be presented with information contradicting a closely held belief. In these instances, we must be open to modifying or discarding one or more of our beliefs.

The peril of embracing false beliefs lies in the potential to overlook crucial truths that God wishes to reveal to you. For instance, if you adopt the notion that hardship or loss signifies

God's abandonment or betrayal, you'll miss out on the opportunity to see how God can use adversity and loss to bring you closer to Him, to foster character and deeper trust within you, and to impart vital lessons. All these benefits can be forfeited by clinging too tightly to a false belief about God's nature or His design for life.

Many non-Christians have encountered religious ideas and religious individuals or have had church experiences that have sown seeds of misconceptions about God and Christianity. Similarly, numerous Christians have absorbed (or formulated on their own) beliefs that are not entirely accurate, and in some cases, completely false. In this chapter, my primary aim is to address some widely held misconceptions that hinder our connection with God. These misunderstandings about God, life, religion, the Church, or Christianity, if they form part of your mental framework, can dampen your desire to seek God and hinder your ability to grasp His true nature and His intended ways of life.

(In the next chapter, I will discuss several fundamental principles of the Christian life that can aid you on your spiritual journey. When present in your mental framework, this second set of principles will enable you to approach God in ways that will enhance your ability to respond appropriately to many of the challenges you will face as you seek to know God and follow His leadership. Together, the content presented in these two chapters can assist you in developing a sound mental framework.)

Our lives are primarily driven by our thoughts, beliefs, and the plans we make for ourselves. While we sometimes think about the deep-seated dreams in our hearts, we usually focus on short-term goals. One of the circumstances that frustrates me most is how our interpretation of life experiences can lead us to hold false beliefs, which in turn hinder us from becoming and experiencing all the amazing things God desires for us. Fortunately, on many occasions throughout our lives, God "intervenes" in ways designed to draw our attention to Him so He can modify those false beliefs and redirect our lives in significant ways. God's "interventions" often occur during a conversation with someone, after we have experienced a great accomplishment, failure, or some tragic event, or when we find ourselves pushed outside our comfort zone. There may also be times when you yearn for something deeper in life. These are just a few examples of the kinds of life events that God uses to draw our attention to Him. I have noticed that the birth of a child, being present at a wedding ceremony, or attending a memorial service are life events that frequently cause people to reflect on their lives globally, wondering if they might be missing something important. In each of these instances, and many more, God reaches out to draw our attention to Him. In John 6:44, Jesus said, "No one can come to me unless the Father who sent me *draws them.*" God is regularly reaching out to you, attempting to get your attention. However, if you hold certain false beliefs about God or spiritual matters, you will be inclined to quickly dismiss these "invitations" to connect with Him.

The following are common false beliefs that can prevent you from responding to God when He reaches out to you. If any of these false beliefs are present in your mental framework, they will likely interfere with your ability to respond to God's "invitations" to draw near to Him. If you recognize that any of these "beliefs" are present in your mental framework, these issues must be resolved for you to connect with God more deeply. If the insights presented cannot remove the false belief entirely, you must seek God with greater intentionality to resolve the issue. God will *always* respond when we seek to know and understand the truths of life. But recognize also that God often directs us to other sources, like books or conversations with informed people, to aid us in our journey to know and follow Him.

False beliefs that can block you from seeking or following God.

I. God is angry and vindictive.

Many people believe that God is a grumpy old grouch who has established a bunch of rules that are supposed to be followed, and He looks angrily upon people whenever they make a mistake, often punishing them for their failure to obey Him. For people who hold this belief, following God means giving up many of the things they enjoy, as well as feeling guilty much of the time because they can't always do what they know is right! If you believe God acts in these ways, you will probably prefer to have nothing to do with Him. But this belief is absolutely false!

God is not angry with you, nor is He disappointed in you! In contrast to this false belief, God is actually kind, gentle, patient, and merciful. People tend to hold inaccurate opinions of God's character because of things they've heard people say about God rather than from personal interactions with Him. You must understand that the only way to really "know" someone is to spend a great deal of time with them – hearing them speak and observing how they react in various situations. Consider the following biblical passages, written by individuals who had personal interactions with God, describing their experiences.

> **Psalm 86:** [15] But You, O Lord, are a God merciful and gracious, slow to anger and abundant in lovingkindness and truth.

> **Psalm 116:** [5] Gracious is the LORD, and righteous; Yes, our God is compassionate.

Ephesians 4: [32] Be kind to one another, tender-hearted, forgiving each other, just as God in Christ also has forgiven you.

As you understand God better and interact personally with Him, you will discover He is a loving, kind, patient, merciful, and compassionate Father who desires that you experience a rich, full, happy life. Every time He intervenes in your life, you will experience greater happiness and fulfillment. *God is always on your side*, longing for you to experience an ever-growing sense of meaning, purpose, and fulfillment. As you personally interact with Him, you will experience these aspects of His character through His words, the strength, peace, comfort, and joy He provides, and the actions He encourages you to take. One of our major problems is that we think we know what is in our best interest. But we are wrong about many, many things. God needs to replace our false beliefs with truth. God is not angry and vindictive!

II. God punishes you for the mistakes you make.

This belief is closely related to the previous one about believing God is an angry old grouch. When God created the heavens and the earth, He also established the principles governing everything He had created. Any activity contrary to those principles is likely to result in less-than-desirable outcomes. However, the outcomes we experience when a life principle is violated are *natural consequences rather than punishments*.

For example, if I jump off the roof of my house, I am likely to be seriously injured or perhaps even killed. God would not have *caused* my injuries; any suffering I experience will be a natural consequence of my stupidity or carelessness. When God designed our bodies, they were built to withstand a limited amount of physical impact. Any force beyond that limit will result in injury. The larger the force of the impact, the greater the injury that will result. This is a truth – a pre-established life principle – that governs how our physical bodies are designed to function. If you understand and abide by this truth, you will avoid injury. If you violate this life principle, you will experience pain and suffering. Similarly, one should expect that violating other life principles God has established will also result in unpleasant outcomes.

We must understand that God created principles that govern not only the physical aspects of His creation but also *how every aspect of His creation functions.* So, God's principles govern not only the tangible physical aspects of our lives but also our emotional, psychological, and spiritual lives. The truth is, rather than punishing us for our mistakes, God often mercifully intervenes in ways that protect us from experiencing the full impact of our actions that are contrary to the principles He has established. In many instances, God allows us to experience some degree of pain, suffering, or sorrow when we violate His principles or standards. However, the negative consequences we experience are not punishments or retribution – a desire for us to suffer a penalty for our misdeeds. Instead, God's intent for any of our sufferings or disappointments is always to instruct us – to help us better understand who He is, how He designed life to be lived, and encourage us to think and act differently.

Romans 8: [28] And we know that in all things God works for the good of those who love him, who have been called according to his purpose.

This promise applies not only to the consequences you experience because of someone else's failures but also to the consequences you experience from your own mistakes – even when you purposely ignore His guidance. The Bible uses the word *discipline* to describe how God intervenes in our lives, much like how we might discipline our own children, intending to help us develop character and the kinds of personal practices that will allow us to experience the "full" life He has planned for us. I will go into greater detail about many of these important principles in the chapter titled "How has God Designed Life to be Lived?" But for now, allow the following passages to help you better understand God's character.

> **Hebrews 12:** [10] God disciplines us for our good, in order that we may share in his holiness.

> **Job 5:** [17] Blessed is the one whom God corrects; so do not despise the discipline of the Almighty. [18] For He wounds, but He also binds up; He injures, but His hands also heal.

> **Proverbs 3:** [11] My son, do not despise the LORD's discipline, and do not resent His rebuke, [12] because the LORD disciplines those He loves, as a father the son he delights in.

III. God wants you to follow many rules that will rob your life of joy.

God has indeed designated a significant number of principles that govern every aspect of life. But everything God created – and the principles that govern them – is designed to empower us to experience a rich, meaningful, productive, and fulfilling life. Recall Jesus' statement about His purpose for coming to earth,

> **John 10:** [10] "I have come that they may have life, and have it to the full."

God really desires for you to experience a meaningful,

purposeful, and genuinely fulfilling life! Our problem is that we often find avenues that bring a *modicum* of pleasure but have totally misunderstood the actions, motivations, and experiences that result in the *most significant* amount of joy, peace, happiness, and fulfillment. That is why we keep looking for something "more" – some experience, possession, or relationship that will not disappoint. We have all experienced the reality of seeking after something we believed would make us happy, and then, after the good feelings begin to dissipate, we embark on a search for something "better." God has plans for our lives that will not disappoint!

In truth, we are prisoners of our own ignorance. Because we have sought to discover the "full" life on our own – without God's guidance – we have created a set of beliefs (mental framework) that fails to accomplish our deep-seated desire for meaning, purpose, and fulfillment. God has the same desires for us that we have for ourselves – even *more* than we could ask or think. However, we will only experience the "full" life when we follow God's design for life, including how we live and interact with Him and others. We *prevent ourselves from experiencing our dream life by refusing to seek and follow God.* The life principles you discover on your journey to know God will result in understandings and actions that will help you better follow God and experience the incredible blessings He desires to release in your life.

Jeremiah 29: [11] "For I know the plans I have for you,"
declares the LORD, "plans to prosper you and not to harm
you, plans to give you hope and a future."

Isaiah 41: [10] "So do not fear, for I am with you; do not be
dismayed, for I am your God. I will strengthen and
help you; I will uphold you with my righteous right hand."

Psalms 32: [9] Do not be like the horse or the mule, which

have no understanding but must be controlled by bit and bridle or they will not come to you.

IV. Christians are a bunch of hypocrites.

This belief, unfortunately, is *not* entirely false! Many, if not all, Christians *are* hypocrites! However, if properly understood, this observation should *not* be a reason to reject God's invitation to seek and follow Him. Why not? In part because Jesus had the same observation while He was here on earth. In fact, Jesus directly accused the religious leaders of His day of being hypocrites. One of the places you'll find Jesus' criticisms of those leaders is in the Book of Matthew. The entirety of Chapter 23 is a criticism of the religious leaders. But verses 23 through 26 are probably the most striking:

> **Matthew 23:** [23] "Woe to you, teachers of the law and Pharisees, you hypocrites! You give a tenth of your spices – mint, dill and cumin. But you have neglected the more important matters of the law – justice, mercy and faithfulness. You should have practiced the latter, without neglecting the former. [24] You blind guides! You strain out a gnat but swallow a camel. [25] Woe to you, teachers of the law and Pharisees, you hypocrites! You clean the outside of the cup and dish, but inside they are full of greed and self-indulgence. [26] Blind Pharisee! First clean the inside of the cup and dish, and then the outside also will be clean."

As you can see from this passage, Jesus was very critical of many people who professed to follow God. The same is true today. Christians are hypocrites in that they profess ideals they often fail to live up to fully. And most Christians know that is true about themselves. The major difference between a Christian and a non-

Christian is that the Christian recognizes their guilt, as well as their inability to live up to their ideals fully. Christians also understand that they need to find a way to overcome the burden of guilt they feel each time they fail to live up to the standards they have adopted. Christians understand that through Jesus' sacrificial death and subsequent resurrection, they are forgiven and set free from their guilt. Their appreciation for God's Grace extended to them creates a deeper desire to know and follow Him.

From a biblical perspective, **everyone is guilty** of violating God's principles for life. And everyone knows this is true of themselves. This reality is highlighted throughout scripture, but one of the places it is stated most directly is in Romans 3:23 – "For all have sinned and fall short of the glory of God." But the verse goes on to say, "And all are justified freely by His grace through the redemption that came by Christ Jesus." So, even though Christians often violate the standards they claim to believe in, God still accepts and forgives them. The proper Christian perspective is to humbly acknowledge one's failures and shortcomings, and many Christians do. But just because some Christians fail to act that way doesn't mean that God's principles are wrong. In other words, the fact that some Christians profess standards they fail to follow doesn't negate the validity of those standards. Jesus provides instructions on dealing with our shortcomings and how we should relate to others in Matthew 7.

> Matthew 7: [1] "Do not judge, or you too will be judged. [2] For in the same way you judge others, you will be judged, and with the measure you use, it will be measured to you.
> [3] "Why do you look at the speck of sawdust in your brother's eye and pay no attention to the plank in your own eye? [4] How can you say to your brother, 'Let me take the speck out of your eye,' when all the time there is a plank in your own eye? [5] You hypocrite, first take the plank out of your

own eye, and then you will see clearly to remove the speck from your brother's eye."

Jesus' encouragement here is to humbly deal with one's shortcomings and find resolution *before* instructing others about God's principles for life. The observation of the hypocrisy of Christians is well-founded, but it's not a reason for rejecting an invitation from God. Don't allow other people's shortcomings to prevent you from responding to God's invitation as He reaches out to you. More mature Christians, who have appropriately acknowledged their shortcomings, are guided by biblical principles like the following and interact with humility and grace when proclaiming God's truths.

Colossians 3: [12] Therefore, as God's chosen people, holy and dearly loved, clothe yourselves with compassion, kindness, humility, gentleness and patience.

Ephesians 4: [2] Be completely humble and gentle; be patient, bearing with one another in love.

Micah 6: [8] He has shown you, O mortal, what is good. And what does the LORD require of you? To act justly and to love mercy and to walk humbly with your God.

V. I could never live up to God's standards.

This is another *true* belief. However, it is *not* a reason to avoid God. **It's precisely the reason why you need Him!** As I have already mentioned several times, each of us has a dream in our hearts that our lives should have meaning, purpose, and fulfillment. However, that's not the only dream we embrace. In the depths of our hearts, we also have a picture of the person we could and should become – a person of strength, dignity, confidence, and integrity, facing and overcoming all life's challenges. And, somehow, we also have the awareness that those two dreams are intricately woven together. But as I examine my own life, I have never been able, on my own, to fully harness the focus, strength, and courage needed to fully become the person I know I could be.

And that's not just my problem. That's your problem, too! None of us, in our power, can ever become the person we could be and experience a life rich in meaning, purpose, and fulfillment. That's because *God designed life so that we need Him*! And *that's why God doesn't reject us* because of our shortcomings! Instead of believing that you must *avoid* God because of your limitations, that belief must be replaced with the understanding that *God wants to empower* you to overcome your shortcomings. Consider the following biblical passages that affirm this truth.

Psalm 32: [8] I will instruct you and teach you in the way you should go I will counsel you with my loving eye on you.

Proverbs 3: [5] Trust in the LORD with all your heart and lean not on your own understanding; [6] in all your ways submit to him, and he will make your paths straight.

John 14: [26] The Holy Spirit, whom the Father will send in my name, will teach you all things and will remind you of everything I have said to you.

Isaiah 40: [29] He gives strength to the weary and increases the power of the weak. [30] Even youths grow tired and weary, and young men stumble and fall; [31] but those who hope in the LORD will renew their strength. They will soar on wings like eagles; they will run and not grow weary, they will walk and not be faint.

VI. God could never forgive me for some of the things I have done.

When we think about living up to God's expectations, another thought that can plague us is that God could never forgive us for some of our past mistakes – especially those we knew were wrong but did anyway. This kind of guilt can block any progress in your life. But the Bible makes it clear that this reasoning is faulty. The truth is that God accepts you – fully and completely – just as you are. Nothing you can do or fail to do will *ever* change His love for you. God offers Himself to you freely and in full measure.

> **Psalm 103:** [10] He does not treat us as our sins deserve or repay us according to our iniquities. [11] For as high as the heavens are above the earth, so great is his love for those who fear him; [12] as far as the east is from the west, so far has he removed our transgressions from us.

> **Isaiah 43:** [25] "I, even I, am he who blots out your transgressions, for my own sake, and remembers your sins no more."

> **I John I:** [9] If we confess our sins, he is faithful and just and will forgive us our sins and purify us from all unrighteousness.

One additional issue can prevent us from responding to God's invitations to connect with Him. And that is the anger, resentment, and bitterness that often comes from being disappointed that God failed to come through for you in some critical way in the past. Most of us have experienced the disappointment caused by God's failure to fulfill a deep-seated desire when we hoped and prayed that He would come through for us. And that disappointment rests on the following false belief.

VII. God "controls" everything that happens.

While it's true that God *can* intervene in our lives in absolutely any way He desires (omnipotence), it doesn't necessarily follow that He *always exercises that ability*. One of the essential principles we need to understand is that God created people to have free will – the ability to decide for themselves how they will act. The exercise of free will has resulted in many of the tragic outcomes that have occurred throughout history. Many people wonder why, if God is all-knowing (omniscient), He would create us with free will instead of just "programming" us to do what was right all the time. I believe God gave us free will because He desires to be loved, and He understands love must be freely given to be genuine.

So, the truth is that God *allows* everything that occurs rather than *causing* everything that occurs. That begs the question, "Why does God allow bad things to happen to good people?" That's a question for which an entire library of books has been written, so I won't try to supply a complete response here. However, the short answer, unfortunately, is that there are no people who are fully good – we all fall short of perfection! Sometimes, people experience suffering or loss due to their own shortcomings, while at other times, they suffer or experience loss as a consequence of the failures of others. However, in all circumstances, God allows suffering or loss so that He can redirect our lives in a particular way. What's essential for us to understand here is that God feels sorrow and grief each time we experience suffering or loss. But He also reaches out to us to provide the comfort we need to heal and move forward. The following are just a few biblical passages communicating God's feelings about our suffering and loss.

Hebrews 4: [15] For we do not have a high priest who is unable to empathize with our weaknesses, but we have one who has been tempted in every way, just as we are – yet He did not sin. [16] Let us then approach God's throne of grace with confidence, so that we may receive mercy and find grace to help us in our time of need.

Psalm 34: [17] The righteous cry out, and the LORD hears them; He delivers them from all their troubles. [18] The LORD is close to the brokenhearted and saves those who are crushed in spirit.

Matthew 11: [28] "Come to me, all you who are weary and burdened, and I will give you rest. [29] Take my yoke upon you and learn from me, for I am gentle and humble in heart, and you will find rest for your souls."

These are just a few of the many beliefs and questions that can prevent us from responding to "invitations" God repeatedly sends us to turn our attention to Him so He can guide and empower our lives in ways that will produce the "full" life we so deeply desire. As I pondered the question of what issues I should include in this chapter, many other thoughts came to mind: I'm not worthy of God's attention; religion is just a crutch; I'm already a good person; all the church wants is my money; God has more important things to do than being concerned about me; God doesn't love me; and God is just an image created by people to control others. You may have other questions or thoughts that prevent you from seeking God or responding to His "invitations." One of life's great paradoxes is this: *The only way you will ever find adequate "answers" to the questions or issues that prevent you from reaching out to God or drawing closer to Him is by <u>seeking</u> and <u>interacting</u> with Him. Because only God Himself can provide the answers you need to satisfy the fears* *and confusion preventing you from moving forward.* And because God deeply understands you, He knows precisely what understanding and knowledge you require to resolve every vital question and concern. But there *are* good answers to each of your questions and doubts!

One of the foundational truths about creation is that humankind was created with the intelligence to recognize the inconsistencies and doubts that reside within them and the motivation to seek meaningful answers to life's profound questions. Finding answers to these questions is a significant part of finding meaning and purpose. *You must accept personal responsibility for finding answers to the questions that prevent you from moving forward in fruitful ways – and God desires to assist you in that process.* No question is "off limits" – God desires to help you find meaningful answers to all life's essential questions. **He _designed_ life to work that way! Pursuing meaningful answers to important life questions is the _core_ of The Great Adventure!**

As you search for answers to the critical questions that arise in your mind, God will guide you to find the answers *you need*. That pattern must be followed because that's one of the ways God designed life to be lived! All learning is the result of finding answers to questions. Each time you complete the process of finding an answer to a significant life question, you gain a deeper understanding of who God is, which enables you to enjoy a deeper relationship with Him. And each of these experiences helps you to develop greater confidence and trust in Him. **Your primary calling in life is to be a student – a truth seeker – searching for answers to the questions you believe are most important, and allowing God to be your teacher and guide.** While there is probably an inexhaustible set of questions and answers, in the next chapter, I will present a set of truths established by God, foundational principles of life, that will aid you in connecting with God in significant and personal ways.

Chapter 4
Understanding Foundational Truths

In this chapter, I will share some fundamental truths that are foundational to how God designed life to function. In sharing these truths, I aim for you to understand how to connect with God in ways that will enable you to discern how God is "at work," directing your life (Philippians 2:13) toward His excellent plans for you. Remember, God's plans are always directed toward helping you grow into the "full life" (John 10:10) He has planned for you – a life rich in meaning, purpose, and fulfillment. Some of the truths I share will make perfect sense, some might seem counterintuitive, and some might even make you wonder if I am completely wrong! But remember, the proper understanding of these truths will come not from intellectual knowledge, but from your personal experiences with God.

For these truths to effectively guide your life, they must be personally validated through the life experiences God guides you through. God will need to personally validate these truths for you as you wrestle with the challenges of understanding what it means to be a Christ-follower. These truths can guide you effectively when used as a basis for directing your life. Even the *awareness* of these truths can assist you on your journey to know and follow God.

The *most significant and essential lesson* you must discover, through examining your own life experiences, is that *the pathway to experiencing the most amazing life possible must be God-directed.* That is, the critical decisions you make in life need to be based on your best understanding of God's will for you. Every step off that pathway will yield less-than-optimal (and potentially disastrous) results. While we may come to accept this principle intellectually, our *natural inclination* will be to plan our own way rather than be guided by God. A significant part of the spiritual transformation process involves developing *the habit of turning to God for guidance and support.* While many scripture passages affirm the necessity of following God's guidance, Proverbs 14:12 seems to be the most direct:

"There is a way that appears to be right, but in the end it leads to death."

When we do what *we* think is best, we should expect less-than-optimal outcomes. However, because God desires that we experience a meaningful and fulfilling life, He regularly intervenes in ways that provide opportunities for us to discover our need for Him and the wisdom necessary to redirect our lives accordingly.

Proverbs 16: [9] "The mind of man plans his way, but the Lord directs his steps" (NASB).

Many of the challenges we face in life are designed by God to redirect our attention to Him so that He can help us discover essential life truths and lead us in ways that will optimally enrich our lives. "I will instruct you and teach you in the way you should go; I will counsel you with my loving eye on you." (Psalm 32:8). Our most

50

significant challenge (and greatest opportunity), then, is to discover how we can best learn the lessons that God desires to teach us.

God truly desires for you to experience a life of meaning, purpose, and fulfillment. The Bible communicates that truth in many ways. As we saw earlier, the most direct statement of this truth was expressed by Jesus Himself:

John 10: [10] "The enemy comes only to kill, steal and destroy; I have come that [you] might have life, and have it to the full."

Through this statement, Jesus is telling us that His very purpose for coming to earth was to make it possible for each person to experience a "full" life. But Jesus also points out that an adversary is trying to block our progress. If we depend only on our own understanding and power, we will miss out on many blessings God desires for us. The answer to this problem that applies to us all is to follow Jesus – allowing Him to reveal life's essential truths and guide our thinking and planning.

In John 8:31-32, Jesus reveals the basic principle of the process we must follow: "If you *hold to my teaching*, you are really my disciples. *Then* you will *know the truth*, and the truth will set you free." In John 16:13, Jesus explains in more detail how these truths will be taught to us. "But when He, the Spirit of truth comes, He will guide you into all the truth; for He will not speak on His own initiative, but whatever He hears, He will speak; and He will disclose to you what is to come."

The Gospel message is simply this: Through the sacrifice of Jesus' death and subsequent resurrection and ascension into Heaven, God has made it possible for you to enter into a genuine, personal relationship with Him. That relationship begins when you ask Jesus to forgive you of your rebellion against God and communicate your desire and intention to follow His leadership. At that point in time, your spirit is "born again," and the Holy Spirit takes up residence within your heart (John 3:5-8). The Holy Spirit's presence within you establishes the communication channel between you and God.

From that point on (salvation), God desires you to connect with Him regularly. As you respond to His promptings to seek Him, engage in honest dialogue with Him about absolutely every-thing in your life, and follow through (to the best of your ability) with the ways He challenges you to think and act, you will grow closer to Him. As you deepen your relationship with God and follow His leadership, you will experience an ever-growing sense of meaning, purpose, and fulfillment. It won't always be fun or easy; there will be many challenges as you struggle to surrender to God's leadership. But the long-term result will move you closer and closer to experiencing the "full" life Jesus desires for you.

As I mentioned in the Introduction, if there is one key to growing as a Christian, it is expressed in the Book of Romans.

> **Romans 12:** [2] Do not conform to the pattern of this world,
> but be transformed by the renewing of your mind. Then
> you will be able to test and approve what God's will is – his
> good, pleasing and perfect will.

We "grow" as Christ-followers as we replace our current mental framework – our beliefs about life and truth – with a divinely inspired mental framework. God replaces what is false – our beliefs, which we developed on our own power ("patterns of this world") – with genuine truths about who God is and how He designed life to be lived. *God designed life to be a journey of discovery – a Great Adventure of learning experiences with the Holy Spirit as your personal guide.* The primary requirement is that *you need to become a seeker of truth.* Your journey of discovering the truths God established for life – a biblically sound mental framework – will be accomplished in four ways.

1. Some things you believe to be true about life are correct. These truths must be reinforced, fully embraced, and used as the foundation for your plans and actions.
2. Some things you believe to be true about life are only partially correct. These truths need to be refined.
3. Some things you believe to be true about life are incorrect. These beliefs need to be abandoned and replaced with corresponding truths.
4. There are some understandings and beliefs that are true about life that you do not know at all. These truths must be discovered, clarified, and integrated into your mental framework.

You must approach your life journey as a student. You are responsible for discovering what is true about life and building your life upon these truths. The Holy Spirit will be your teacher and guide. As you seek God, He will teach you through all your life experiences – always attempting to direct your attention to truths in one or more of the abovementioned ways.

Romans 8: [28] And we know that in all things God works for the good of those who love him, who have been called according to his purpose. [29] For those God foreknew he also predestined to be conformed to the image of his Son, that he might be the firstborn among many brothers and sisters.

Based on this general overview, the following is a list of foundational truths, understandings, and practices that will enhance your journey of discovery. Over time, God will reinforce the validity of these truths for you.

Truths that undergird the journey to know and follow God

I. Life is primarily about relationships.

When Jesus began His earthly ministry, He often spoke and acted in ways that contradicted the views of the religious leaders of His day. The truths He revealed through His words and actions were so profound that He captured the hearts of many people. In fact, Jesus became a celebrity among the ordinary people; they flocked around Him everywhere He went. This challenged the authority and influence of the religious leaders, prompting them to seek ways to discredit Jesus. On one particular occasion, the religious leaders attempted to embarrass Jesus by posing a question they thought He would be unable to answer, thereby weakening His stature before the people.

One account of this interaction between Jesus and the religious leaders is captured in Matthew 22. In verse 36, one of the religious leaders challenged Jesus with this question: "Teacher, which is the greatest commandment in the Law?" It's important to understand that the Pharisees had established 613 commandments and taught that all must be obeyed. In their mind, they were all equally important. Surely, they thought, Jesus could not answer this question. But Jesus surprised them. In verses 37-40, Jesus instructs them as follows. (This passage is called The Great Commandment.)

Matthew 22: [37] Jesus replied: "'Love the Lord your God with all your heart and with all your soul and with all your mind.' [38] This is the first and greatest commandment. [39] And the second is like it: 'Love your neighbor as yourself.' [40] All the Law and the Prophets hang on these two commandments."

Jesus not only identified the Greatest Commandment, but He also pointed out the second greatest commandment. He further showed them (verse 40) that all of the other 611 commandments flowed out of these two: their relationship with God and their relationships with others. Since following God's leadership produces the "full" life and seeing that relationships are the most critical issues in life, establishing and maintaining healthy relationships is fundamental to experiencing a life of meaning, purpose, and fulfillment.

As you seek to understand what it means to be a Christ-follower, *your relationships with God and others should always be a major priority.* However, establishing and maintaining healthy relationships will always be a struggle. Consequently, your key relationships will simultaneously be the source of your greatest enjoyment and your most significant conflicts and challenges. God designs this dual nature of relationships to bring us happiness and to challenge us to develop character.

You will grow in meaningful and fruitful ways as you allow God to use these relationships as a focal point for your interactions with Him. Therefore, it will always be essential for you to give special attention to your relationships – starting with God and moving "outward" to family, friends, work associates, and others with whom you interact. *The more significant a relationship is in your life, the greater its impact on the overall quality of life you experience.* For example, strengthening relationships with your spouse and nuclear family will impact your life more significantly than improving your relationship with someone you occasionally interact with at work.

One of the primary applications of this first life principle is that as you connect with God, He will often bring issues related to significant relationships (including your relationship with Him) to mind. The issues God leads you to focus on often impede the "full life" He desires for you. As you allow God to give you insights and understanding into the key relationships in your life, He will reveal truths you need to embrace and act on. This process of reflection is an integral part of the spiritual transformation process. Life is primarily about relationships.

II. Your relationship (interactions) with God must become your foremost priority.

This is probably obvious, but it's so important that I thought it worthwhile to point out. Because God is the source of everything good (James 1:17, Every good thing given and every perfect gift is from above, coming down from the Father of lights, with whom there is no variation or shifting shadow.), the way you connect and interact with God is of supreme importance. I understand, however, that approaching God can be very intimidating. How does one approach God? How can I even show my face before Him, let alone converse with Him? When you stop to think about how flawed you are compared to God's holiness, majesty, and power, the thought of even approaching Him can be fraught with fear and intimidation. But that's where Jesus' sacrifice comes into play. When you are born again (salvation), God sets you free from any fear of punishment for your rebellion against Him.

> **Jeremiah 31:** [34] "No longer will they teach their neighbor,
> or say to one another, 'Know the LORD,' because they will
> all know me, from the least of them to the greatest,"
> declares the LORD. "For I will forgive their wickedness
> and will remember their sins no more."

Justification is the theological term that describes our "position" before God – we can stand before God knowing He accepts us for who we are without fear of judgment. So, we can approach God at any time and converse with Him openly. However, for our interactions with God to be optimally beneficial, *the nature of our conversations must always be conducted with complete transparency and honesty*. We must always be totally honest before God. Since He knows everything about us, there would appear to be no need for us to say anything. But *we benefit* from honestly owning up to our anger, fears, doubts, shortcomings, rebellion, and regrets when we come before God.

Our honest "confession" lays the foundation for God to interact with us and for us to be able to receive His grace and wisdom. The humble recognition and confession of our ongoing need for God opens our hearts to receive all He has for us. King David expressed this truth in Psalms 51:6 (NASB) – "Behold, You desire truth in the innermost being, and in the hidden part You will make me know wisdom." As we interact honestly with God from the depths of our hearts, God gives us wisdom – the ability to understand the truths for living that He established at the very beginning of time. And as we spend time in His Presence, He transforms our hearts and empowers us to live our lives more fully aligned with His will. However, despite the amazing benefits we derive from spending time in God's Presence, developing the pattern of regularly spending fruitful time with Him often becomes one of the most significant challenges for Christians.

Fruitful interactions with God will follow this simple pattern. First, we approach God with an open heart and mind, speaking honestly from the depths of our hearts. Second, God dispenses His grace to us in some way. (Grace is a HUGE topic, but for now, let's say that grace is an outpouring of some "blessing" or benefit from God.) His grace might come as a feeling of acceptance or empowerment to move forward. God's grace might appear as a feeling of being comforted or encouraged, or as a word of correction, where He gives you an insight into your behavior you were not previously aware of. His grace might be a challenge to do something. Regardless of the *form* that God's grace takes, our interactions with God will always result in some *"course correction"* to our mental or emotional framework. God will permanently implant some wisdom to help us better understand one or more truths He has established for life

Following our interactions with God, we become responsible for incorporating the truths He reveals into our daily lives. And that's step three: we begin to think, feel, and act differently. We respond to God's interactions by allowing Him to change us. That's the transformation that occurs by "the renewing of your mind," expressed in the passage from the Book of Romans, Chapter 12. In condensed form, these three steps should define most of your interactions with God.

1. Come before God with an open heart and mind, speaking honestly from the depths of your heart.
2. Receive whatever God wants to give or reveal to you and clarify how you should respond.
3. Follow through to the best of your ability.

There is actually a fourth step: repeat this pattern as often as possible! This is the essence of prayer – connecting with God in a personal and meaningful way. The entirety of the Christian life is built on this practice of interacting with God. However, God will often direct you to interact with others. (Remember the second part of Jesus' Great Commandment!) So, unless God gives you the particular calling to do so, your life doesn't have to be that of a monk who spends their entire day apart from people and the everyday rhythms of life. You still live a "normal" life; it's just one that is increasingly God-directed rather than being self-directed.

And our interactions (relationship) with God become the "fuel" that moves us forward healthily.

Understanding the importance of regular interaction with God does not automatically translate into practicing it. It is frequently a significant challenge for Christians to establish this spiritual discipline. Most believers I have known have struggled, often for years, with consistently connecting with God in meaningful and productive ways. The spiritual practice of regularly connecting with God will likely take many different forms over time, often requiring modification in some way. However, asking God to help you grow in the practice of connecting with Him and following His lead will ultimately lead to greater and greater success.

III. God's goal for your relationship with Him is to help you grow in faith and trust.

Many people think that if God exists, He is primarily concerned with our adherence to a stringent set of rules and practices. That mindset reduces Christianity to a form of slavery, where God "imposes" His will on you, restricting your freedom rather than developing a relationship with God that leads to a life of liberty and freedom.

> John 8: [31] To the Jews who had believed him, Jesus said, "If you hold to my teaching, you are really my disciples.
> [32] Then you will know the truth, and the truth will set you free."

It is indeed true that the principles God designed for living – ones that produce the "full" life – are different than the principles for living that you would embrace left to your own designs. In this sense, we must surrender a significant degree of self-will to follow God. However, a genuine relationship, characterized and motivated by love, produces a desire to please Him. So, rather than feeling duty-bound to force ourselves to obey God, **Christianity is an invitation to be transformed by a loving God who creates a "new" heart within us so that we are genuinely motivated to align our lives to the truths for living that God established at the beginning of time.**

> **Ezekiel 36:** [26] "I will give you a new heart and put a new spirit in you; I will remove from you your heart of stone and give you a heart of flesh. [27] And I will put my Spirit in you and move you to follow my decrees and be careful to keep my laws."

However, such a heart transformation only occurs as we spend time in His Presence and grow in faith and trust.

By definition, faith is believing in something for which there is no absolute proof. As I wrote in Appendix A: "The God Thing," we all hold many beliefs for which we have no proof. (Like believing that getting married and having children will automatically result in a happy and fulfilling life.) There may be *evidence* that leads us to embrace our beliefs, but definitive proof is often absent. **From a biblical perspective, growing in faith means becoming increasingly confident that everything God says is true.** The more confidence we have in God's truths, the more our faith grows. And that faith comes directly from our interactions (relationship) with God – seeing how He faithfully delivers on His promises.

Trust is a similar but slightly different idea. While faith is a belief that some statements or ideas are true, trust in someone means that we have confidence they will reliably care for something of value we place in their possession. **Trust in God means we are confident He will take care of everything we surrender to Him.** God's desire for us to trust Him with our entire lives means that He intends for us to have confidence that He will use everything that happens in our lives for our good.

> **Romans 8:** [28] And we know that God causes all things to
> work together for good to those who love God, to those
> who are called according to His purpose.

But we need faith to believe this statement is true. One of the primary reasons our relationship with God is so important is that it is through this relationship that we grow in both faith and trust. The more we believe that biblical standards are trustworthy, the more our faith grows. And the more we follow God's directives and see that our lives are better for following His leadership, the more our trust in God grows. As our relationship with God deepens, so does our confidence in the validity of God's truths (faith), and we become increasingly convinced that obeying God will yield beneficial outcomes for us (trust). That is why God's goal for our relationship with Him is to help us grow in faith and trust. And that is how our lives grow in meaning, purpose, and fulfillment, precisely what God desires.

> **Hebrews 11:** [6] And without faith it is impossible to please
> God, because anyone who comes to him must believe that
> he exists and that he rewards those who earnestly
> seek him.

> **Proverbs 3:** [5] Trust in the LORD with all your heart and do
> not lean on your own understanding. [6] In all your ways
> acknowledge Him, and He will make your paths straight.

IV. Solitude and Silence are essential processes for growth.

The premise of this book is that the "full" life – a life rich with meaning, purpose, and a deep sense of personal fulfillment – is one that God truly desires for us but is only experienced as we *follow Him*. Following God has two necessary components: first, we must adequately understand (discern) what God is asking us to do, and second, we must follow through (to the best of our ability) with whatever God asks us to do. So, following God relies on our relationship with Him because that is how we understand what He asks us to do at any given time. But I have also argued that the Bible (in its original languages) is the only source of objective truth and God's divinely inspired communication to and with humanity.

> 2 Timothy 3: [16] All Scripture is God-breathed and is useful
> for teaching, rebuking, correcting and training in right-
> eousness, [17] so that the servant of God may be thoroughly
> equipped for every good work.

The existence of biblical truths can sometimes make it difficult for us to understand what God is asking of us. Many people take biblical statements as "rules" that *must always be followed*. That viewpoint, I believe, frequently removes a genuine personal relationship with God from the picture because it causes us to think that we already know what we are supposed to do! But that is the same mistake made by the religious leaders of Jesus' day. They taught people that they must follow all 613 commandments. Instead, as Jesus communicated in the Great Commandment, the most essential thing in life is loving God (which speaks of relationship) rather than trying to "follow all the rules." Our relationship with God and our behavior are closely related. However, I would argue that **deepening *our relationship with God precedes obedience, rather than obedience leading to a deeper relationship with God.***

As we deepen our relationship with God, He transforms us in ways that enable us to live more closely aligned with biblical truths. *We cannot fully align our lives with God's ways unless He empowers us.* And that empowerment comes directly from Him as we connect with Him, on a personal level, and experience His Presence. So, the question needs to be, "How can I best connect with God on a personal level so that I can receive the wisdom concerning what He wants me to do and the power to follow through?"

There are many ways to personally "connect" with God. Prayer, worship, meditation, service, reading or memorizing scripture, and journaling are among the most common practices people utilize (spiritual disciplines) to connect with God. Although I have personally practiced these activities, there are two potential problems with creating such a list. First, we can begin to think (erroneously) that practicing these activities will get God to "do" what we want, which is the opposite of the goal. (We need to follow God's plans rather than trying to get God to follow ours!) The second potential problem is that we may get the idea that we are "earning" God's approval, rather than recognizing that God fully loves and accepts us just as we are, regardless of how we behave. So, it's possible to practice spiritual disciplines in a way that *fails* to connect us with God in meaningful ways. But these same activities can be very productive and meaningful when practiced with the right attitude, motivation, and understanding – to connect with God on a deep, personal level and receive whatever He desires to impart to us.

The two practices that have become most meaningful and helpful to me are solitude and silence. Solitude is simply the act of entering a "space" alone, coupled with the primary motivation to connect with God on a deeply personal level. Silence means eliminating as many sounds and visual distractions as possible that might divert your attention from connecting with God. When I first discovered the benefits of these practices, my primary place of solitude was sitting alone in my car in a large, empty parking lot very early in the morning before most people were awake and going about their daily activities. My goal as I practiced solitude and silence was to quiet my mind and emotions and create a "space" where I could focus on seeking God's Presence. I was *hungry* to connect with God and for Him to "speak" to me – to help me understand what He wanted to accomplish in and through my daily activities and plans.

Because I had come to understand that following God was the primary way God designed for us to live, my deepest desire was to understand what God specifically wanted me to do. While I knew that many issues in my life fell short of all God desired, I also knew I couldn't change everything at once. So, there needed to be priorities for these changes, and I believed that God had a "plan" for me to follow. Whatever that plan might be, I needed to receive direction from Him. I also understood that I could not make many of the changes God desired unless His power was released within me. In fact, some of the changes God desired to accomplish – especially changes of attitude and perspective – could only be done by God Himself. This realization of my deep need for connecting with God motivated me to make whatever changes were necessary to create this "space" in my life.

While I had long been *aware* of my need to connect with God more deeply, I lacked the motivation to make the necessary changes. It took many years before the motivation became strong enough to make the life changes required to create the "space" (time and location) necessary for connecting with Him deeply. I believe God used the many years of *trying* to connect with Him to change my heart and create the *hunger* to connect with Him on a deeper level.

I believe that's part of the spiritual journey for each of us. As we attempt to connect with God and fail to find sufficient fulfillment, He directs us to and through other experiences. The totality of those experiences helps to develop a deeper hunger for Him and motivates us to search for additional ways to know and love Him more. My journey led me to create a "space" in my car early each morning; your journey might look different. God may lead you to the beach, a forest, a walk around the block, or some other place that will become your "holy space." You need to allow God to guide you to a "space" where you can connect with Him deeply and personally to receive what you need to know and follow Him more fully. We each need to discover the "way" that can help us effectively practice solitude and silence, and God will guide and empower you if you seek His assistance.

However, it's essential to understand that it's not the "act" of solitude and silence that is important – it's what happens during that time that is most significant. As we learn to quiet our hearts and minds, God "fills" that space with Himself. God engages in a "conversation" with you (usually just thoughts in your mind or emotions that arise), where He brings to your recollection (past or current) experiences of your life. And throughout the "conversation" – the honest, back-and-forth exchanges between you and God – He purposefully weaves your thoughts and emotions.

God intends to transform your understanding of Him and yourself, your thinking patterns, and your feelings in such a way as to modify your mental and emotional framework. His main goal is for your life to become more aligned with the truths He established at the time of creation (Romans 12:2). Practicing times of solitude and silence is an essential component of God's design for living.

Psalms 23: [2] He makes me lie down in green pastures, he leads me beside quiet waters, [3] he refreshes my soul.

Isaiah 30: [15] "In repentance and rest is your salvation, in quietness and trust is your strength."

Psalms 46: [10] He says, "Be still, and know that I am God".

Luke 5: [16] But Jesus often withdrew to lonely places and prayed.

I have introduced several significant ideas in this chapter. If you feel somewhat overwhelmed and there is more you need to know about these ideas (as well as questions and concerns I haven't addressed), that's okay. My purpose in writing this chapter is twofold. First, I hope you've become aware that your current mental framework requires much attention to weed out false beliefs and discover critical new truths. Second, I hope God has awakened a hope within you that there might be much more to this "God thing" than you previously imagined. You're probably eager to learn more if I accomplish either of these objectives. I hope the following chapters will help answer many of your questions. However, seeking answers to essential questions *is precisely* the pattern of the spiritual journey God calls us to live.

Let me summarize the argument that I have been presenting thus far. At the beginning of time, God designed human life to be lived in partnership with Him. In much the same way as good parents desire to share their lives with their children, God, as our perfect Heavenly Father, desires to share His life with each of us. He is the source of all wisdom, power, and truth, and He wants to impart wisdom, understanding, courage, and strength to enable us to experience lives of deep meaning, purpose, and fulfillment. He genuinely desires that each of us would find joy and peace in all that we do. But for those amazing outcomes to be manifested, we must discover the secrets of how God designed life to be lived. And that wisdom and understanding, as well as the courage and strength we need to live by those truths, can only come from God Himself.

I share these truths to help you understand that the most

significant focus for our lives is to *follow God's leadership*. He is not only our Father but our counselor, protector, coach, comforter, friend, guide, and teacher. The Great Fall in the Garden of Eden severed the relationship between God and humankind. And because of that Fall, we are born cut off from our connection with God. During all the years we live separated from God, we develop many false beliefs about life. We each construct our own mental and emotional framework – a unique and personal set of beliefs and feelings about what we think is right, true, and good. Based on our framework, we strive to build a life that is meaningful, purposeful, and fulfilling. But we can never achieve the "full" life on our own. And that's because we will never experience a truly "full" life unless it conforms to the way God designed life to be lived. We can only discover all we need to know and do by learning how to connect with God and how to follow Him most effectively.

To follow God means to both seek His input – His "instruction" and "directions" for living – and implement (to the best of our ability) what He directs us to do. While much of our lives on earth are characterized by our own efforts, we must discover how we can best "connect" with God to receive the guidance and support we so desperately need. This means we are responsible for our lives while simultaneously wholly dependent on God. This might seem to be a contradiction, but it's one of the great paradoxes of life. *We are entirely dependent on God and simultaneously fully responsible for ordering and directing our own lives.* This is only one of the many truths God established for life that can only be learned and resolved with God's assistance.

What I have discovered on my own journey to know and follow God is that as I came to understand truths in four specific domains – and sought to live by those truths – my life grew exponentially in meaning, purpose, and fulfillment. The purpose of the next chapter is to explain these four areas of truth in a way that can aid you in your journey to know and follow God. But before we move on, I would like to share the most essential ingredient of a life that "follows God" – establishing your "initial connection" with Him.

The Bible teaches that we are born separated from a personal relationship with God. That separation was initiated by the Fall in the Garden of Eden and extends to each of us as we are born with the "self-will" to act as our own gods – deciding for ourselves what is right, true, and good. This self-will is sometimes called a "sin nature." On our own, we are all inclined to take charge of our own lives.

> **Romans 5:** [12] Therefore, just as sin entered the world through one man, and death through sin, and in this way, death came to all people, because all sinned.

The "death" that occurred was that of our **spirit** – the pathway through which God connects with us. And the "cure" for that condition – what reconnects us with God – is to be "born again."

> **John 3:** [5] Jesus answered, "Very truly I tell you, no one can enter the kingdom of God unless they are born of water and the Spirit. [6] Flesh gives birth to flesh, but the Spirit gives birth to spirit. [7] You should not be surprised at my saying, 'You must be born again.'"

To connect with God personally, we must each be born again (have our spirit come to life). The Bible explains that we are born again (saved) by following two steps. First, we need to believe that Jesus is the Son of God who came to earth to sacrifice His own life to pay the penalty for all sins for all time. Second, we must acknowledge our own sins, ask Jesus for His forgiveness, and express our desire to know and follow Him.

Romans 10: [9] If you declare with your mouth, "Jesus is Lord," and believe in your heart that God raised him from the dead, you will be saved. [10] For it is with your heart that you believe and are justified, and it is with your mouth that you profess your faith and are saved.

So, the first step in your ability to connect with God on a personal level is to be born again (saved). If you have not already been born again, your journey must begin with addressing what separates you from completing the steps outlined above. If you believe that Jesus is the Son of God who came to forgive the sin that separates you from God, all you need to do is ask Him to forgive you and express your desire to know and follow Him. If you lack the faith necessary to make that commitment, your journey must begin by finding meaningful answers to the questions or concerns that prevent you from having faith in Jesus and surrendering to His leadership. (You might need to refer to "The God Thing" in Appendix A for assistance in that journey.)

If serious doubts persist, I hope these opening chapters have provided a sufficient rational foundation to motivate you to resolve the questions or issues that prevent you from declaring faith in Jesus. But if you already believe God is real, that Jesus is God's Son sent to pay the penalty for your sins, that the Bible is God's Word sent to help you discover and understand truth, and you desire to know and follow God, then you are ready to proceed! The information presented in this next section (Part 2) is designed to provide a framework to find meaningful answers to the important questions about God, His ways, and how you can find more significant meaning, purpose, and fulfillment.

Part Two

Preparing for Departure

After selecting and paying for your cruise vacation, you usually have several weeks before you board the cruise ship. During this time, you can research the ship you will sail on and the ports you will visit on your journey. You might consider questions like: "What entertainment activities and eating venues are available while I'm onboard the ship?" "Where is the pool located in relation to my cabin?" "What vacation activities, excursions, and eating establishments are in each port city? Any knowledge you gain from this research before departure will help ensure your journey is optimally peaceful and enjoyable. Similarly, before departing on "The Great Adventure" of Following God, gaining additional knowledge about the faith journey will be extremely helpful.

In Part 2, I will present a framework to help you process the many experiences you will encounter as you seek to know and follow God. Specifically, I will present four Essential Questions that will serve as a "filter" for processing your significant life experiences – past, present, and future. The knowledge and understanding you gain as you find meaningful answers to each of these Essential Questions will serve two extremely significant purposes.

1. You will gain insight, understanding, and wisdom about how God designed life to be lived.
2. You will experience an ever-increasing sense of meaning, purpose, and fulfillment.

Chapter 5
How We Process Life

God, in His infinite wisdom, recognizes that our thinking greatly influences who we are and how we live. Therefore, He places significant attention on transforming the way we think.

> **Isaiah 1:** [18] "Come now, and let us reason together," says the LORD. (NASB)

> **Romans 12:** [2] Do not conform to the pattern of this world, but be transformed by the renewing of your mind. Then you will be able to test and approve what God's will is—his good, pleasing and perfect will.

> **1 Corinthians 14:** [20] Brothers and sisters, stop thinking like children. In regard to evil be infants, but in your thinking be adults.

Before exploring the four Essential Questions and their role in finding meaning, purpose, and fulfillment, I would like to explain how our thinking progresses from simple to more complex, or from less to more mature. I have come to realize that my thinking shifts between four distinct levels of reasoning as I respond to life's experiences and challenges. Recognizing this hierarchy of thinking can help you better process your thoughts and feelings. It is also worth noting that the highest levels of spiritual growth and transformation occur at Levels 3 and 4. However, most people – even Christians – typically operate at Levels 1 and 2. In the following explanation, I will interchangeably use various terms such as thinking, questioning, reasoning, and rationality.

Levels of Rationality

Level 1 thinking (reasoning) happens naturally throughout each day. "What should I wear?" "What's the weather going to be like?" "I wonder how bad traffic will be on my morning commute?" "What should I plan for dinner?" Thousands of questions like these come to mind automatically as we go about our day. However, Level 1 thinking can also be caused by our emotions when we face life situations. "I hate that she did that; how can I get even with her?" "I wonder why he's acting like that?" "What's *his* problem?" Our minds automatically respond to many life events by creating questions that often steer our reactions. The thoughts that come to mind in response to these questions often determine our actions. In general, Level 1 reasoning is just reacting instinctively from our "gut." Depending on our emotional, mental, and spiritual maturity, or our current mood, our "gut" reaction can range from fairly "ugly" to socially acceptable. When you find yourself functioning on "autopilot," you are using Level 1 rationality. But sometimes a "filter" kicks in and you wonder how you *should* respond. That shift, when it occurs, moves you to Level 2 thinking.

Level 2 reasoning often happens when we realize that we are motivated to react to a situation in ways we suspect might not be suitable. For example, we know from experience that when strong emotions like anger, fear, frustration, or jealousy surface, they can cause us to act in ways we will later regret. Based on these experiences, people often pause when they start feeling intense negative emotions to consider whether a more reasonable response might be better. Level 2 reasoning involves living by a "life principle." Life principles are personal beliefs about how life works – or *should* work. Our families and culture reinforce these principles by emphasizing certain behaviors as "acceptable." For Christians, most sermons focus on one or more biblical truths (principles) that should guide our actions. Replacing behaviors driven by your "gut" feelings with ones aligned with biblical truths shows spiritual growth – a shift from living a self-focused life to striving for a more God-centered life.

The more we read, understand, and desire to follow the Bible, the more our actions will reflect our understanding of biblical truths. The more often we practice Level 2 thinking, the better we become at living in accordance with those truths. However, as we grow in our faith, we realize that God cares more about our **relationship with Him** than our behavior. The desire to truly "know" God and connect with Him personally motivates us to progress to Level 3 thinking. (Before we move on to the next level of thinking, I want to mention that non-Christians and less mature Christians rarely go beyond Level 2 thinking. They are often stuck trying to simply align their behavior with a set of "standards" they have accepted as "true" or "right.")

As Christians become more aware of biblical truths – by reading Scripture, attending a biblically "healthy" church, interacting with mature Christians, and other biblically sound practices – they become aware that God desires a personal relationship with them. This awareness prompts them to begin the process of personally and intentionally reaching out to God in the search for a deeper understanding of who He is and how they should plan and live their lives. The change from "rules-based" reasoning to a God-focused "relationship-based" reasoning initiates Level 3 thinking. **Level 3 thinking should become the "heartbeat" of life for a Christian!** (Non-Christians are incapable of engaging in Level 3 thinking due to their lack of a relationship with God, which is established when one is born again.)

Level 3 thinking involves a three-step process as we try to interact with God on a personal level.

Step 1: "Switching" your focus from yourself to God and directly asking Him what He wants you to do.

Step 2: Pausing until some "answer" is received.

Step 3: Obeying (to the best of your ability) whatever you believe God is directing you to do.

Although this may seem like a simple and quick process, it can sometimes take several months to complete all three steps for a particular issue or life experience. For example, before we are ready to receive God's "answer" about what He wants us to do in response to a conflict with someone (Step 2), we often need to work through several powerful feelings "attached" to that conflict, often from past relational disputes. It will be hard for us to understand (discern) what God is guiding us to do until we have properly addressed these past issues. Only then can we receive God's direction with calmness and humility. Sometimes we need to ask a trusted friend for help or wait for God to "walk us" through more life experiences before we can fully understand and accept His guidance. Obeying (Step 3) can also be very difficult, and we often fail, which leads us to return to God (Step 1) to process the feelings that come from our failure to fully follow His previous instructions! Unfortunately, many Christians only use Level 3 reasoning as a "last resort" when they feel overwhelmed. *However, when Level 3 reasoning is practiced regularly, it leads to enhanced spiritual growth and transformation because we are interacting directly with God Himself and following His plans!*

As we become more spiritually mature, we begin to realize that the ongoing process of reflecting on our thoughts and feelings with God is a crucial part of how He transforms us. Every moment we spend seeking God's guidance and support and aiming to follow His leadership strengthens our relationship with Him, and God increases our capacity to love Him. An encouraging result of these interactions with God (Level 3 thinking) is that we find greater meaning and purpose in our lives. We notice ourselves spending more time interacting with God and experiencing deeper levels of joy as He transforms our thoughts and, in turn, how we live. We also start to feel more fulfilled as God guides our lives. Still, we can reach even higher levels of meaning, purpose, and fulfillment by directing our thoughts toward **Level 4** reasoning.

Using Level 1 and 2 reasoning, we rely only on our own resources; with Level 3 reasoning, we turn to God and are open to receiving His guidance and resources. However, in all three levels, we are reacting to a life situation or circumstance – we are functioning from our own agenda. **In Level 4 reasoning, we rely on God to set the agenda!** Level 4 rationality is best experienced in silence and solitude.

In Chapter 4, I explained that God's main goal for you is to build a deep, personal relationship with Him. It's important to realize that relationships grow closer and more intimate as people spend time together, sharing thoughts, feelings, and experiences. The same principle applies to our relationship with God. **Level 4 Rationality involves spending time with God, allowing Him to direct and guide our interaction.** The best way to do this is to set aside an extended period (15 to 45 minutes or more) with the specific purpose of letting God steer our thoughts. Sometimes, God will lead us to worship Him; other times, He will direct our attention to a past or present situation where He wants to give us insight or guidance. Sometimes, God will reveal aspects of our current mental or emotional framework to help us make needed changes. When we give God the chance to "set the agenda," He moves in ways that are vital for our ongoing growth and transformation. **Practicing Level 4 Rationality results in the greatest spiritual growth and change because you focus on God's priorities for your life!**

As Christians increase their capacity to understand God's ways and seek to follow them, they acquire an ever-growing mountain of knowledge. However, large amounts of information can often create confusion and frustration if we cannot organize and synthesize the information we accumulate into a structured knowledge base. The Bible uses the term *wisdom* to denote the process of synthesizing knowledge into a usable framework for guiding decision-making. Scripture challenges us to connect with God to grow in understanding and wisdom.

> **1 Kings 3:** [9] So give Your servant an understanding heart ...
> to discern between good and evil.

> **Proverbs 2:** [6] For the LORD gives wisdom; from His mouth
> come knowledge and understanding.

> **James 1:** [5] If any of you lacks wisdom, you should ask God,
> who gives generously to all without finding fault, and it will
> be given to you.

But the "full life" – the life Jesus came to enable us to experience – involves much more than merely "controlling" our responses to daily life experiences. In addition to finding meaning, purpose, and fulfillment in our daily activities and experiences, God desires that we experience those same blessings in a "global" way – that the entirety of our lives would be richly and "fully" rewarding!

Jeremiah 29: [11] For I know the plans that I have for you,' declares the LORD, 'plans for welfare and not for calamity to give you a future and a hope.'

Proverbs 10: [22] It is the blessing of the LORD that makes rich, and He adds no sorrow to it.

Isaiah 35: [2] They will see the glory of the LORD, the majesty of our God. ... [7] The scorched land will become a pool and the thirsty ground springs of water ... [8] A highway will be there, a roadway, and it will be called the Highway of Holiness.

This last passage speaks to God's vision for the lives of "His people" – those who choose to know and follow Him. The "full life" Jesus spoke of in John 10:10 is lived on a "highway" – a *"high way"* of living – a life with meaning, purpose, and fulfillment that progressively develops as we seek to understand and live according to God's ways. And God's "ways" include – and are based on – knowing, loving, and following Him on a deeply personal level. That approach to life leads to maximum joy, peace, and gladness of heart. I have spent the past 40+ years doing my best to know and follow God. As my knowledge of God and His ways increased (often through my own failures), I frequently felt frustrated by my inability to synthesize all the information into a coherent and understandable whole. However, despite my frustrations, I persevered despite being unable to accomplish that task.

Over time, my life became increasingly God-centered and

grew in meaning, purpose, and personal fulfillment. (In all honesty, I can still be a jerk sometimes; it just seems to happen less frequently!) In the several months preceding my retirement from teaching and ministry, I wondered what my life might "look like" in this next chapter. I began reflecting on all God had helped me understand and how He supernaturally changed me over time. God helped me see that all the knowledge He revealed and helped me process "fit" nicely into four categories. He also helped me realize that as the amount of knowledge and understanding increased within and among these four categories, and I aligned my life accordingly, the overall levels of meaning, purpose, and fulfillment I experienced also increased! All the information about God and His ways fit nicely as "answers" to four specific questions. **Reflecting on these questions is an important part of Level 4 thinking. These are the most important questions in life!**

1. Who is God?
2. How Has God Designed Life to Be Lived?
3. Who Am I? (And Who Does God Want Me to Become?)
4. What is God Calling Me to Do?

As you reflect on these *Essential Questions*, find the "right" answers, and allow God to use those insights to guide your life, you will ***supernaturally experience increasingly deeper levels of meaning, purpose, and personal fulfillment.*** The rest of Part 2 (Chapters 6-10) will be focused on developing a deeper understanding of these Essential Questions. However, before moving forward, let me share an example of how I have seen my mind "navigate" between the four levels of rationality.

Near the end of my teaching career, the education bureaucracy in America began pushing for the implementation of "Common Core Math." (Before proceeding, I sincerely apologize if the reference to mathematics causes you any anxiety. I also want to apologize for any embarrassment or other mistreatment you may have suffered at the hands of math teachers in the past. Try to suppress all those feelings generated from your problems with mathematics throughout your life – or schooling in general – and turn your focus, instead, to the explanation of how my thinking moved between the four levels of rationality!)

As a trained professional with over 40 years of experience teaching mathematics at various levels, I recognized that many aspects of the Common Core "movement" were problematic for the teaching and learning of mathematics. However, my building principal and district administrators (who had almost no knowledge of teaching and learning mathematics) thought it was a great idea and pushed for full implementation of every-thing the "experts" suggested. In the minds of my "superiors" (perhaps because they never really experienced much success in mathematics), the Common Core initiative would help students better understand and learn mathematics. Because I knew better, my immediate reaction was to resist, and I did so, first in dialogue with my principal and later at the district level. Not surprisingly, this created great conflict – within me, and with my superiors.

The conflicts that arose generated many strong feelings and caused me to spend a great deal of time deciding how to respond to the challenges I faced. First, I needed to pay attention to the strong negative emotions I discovered rising in my heart. My anger, resentment, and disgust prompted numerous thoughts about how foolish my superiors were and how I might be able to exert greater influence over the proposed changes. I wondered how I might show them how ignorant it would be to unthinkingly implement strategies and curricula pushed by people they didn't even know. I automatically started to think: "How can I show them their lack of understanding and the errors in their reasoning?" "How can I find ways to help them understand how the changes that are being suggested violate basic principles of how students learn mathematics?"

Since these questions arose from strong negative emotions, I knew I was looking for ways to embarrass my superiors and "help" them understand how stupid they were! *This was Level 1 thinking*, and I instinctively knew that any decision arising from these strong negative emotions would likely be unproductive and probably cause further damage to my relationships with my superiors. I'm embarrassed to admit it, but I sometimes allowed Level 1 thinking to influence my behavior. *This awareness caused me to shift to Level 2 thinking.* What are the "rules" that govern relationships? What kinds of behaviors and attitudes (on my part) would please God and be more likely to result in positive outcomes? I recall pondering many questions like these for a long time before I realized I was still processing these issues in a less-than-mature way. I was focusing on the "small picture" and ignoring the reality that many problems in life were more important than how students were taught mathematics. I was focusing almost exclusively on my concerns rather than on God's. I was guilty of "seeing the trees but not the forest" – and both were important! *This new awareness prompted me to move my thinking to Levels 3 and 4.*

From the perspective of my *actions*, I would ask God *Level 3 questions* like, "What's the best way for me to point out potential problems (with a given proposal) in a way that demonstrates both personal as well as professional respect for my superiors?" "What are my responsibilities as both a math teacher and a department chairperson, and how can I fulfill those responsibilities in a way that honors You?" Those are just two examples of the Level 3 questions I began processing with God, each time navigating all three processing steps. *As I pondered the issues I faced, many Level 4 questions surfaced.* "What do these strong negative emotions tell me about who I am?" "How does my teaching mathematics fit into my life calling as a Christian and my personal calling to help people

82

discover how God is at work in their lives?" "What can these experiences teach me about how God designed the superior-subordinate relationship to best function?" "Are subordinates supposed to submit to their superiors blindly, or is there a responsibility for the subordinate to be more involved in the decision-making process?" "How might a subordinate effectively appeal to an authority figure and provide information the superior may not be aware of or understand?" "When I see all You allow to happen – to me, my students, the American educational establishment, etc. – what does that teach me about Your character? Your plans?" "What does all I am experiencing in this situation tell me about Your plan for me?" These are examples of Level 4 questions I often pondered and continue to reflect on today.

I would often see myself fluctuating between the four levels of rationality, moment by moment and day by day, depending on "where my head was" at any given time. I hope this example helps you better understand the four levels of thinking and how one might "navigate" between them. In my experience, the most effective way to process Level 3 and Level 4 questions is during extended periods of solitude and silence. For the last ten years of my teaching career, I would spend between 30 and 60 minutes every school-day morning parked in my car in a large, empty parking lot about a quarter mile from the school where I taught. Those times in solitude each day contributed profoundly to my transformation and spiritual growth. *Times of solitude and silence continue to be the "best" part of every day for me, producing the highest levels of meaning, purpose, and fulfillment!*

Before moving on, I should point out a **5th Level of Rationality** (consciousness might be a better term) that transcends the other four levels of thinking. This 5th level of consciousness – *experiencing God's Presence* – occurs when your spirit is awakened to the realization that God is present with you and desires to "connect" with you on a deeply intimate level. This 5th level of "consciousness" only occurs if you pause and allow God to "draw near to you" (James 4:8 – "Draw near to God and He will draw near to you.). As you "suspend" thinking (put your mind in "neutral") and just wait for God, He will often "break through" in a powerful way. Sometimes you'll be overwhelmed by His Presence and weep as He releases mercy, compassion, and grace, ministering to you on a deeply personal level. At other times, God will "implant" a deeper, more wholistic understanding of an important issue you are attempting to resolve, or a deeper understanding of who He is or who you are.

In whatever way God "reveals" Himself, you'll walk away from the experience with greater confidence, peace, and hope. These kinds of experiences happen to me, mostly during solitude or deep worship. But God has sometimes broken through like this while I was driving my car or doing laundry! The goal – always, always, always – is to seek Him to the best of your ability. Everything that occurs after that depends entirely on Him. As you continue to do your best to know and follow God (which is all anyone can do), you will find yourself more quickly (and with greater frequency) directing your thoughts toward God rather than relying on your own capabilities, functioning more frequently at Levels 3 and 4 in your thinking. As you see it occurring in your life, recognize it as a mark of a deepening spirituality! The following five chapters will help you better understand each of the Level 4 Essential Questions and how the "right" answers to these questions will grow your life in meaning, purpose, and fulfillment.

Chapter 6
Essential Question
#1: Who is God?

Overview: Essential Life Questions

The deepest levels of learning occur as we reflect on our life experiences. You've probably heard the saying that "hindsight is always 20-20". That is, we see and understand life experiences more clearly as we "look back" on issues that have occurred in our past. That's probably because we can "look back" more objectively – when strong emotions are tempered or removed from our experiences – and we are (hopefully) wiser and more mature. Developing the habit of reflecting on the critical issues and significant events in your life is a wise practice. It has been my experience that times of reflection have produced the most profound learnings, especially in finding the "right" answers to the Essential Questions (Level 4 Thinking). I recommend the following process.

As you reflect on a given experience, use the Essential Questions as a "filter" for learning. Ask God, "What do You want this experience to teach me about You?" "What life principles can I discover?" "What do my reactions to this experience – past and present – teach me about myself?" "How do You want me to respond to this?" Virtually every life experience is "pregnant," with the possibility of gaining essential knowledge and understanding. And when you reflect on emotionally charged experiences from your past, you open the door to healing and closure, guided by God's Grace.

I'd like you to consider these four Essential Questions as separate *containers* of knowledge (see Figure 6-1).

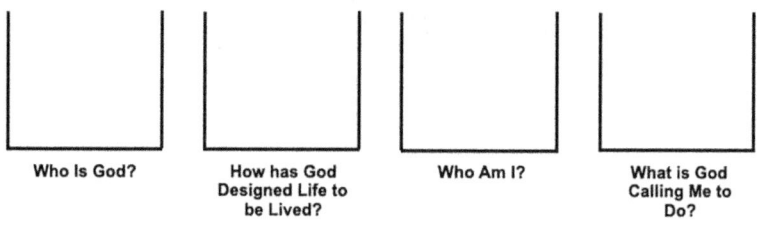

| Who Is God? | How has God Designed Life to be Lived? | Who Am I? | What is God Calling Me to Do? |

Figure 6-1: The 4 Essential Questions

As you reflect on past or present life experiences and engage in the four-step Level 4 thinking process previously outlined, God will reveal important insights that will become "answers" to one or more of these questions. In your mind, "sort" the insights God provides into one or more of these four containers. Over time, the amount of information in these areas will increase significantly. As the amount of information expands, allow the Holy Spirit to direct your mind to search for synthesis among the various pieces of information within each container. This practice will enable you to discover valuable *life principles* within each container. Additionally, as the Holy Spirit guides you, allow your mind to search for synthesis amongst the four containers. You will experience an increased sense of direction, meaning, and purpose as you allow the Holy Spirit to accomplish these synthesizing tasks. And as your thoughts, plans, and actions are guided by these insights and understandings, you will also experience an ever-increasing sense of fulfillment.

Even though the growth of meaning, purpose, and fulfillment unfolds supernaturally, the process is not something "magical." The development of these powerful life experiences has a rational foundation. The more we engage in Level 3 and Level 4 thinking, the more each life experience becomes pregnant with the potential for significant meaning and purpose. If the insights gained enable you to better understand and surrender to God's leadership, then all your life experiences can contribute to your future, bringing you ever closer to fulfilling God's unique purposes for your life. This is how meaning, purpose, and fulfillment grow as we find answers to these Essential Life Questions and allow them to guide our lives. *And this is how the singular life focus to "know and follow God" causes everything of value in life to unfold.*

Given this brief outline of the role of these four questions in helping us to know and follow God, I also want to communicate why these Essential Questions are vitally important. When I came to faith at the age of 29, the commitment I made at that time was to seek to know and follow the truth, wherever it might lead me. My faith then was that God was real and that He had created everything that I had come to accept as real. Influenced by my upbringing in Catholicism, I began with the idea that God was all-knowing (omniscient) and all-powerful (omnipotent).

In Appendix A: "The God Thing," I explain my early journey to believe that God was real. My confession of faith (that is, accepting Jesus' sacrifice on the cross for the forgiveness of my sins – my failure to follow what I really believed to be *right* – and seeking to surrender to God's leadership in my life) was just the next step in my spiritual journey. At that time, I believed that if God was powerful enough to have created all of life, He certainly was worth knowing and following. If God is powerful enough to create the "heavens and the earth," it would be stupid to ignore *anything* He might have to say! My previous 29 years of life experience taught me that ignoring people with great power and knowledge can only lead to disappointing outcomes. If for no other reason than self-preservation, I should at least listen to what God might have to *say* about life!

I pressed on in my journey to understand and follow what was right and true to the best of my ability, but this time, I sought God's assistance and guidance. My journey quickly brought me to explore the Bible and the Church. I began reading the New Testament (Phillips Translation), starting with the Gospel of Matthew and reading my way through to the end of the Book of Revelations. While many issues were confusing – some even seemed to be contradictory – my overwhelming response was that God's Word was *true*! I came to realize this Book contains words of wisdom and truth! The more I learned, the more I became convinced that the Bible (in its original languages) is the *inspired* Word of God and must serve as the foundation upon which all truths are to be examined and understood.

> **2 Timothy 3:** [16] All Scripture is God-breathed and is useful for teaching, rebuking, correcting and training in right-eousness.

As I acknowledged earlier, the accumulation of knowledge and understanding often became confusing as I tried to organize and synthesize all I was coming to believe was true. Only in the past year or so (after 40+ years of trying to know and follow God) have I realized the significance of the four Essential Questions. In the remaining chapters of Part 2 that follow, I aim for you to understand the *essence* and *importance* of these four questions, and *not* to provide all the answers. ***Finding answers to these Essential Life Questions is the journey God asks YOU to take with Him.*** As you follow God's leadership – and attempt to do what God asks you to do to the best of your ability (Level 3 thinking) – He will teach you an incalculable number of truths. As you organize and synthesize these truths among the four Essential Questions (Level 4 thinking) – and allow them to influence how you live – you will experience an ever-growing sense of meaning, purpose, and fulfillment! Now, let's explore those questions!

Essential Question #1: Who is God?

It seems a bit presumptuous even to ask such a question. If God can create everything we understand to be real, then He is undoubtedly unlike anything or anyone we have ever known. How can one really *know* someone or something that is so entirely different? With these thoughts in mind, I embark on the journey to find answers to this first Essential Question with humility, a little fear, and the recognition that I will probably never fully comprehend the magnitude of His Being.

> **Romans 11:**[33] Oh, the depth of the riches of the wisdom
> and knowledge of God! How unsearchable his judgments,
> and his paths beyond tracing out.

Despite the limitations that may be present in our search, we are still encouraged to know Him.

> **Jeremiah 9:** [23] This is what the LORD says: "Let not the
> wise boast of their wisdom or the strong boast of their
> strength or the rich boast of their riches, [24] but let the one
> who boasts boast about this: that they have the under-
> standing to know me, that I am the LORD, who exercises
> kindness, justice and righteousness on earth, for in these I
> delight," declares the LORD.

> **Philippians 3:** [10] I want to know Christ – yes, to know the

power of his resurrection and participation in his sufferings, becoming like him in his death.

Proverbs 8: [17] I love those who love me, and those who seek me find me.

Essential Question #1 is designed to discover answers that will help us know God similarly to how we come to know others. This question does not seek to understand what it means to be God, that is, how God is different from His creation. Neither is it seeking to understand what "life" might be like on God's plane of existence. Those might be interesting questions, but they are distractions from genuinely wanting to comprehend what it means to know and follow God.

Asking the question "Who is God?" is born out of a deep desire to experience a genuine relationship with Him: Does God have feelings like mine? What does God think or feel about me? Does God get angry? If so, what makes Him angry? Does God act differently when He is angry versus when He is pleased? What makes God sad? What are God's goals for humankind? For me? Any information that would help you understand another person is the same type of information that can assist you in better understanding who God is.

This first essential question is also motivated by a desire to *live out* the "Greatest Commandment" that Jesus identified in **Matthew 22:**

[37] Jesus replied: "'Love the Lord your God with all your heart and with all your soul and with all your mind.' [38] This is the first and greatest commandment."

We are called to develop an all-encompassing, loving relationship with God. The Essential Question, "Who is God?" is designed to provide answers that will help us understand God in a way that will enable us to enter more fully into a loving relationship with Him.

A simple "Google search" would provide many insightful answers to this Essential Question, but such a search would not be a truly fruitful process for two crucial reasons. First, the goal is not to arrive at a cognitive (or academic) understanding of God. Instead, this question (as well as the remaining three Essential Questions) is designed to elicit insights contributing to a holistic spiritual, intellectual, emotional, and relational *connection* with God. Each "right" answer you discover – answers God *leads* you to – should derive from a sense of being drawn closer to God. The second way this search is unlike most other learning experiences is that you must *own* each answer. These answers are not merely pieces of information that might become lost or misplaced. These learnings become a part of you, and that occurs because the insights come directly from experiences that *connect* you with God – they emerge out of your own life experiences as you search for meaningful answers from God Himself.

If I were to provide some of my answers to the question, "Who is God?" I would rattle off a list of descriptors, such as 'He is good, kind, and loving.' He is my protector, provider, teacher, and guide. He comforts, consoles, strengthens, and encourages me. Each of these descriptors is supported by scripture, but neither the list of virtues nor the scripture references are what makes those attributes of ultimate value. *What is of primary importance is that God has demonstrated Himself to actually be each of these things in my life.* God has comforted me, God has encouraged me, and God has carried me when I didn't know if I could go on. God has embodied each of these descriptors – and many more – and that *experiential knowledge is what matters*. That's how I *own* my understanding of who God is, rather than just being intellectually aware of some reliable information about Him. And that's how you must find answers to each of the Essential Questions. While there are many ways to gain *experiential knowledge* of God's identity, I will provide three examples.

The first example is illustrated through the experience of reflecting on scripture reading. Over the past several months, my devotional readings have included Old Testament stories of God's interactions with the Nation of Israel. Without recounting those stories here, I will list some questions that popped into my mind as I read. Among these readings, I noted the period between God's first call to Abraham (Genesis 12) and when God changed Jacob's name to Israel and began "building" the 12 "tribes" (Genesis 32), which was roughly 200 years. I wondered why it took God so long to move in this way. Later, I noted that the Nation of Israel was enslaved in Egypt for about 400 years. Why, I wondered, would God allow His people to suffer for so long before freeing them? What do these and other examples teach me about God's timing? His patience? Does He care when people are suffering? What, if anything, is He *doing* during this period of time?

Additionally, when I considered the transition of God's leadership over Israel from using judges (1 Samuel) to anointing their first king (Saul), why would God grant His people's desire for a king when that wasn't what He genuinely wanted for His people? (See 1 Samuel, Chapter 8) Later, I thought about how God removed His anointing from Saul and anointed David in Saul's place (but did not *make* David king at that time). Why would God allow so much time to transpire before allowing Saul to be killed in a battle so David could take his rightful place as king? These and many additional questions all caused me to reflect on the Essential Question, "Who is God?". As God gave me insights, additional truths were added to that *container* in my mind. These are just a few examples of how reading scripture can aid in finding meaningful answers to the Essential Question, "Who is God?"

The second example of how one can develop experiential

knowledge of God's identity is by reflecting on events as they unfold in the world around us. As I write these words, we are just beginning to come out of an extended period of "lockdown" associated with the COVID-19 coronavirus pandemic of 2020. Except for "essential services," the entirety of the American economy has been shuttered for approximately two months (so far). During this time, it is unclear how many people might die from the virus, as well as what the financial consequences might be. The American government has spent several trillion dollars to support the vast number of people who are currently unemployed, as well as the many businesses that have closed and may never reopen. Throughout this time, I wondered how God views America and the world. Why would God allow such a destructive virus to be released? Is this God's judgment? Is God "finished" with America? Is this the consequence of millions of abortions and America's drifting away from God? Is this the beginning of the "end times"? Each thought and the insight God provided added information to the "Who is God?" container. So, using Level 4 reasoning regarding current life events is a second way to gain experiential knowledge of God's identity.

The third and most impactful example of how one gains experiential knowledge of God's identity is through reflecting on personal life experiences. The more significant a given life experience is to you personally, the more profound the learning will be for you. When our deepest thoughts, emotions, and motivations are brought into the light of God's Presence, we enter into an exchange with the potential for extreme levels of insight, wisdom, and transformation. One such incident occurred for me in July of 1985. I had just completed my first year of ministry experience as a youth pastor and serving as the founding principal of the K-12 church school we had launched. It was an incredibly hard yet fulfilling and thoroughly exhilarating year. Not only did I enjoy being invited into an extremely meaningful ministry experience, but we also just started our family in June of the previous year with the birth of our first child. When you add the excitement and challenges of starting a family, moving into a new home, and launching a new career, it was almost overwhelming in every positive way!

When we were just days away from our first family vacation, our 13-month-old daughter began to exhibit flu-like symptoms. My wife took her to our pediatrician, who prescribed some over-the-counter medications to deal with the fever and encouraged her to consume plenty of liquids. However, a few days later, our baby seemed to be getting worse rather than better. My wife and I returned to see our pediatrician. This time, when he looked into our daughter's eyes, the doctor turned to us and said, "This is something serious; head over to the hospital. I'll call ahead for them to reserve a room for you, and I'll meet you there shortly." Those were the scariest words we had ever heard. (I'm emotionally overwhelmed just recounting this incident.)

We drove the short distance to our local hospital and, upon entering, provided our names, which led to our being escorted into a small, private examination room. We knew this was very serious based on our doctor's tone. My wife immediately sensed we needed prayer support and left me alone with our daughter as she searched for a public phone to call some of our closest friends and ask them to pray for our baby and us. (Cell phones were not in existence at this time.) As I stood there alone, holding our very sick little girl, scenes from the past many months flashed through my mind. I recalled the excitement of my wife's pregnancy and the many times I had read to my child as she was growing within my wife's womb. I remembered our hopes and dreams; I recalled the excitement of her birth and all the "wins" during her first year of life. I remembered her learning how to turn over, crawl, stand up, begin to take her first steps, and even speak her first words. All those thoughts and dreams filled my heart and mind as I held my sick baby, wondering what was about to unfold.

As I quieted my mind, the thought entered: "God, would you take our baby?" "Is it really possible that you might remove this great blessing from our lives?" After a quiet moment, I sensed the Holy Spirit asking me in return, "If I did take her, would you still love and serve Me?" "Would you still believe that I am a loving and caring God even if I were to take your baby from you?" After another pause – I'm not sure how long it took – I remember responding, "Well, I know she would be better off with You than with me. So, if it is Your will to take our little girl, then yes, I will not allow the outcome of this experience to undermine my commitment to know, love, serve, and follow You. I will still confess that You are a kind, compassionate, and loving Father."

Those interactions with God during that very tender time solidified something deep within my heart. I probably failed to capture it adequately, but God's dealings with me were tender, sweet, and comforting during those moments. Through those interactions, as well as the three weeks our baby spent in the hospital recovering, and the months and years that followed in dealing with the deafness caused by our daughter's battle with spinal meningitis, God has only further shown Himself to be a kind, loving, compassionate, and faithful Heavenly Father. That's the kind of experiential knowledge we seek when we ask the Essential Question, "Who is God?" That is also the kind of experiential knowledge we desire as we search for answers to the other three Essential Life Questions.

Let me close this chapter with these thoughts: We wish to achieve two critical goals in finding answers to Essential Question #1: Who is God?

1. We want the insights we gain to aid us in connecting with God in ever-increasingly personal ways, and allow

these Divine interactions to bring about all the
transformation God desires to accomplish within us.

2. We want the insights we gain to transform how we
interact with others, especially those with whom we
interact most deeply and frequently.

These two goals also apply to the remaining three Essential
Questions. The next chapter will examine Essential Question #2:
"How has God Designed Life to be Lived?" We will search for
God's foundational principles for our spiritual, psychological,
relational, social, and emotional well-being. The more we discover
about who God is, the easier it will be for us to embrace the idea
that God has established truths upon which ALL of life is to be
lived! And integrating these truths into our lives will provide
increasing stability and peace, and contribute to the growth of
meaning, purpose, and fulfillment.

Chapter 7
Essential Question #2: How has God Designed Life to be Lived?

When one considers the existence of God and His rightful claim as the ultimate authority over everything He has created, one obvious conclusion is that we, as part of His creation, should yield to His authority. Every subordinate intuitively understands the need to submit to the leadership of superiors. So, submitting to God – the ultimate authority – is a no-brainer. But what is it, exactly, that God desires from us? How am I supposed to order and direct my life? Given that the Bible is God's revelation of Himself to humankind, it seems reasonable to search Scripture to gain insights into God's plans for His creation. The challenge, however, is that the Bible is not organized like the user manuals or textbooks we are used to studying. Discovering biblical truths requires a unique approach. This investigative methodology is also how we learn most about life – by searching for logical connections between and among the things we see and experience.

The Bible is a compilation of 66 relatively short books – including historical accounts, poems, songs, personal letters, religious instructions, and prophesies – penned by approximately 40 different writers over about 1300 years. Due to its unique composition, one often needs to read substantial portions of text to gain insights, searching for threads of commonality and then synthesizing the information to grasp a given principle or truth. I am convinced that God's intention behind this design will soon become clear. As I've journeyed through the entire Bible numerous times, the central theme of scripture, from start to finish, is encapsulated in one straightforward life objective: to know and follow God. Moses articulated this principle when he gave the Nation of Israel their "marching orders" before his passing. As with many biblical truths, this statement is not limited to the Nation of Israel but applies to each of us individually.

> **Deuteronomy 28:** [1] If you fully obey the LORD your God and carefully follow all his commands I give you today, the LORD your God will set you high above all the nations on earth. [2] All these blessings will come on you and accompany you if you obey the LORD your God.

Most of the Old Testament is a historical account of God's interactions with His people, the Nation of Israel. One pattern emerges repeatedly: when Israel sought to follow God, they prospered and lived in peace, and when they strayed from following God (especially worshipping other gods), they suffered all sorts of harm. When Jesus came on the scene, He also reinforced this central idea of following God.

> **Matthew 4:** [4] Jesus answered, "It is written: 'Man shall not live on bread alone, but on every word that comes from the mouth of God.'"

Following God means, quite simply, that we need to understand what God is asking us to do and then show deference to His leadership by doing our best to align our lives to His expressed will. One challenge we often encounter when reading scripture is that it is not always clear to us precisely what we should do. In those instances, we must search for the *principles* that encapsulate the stories and words we read and then allow these principles to *guide* our lives. However, an additional challenge often arises: the details of how, what, when, why, how often, how much, and with whom we need to direct our lives are frequently missing. To complicate matters further, as we *try* to live by biblical principles, we often lack the courage and determination to comply fully.

The singular idea of "following God" seems inadequate as a sole focus for life. And that's primarily because a significant part of God's design for life is not made abundantly clear by a simple reading of scripture. One critical aspect of following God, often misunderstood, is our responsibility for connecting and interacting with God on a deeply personal level. *Our responsibility is to discover – by intentionally seeking His insight, guidance, and support – all God desires from us.*

1 Chronicles 16: [11] Look to the LORD and his strength; *seek his face always.*

Hebrews 11: [6] And without faith it is impossible to please God, because anyone who *comes to him* must believe that he exists and that he rewards those who earnestly *seek him.*

By personally seeking God and asking Him to teach, guide, and empower us, we discover a significant dynamic: *God designed life to be lived in partnership with Him.* From the very beginning of time, God apportioned a set of responsibilities to humankind and also to Himself. In Genesis 2:15, God assigns Adam the responsibility of "caring" for the Garden of Eden. ("The LORD God took the man and put him in the Garden of Eden *to work it and take care of it."*) Earlier, in Genesis 1:26, God makes it clear that humankind has been tasked with providing stewardship over His Creation.

> **26** Then God said, "Let us make mankind in our image, in our likeness, *so that they may rule over* the fish in the sea and the birds in the sky, over the livestock and all the wild animals, and over all the creatures that move along the ground."

However, God remains present, personally involved in Adam and Eve's lives. In Genesis 3:8, we see God approaching them to initiate an exchange.

> **8** Then the man and his wife heard the sound of the LORD God *as he was walking in the garden* in the cool of the day, and they hid from the LORD God among the trees of the garden. **9** But the LORD God called to the man, "Where are you?"

This scene presents the idea that God walking through the Garden of Eden and interacting with Adam and Eve is just a regular part of the day. The interaction captured here in Genesis 3 is even after Adam and Eve have disobeyed God's one requirement – to not eat "from the tree of the knowledge of good and evil" (Genesis 2:17). As one reads through the account of The Fall, and humanity's expulsion from the Garden of Eden at the end of Genesis 3, Adam and Eve retain their responsibility to care for God's Creation. The rest of the Bible consistently shows God interacting with humankind. So, this **partnership between God and humanity is a significant aspect of how God designed life to be lived.** Understanding this dynamic – and learning how to function in a relationship with God – is simultaneously the *foundational principle and the central challenge of The Great Adventure!*

Essential Question #2: How has God Designed Life to be Lived?

As we endeavor to gain a deeper understanding of how God designed life to be lived, it's clear that God would have some *rules* or *practices* people should follow. The very nature of all forms of leadership is to establish a framework within which subordinates are to function. The idea of providing some structure to help subordinates understand their performance responsibilities follows from the very definition of leadership. The search for answers to this Essential Question, however, is not to create a list of *rules* that must be followed to avoid some punishment. The forgiveness and grace we experience due to Jesus' life, death, and resurrection dispel such a notion. **The goal is not to avoid punishment but to *order* our lives according to God's *design* because doing so honors God and results in the best life possible.**

While the 10 Commandments might come to mind as we search for answers to this Essential Question, that's not the type of "answer" we seek. (However, the *existence* of the 10 Commandments certainly provides some vital information for consideration.) The "answers" I'm suggesting we search for will be less *directive* and more like *guidelines* as we seek to understand how to plan and live our lives. Once a principle is identified, understanding how it should be implemented must be discerned through personal interactions with God. Therefore, given the understanding of God's role as our Supreme Leader, this Essential Question requires us first to discover God's *principles* for how we should live our lives and then learn how to apply these principles through ongoing interactions with Him.

For example, the natural sciences, such as Biology, Chemistry, and Physics, seek to understand how God's physical creation functions. Each discipline aims to identify the components that exist within a particular system (e.g., the human body), how each component (e.g., organ) is designed to perform, how the various components work together to form larger systems (e.g., digestive system), and how various conditions or experiences (e.g., diet) can alter the performance of individual components as well as the different systems and subsystems present within the whole.

Similarly, the intent of this Essential Question: "How has God Designed Life to be Lived?" seeks to examine the totality of life in a way that would help to establish *guidelines for how God intends for humans to live in all the various aspects or components of life.* This Essential Question is searching for answers that can serve as principles to inform and guide the individual plans or behaviors we consider. In addition to identifying the broader principles of God's design for life, such as living in partnership with God, we are also interested in understanding how these principles inform how our lives should be lived at a profoundly personal level.

Given the extreme importance of interpersonal relationships that Jesus emphasized through The Great Commandment (Matthew 22), our understanding of how God designed life to be lived will be deepened as we find answers to more focused questions, such as: What are the principles God has established for marriage and family life? What are the responsibilities of the husband? The wife? How am I supposed to parent my children? What does it really mean to honor your father and mother? How does the parent-child relationship change with each person's age and stage of life? What are the proper purposes of friendships? And what is the role of each person? Are there some boundaries needed to maintain personal mental health and establish healthy relationships? How have You designed the authority-subordinate relationship to function?

The "How has God Designed Life to be Lived?" Essential Question seeks to understand the principles God has designed for every area of life **and how those principles are to be applied on a profoundly personal level.** In particular, the principles God has established for relationships are of utmost importance for us to understand. Violating relational principles – especially within the

nuclear family – will negatively impact ALL the important relationships in your life! This Essential Question also desires to
understand the *relative importance* of various principles when they
appear to conflict or compete with one another. That is, we also
need to comprehend the *hierarchy* of God's principles for life.

Since there is virtually an infinite number of questions one
might ask about how life is to be lived, there is no expectation that
we will ever fully understand everything there is to know. Our goal
here is **not** to be so wise that we know (in our own power) what to
do in every situation. Instead, **we desire to understand the principles of God's global design for life, discerning with greater
specificity how God guides us in responding to the challenges
we face.** That is, instead of functioning independently from our
own knowledge base, we should seek to develop the habit of
frequently connecting with God on a personal level to receive His
guidance as we make decisions in life. Our understanding of God's
design principles for life empowers us to discern with greater
accuracy what He is encouraging us to do.

Design Elements

To best understand God's design principles for life, it is helpful to
recognize that there are two dimensions to life within which we
must learn to function effectively. Aligning our lives with the
biblical principles that govern each dimension will enable us to
experience the greatest overall peace, confidence, stability, joy, and
success. Those two dimensions are the Spiritual and the Natural.
The Spiritual Dimension encompasses our interactions with God,
while the Natural Dimension encompasses our interactions with
others and the world. As we consider these two dimensions, it is
essential to understand that the Spiritual Dimension transcends
the Natural Dimension, and it is optimal for us to be as attuned to
it *as possible.*

. . .

Spiritual Dimension: First and foremost, we must recognize that our individual lives are meant to be lived in ongoing fellowship with God, where He leads, guides, empowers, and directs us toward His unique plan for each of our lives. Because God is a spirit, we must interact with Him in the Spiritual Dimension.

> John 4: [24] God is spirit, and his worshipers must worship in the Spirit and in truth."

I'll address the nature of our Spiritual Self in more detail in Essential Question #3: "Who Am I?", but part of what needs to be understood in Essential Question #2 is how God designed us to function in the spiritual realm. So, some of the questions we must consider in this Essential Question include: What is the spirit? How do I function in the spiritual realm? What does that even mean? Recognizing that life is to be lived in partnership with God, what is my role in the transformation process, and what is God's role? How does my *spiritual self* interact with my *natural* self? Is there some balance I should maintain between the two dimensions? If so, how can I do that? How does one switch from the Natural Dimension to the Spiritual Dimension? And when is it essential to distinguish between the two dimensions? Because our interactions (relationship) with God are foundational to how God designed life, we must always seek to understand our spiritual nature at a deeper level. Since the focus of this book is to help the reader better understand how to know and follow God, it should be evident that much of the book's content is devoted to helping you better understand the Spiritual Dimension.

. . .

Natural Dimension: The natural dimension is where we function most of the time – eating, working, interacting with others, etc. Most of our interactions with God (which occur in the Spiritual Dimension) focus on seeking His assistance for living in the Natural Dimension. Our understanding of the existence of the Natural Dimension comes, well, quite naturally! One of the things we need to understand about the Natural Dimension is that there are several "components" that must each be present and functioning properly for us to maintain spiritual, mental, emotional, and physical equilibrium. People often wonder, "What does God want from me?" And "What am I supposed to do?"

> **Micah 6:** [8] He has shown you, O mortal, what is good. And
> what does the LORD require of you? To act justly and to
> love mercy and to walk humbly with your God.

Acting justly and loving mercy speaks to attitudes of our heart that drive how we live our lives; walking humbly with God refers to our willingness to connect with God and follow His design and guidance. As we discover the "right answers" to Essential Question #2 and allow those truths to inform how we plan and live our lives, we will experience a life more aligned with God's design, which, in turn, will produce greater levels of stability, predictability, joy, and peace.

At a very foundational level, six components of the Natural Dimension must be understood, planned, and managed. As you press into God and seek His guidance in understanding how He would like you to move forward, it would be appropriate to examine your life and consider what (if any) changes might benefit you in each of these components. While engaging in this practice of reflection, you should consider each component individually. In most instances (and in most "seasons" of life), a healthy, well-balanced life will include one or more activities in each of the following six components. As we gain a deeper understanding of each component and implement any changes God encourages us to pursue, our lives will become more closely aligned with God's design, and we will experience greater emotional, psychological, spiritual, and physical harmony.

The Six Components of the Natural Dimension

1. **Connecting with God** – doing anything *with* God. (This component was previously identified as belonging to the Spiritual Dimension, but some aspects must be planned and executed in the Natural Dimension.)
2. **Work** – activities that *must* be done for survival and orderly living.
3. **Rest** – *disengaging* from activities with any other identified purpose.
4. **Recreation** – experiences or activities planned for *enjoyment*.
5. **Social Interactions** – experiences or activities done *with others*.
6. **Service** – activities done with the intent *to serve the needs of others*.

Connecting with God. Because the primary call on each of our lives is to follow God, and because the only way we can follow God is by first discovering what He is asking us to do, *connecting with God is the most important and utmost consequential component of all*. The ultimate goal of our endeavor to connect with God is to fulfill the Great Commandment – to "love the Lord your God with all your heart and with all your soul and with all your strength and with all your mind" (Luke 10:27). While it is highly beneficial for us to connect with God frequently throughout each day, we should establish the practice of connecting with Him deeply during a time designed solely for that purpose.

During this special time, we must allow the Holy Spirit to disarm us from pursuing our own agenda. The goal is for God's Presence to wipe our hearts and minds from all preoccupations and to be "washed" of all our fears, worries, priorities, and plans. When we connect with God during this time, we need a *reset* – a renewal of our confidence, trust, and commitment to surrender to His leadership. Only as we re-center and re-focus ourselves in this way can we fully receive God's Grace for meeting our every need. And it's only from this place of renewed surrender that we can accept His correction and the directions we need to move forward.

Instituting this special time to connect with God is often the most challenging component for us to establish in a way that accomplishes the intended goal. Therefore, we must continually seek God for His assistance in understanding the kinds of activities or experiences we should plan, as well as the strength and determination we need to follow through. Don't let anyone prescribe the time, place, or manner you should connect with God. Allow the discovery of how to connect with God most effectively to become a regular part of your spiritual journey.

As much as we would like to think of ourselves as intelligent and planful people, our actions are often based on a minimal amount of thought. Indeed, people frequently make significant decisions, such as choosing a career path, a life partner, and many lifestyle choices, based on feelings rather than a well-defined decision-making process. Our daily actions often result from very little conscious thought. The food we choose to eat, the people we tend to associate with, and the routes we choose to follow as we navigate our lives are just a few examples of the many "decisions" we make that are often based more on habit or emotion rather than any conscious planning on our part.

Sometimes, our actions are merely reflexive. When we are criticized, for example, we often respond defensively rather than taking time to consider the best response. In fact, we can sometimes live a substantial portion of our lives by habit rather than careful planning. It sometimes requires a significant life event (such as a major conflict or severe loss) to jar us from our daily patterns of living and cause us to evaluate our lives seriously.

The more our lives are self-directed rather than God-directed, the more likely we are to fall into this pattern of self-centered, habitual living. The only way we can protect ourselves is to set aside time for personal reflection and seek God's insights, wisdom, and direction. This is why we need some regularly scheduled "quiet time" each day. However, we should not set aside such a time because God *requires* us to do so. Instead, we should plan to connect with God regularly because we *need* Him. **The transformations *that produce the most significant value and benefit will flow from your connections with God.*** If you fail to address this area of your life – if you do not make connecting with God a pattern – you will never find personal fulfillment, and you will never fulfill your God-given destiny.

Because of the ultimate importance of regularly connecting with God, Satan will do everything he can to discourage you and prevent you from fulfilling this critical need. It is helpful to understand that it will regularly be challenging for you to make your connection time with God meaningful and productive. It will likely take great effort to successfully plan and execute a quiet time each day. Remember, this is not a religious requirement; you **_need_** to connect with God in a substantive and meaningful way each day.

Your connection time with God is to *receive* what you *need* from Him. And we each need very much from Him. We need insight into our own hearts and minds. We need God to reveal to us the issues that require attention and how we should address them. We need strength and courage to yield to His leadership. Most importantly, we need God to change our hearts and minds. The most important focal point of life is to know and follow God. However, our natural inclination is to follow our own desires and plans. We need God to transform our hearts so that we more fully desire to know and follow Him. Heart transformation, not surprisingly, flows directly from our connections with God. This is why we must make connecting with God our highest priority. Expect a battle, and recognize that you will need God to guide and empower you in establishing and maintaining a regular time of connecting with Him.

Below are several parameters that I have found helpful for connecting with God at a deeper, more "surrendered" level. These principles have made me feel more confident that I am genuinely attempting to follow God's leadership rather than my own plans (although I know I will frequently "fall short").

1. Be intentional about arranging your schedule so you can be **fully present** to connect with God. (Select a location without distractions and at a time of day when you can be most "present" intellectually and emotionally and free from pressure to respond to other demands.)
2. Present yourself before God as one ready to deal with any item on His agenda.
3. Pause and ask God how He would like to use the time.
4. Wait as long as necessary for God to "bring the meeting to order."
5. Allow God the freedom to direct your attention in any way He desires. (He may move you to pray for someone, He may encourage you to listen to worship

music, He may lead you to read or research some portion of scripture, He may draw your attention to a particular relationship, He may bring an experience to your attention, or He may move your attention toward some future endeavor or goal. He is God; humbly allow Him to "lead you" in any direction He desires. Let your thoughts and emotions be fully present to whatever He brings to your mind. He may enable you to see some shortcomings in yourself that you hadn't seen so clearly before, He may applaud you for some actions you took, He may provide some insights that will encourage you to pursue a different approach to some of your plans, or He may encourage, comfort, or console you. Whatever God chooses to "do" should be recognized as an outpouring of His Grace designed to "enrich" your life.

6. If you think your mind might have been distracted from important issues and your thoughts are now just "wandering," ask Him about that possibility. (I believe you'll discover that type of "wandering" is often God redirecting your attention to another issue. Let God decide what's "important" for you to think about!)

7. If your practice involves selected readings, leave some time at the end for quiet reflection.

8. When the time you have set aside is completed, feel free to go about your everyday life practices. You should exit the experience feeling that your life is on a more solid and stable foundation than when you initiated the connection with God.

9. Over time, God will move you to find ways to expand and improve your connection times with Him. You will discover those experiences so rewarding and fulfilling that your hunger for more of God will grow.

Essential Question #2: How has God Designed Life to be Lived?

Over the years, I have frequently adjusted the timing and content of the spiritual disciplines I practice. Sometimes, I could consistently practice a particular spiritual discipline; at other times, it was difficult. For much of my early years as a Christian, I would devote about 15-30 minutes to some devotional activity. In recent years, however, both the timing and the practices I have followed have remained relatively constant. As I entered retirement, it took some time to establish a new pattern; the amount of time spent connecting with God increased, and some of my practices changed. My daily practices will typically include several of the following: devotional readings, quiet reflection, listening to worship music, reading scripture and other Christian writings, personal writing, and prayer. Whatever practices you feel led to pursue, including the timing and location, are not the most critical issue. **What *is* essential is that you are doing your best to follow God's directions for you.**

> **1 Samuel 15:** [22] But Samuel replied: "Does the LORD delight in burnt offerings and sacrifices as much as in obeying the LORD? To obey is better than sacrifice, and to heed is better than the fat of rams.

While I must address the following two components individually, one biblical passage establishes validity for both.

> **Exodus 20:** [9] "You have six days each week for your ordinary <u>work</u>, [10] but the seventh day is a Sabbath day of <u>rest</u> dedicated to the LORD your God." (NLT – emphasis added)

Work is any activity involving mental or physical effort to make it possible for you to maintain or advance your lifestyle. Work includes activities such as earning wages for your living expenses, completing household chores, attending school, shopping for groceries, cooking, and doing laundry. God designed work as an essential part of Adam's and Eve's life in the Garden of Eden (Genesis 2:15), but work became "corrupted" when they were cast out of the garden (Genesis 3:17-19). As you mature spiritually, intellectually, and emotionally, work will become more enjoyable and fulfilling, but there will always be some part that will just be *work*! When we consider **Work** as a component of the Natural Dimension, we should discern the degree to which we are following God's plan for our lives. We should reflect on questions such as: Am I doing the kind of work God desires for me? Am I working too much or too little? Am I avoiding any work that God wants me to do? Am I honoring God in the *way* I do my work? What changes, if any, should I make in this area of my life?

By dictionary definition, **Rest** is the bodily state characterized by minimal functional and metabolic activities, the freedom from activity or labor. Prioritizing Rest means planning for detachment from engaging in activities that require physical and mental effort. Rest is what you do when you're not at Work or engaged in another activity designed to accomplish a specified goal. Rest, then, is the intentional use of a period of time to disengage from any activity that requires concentration or effort. Sleep is a form of rest, but we often benefit from engaging in rest during our day. We need to rest sometimes, which is very difficult for some people. You should not feel guilty for taking time to rest; it is an integral part of God's design for life! When we consider Rest as a component of the Natural Dimension, we need to discern the degree to which we address this component according to God's plan. It would be appropriate to reflect on questions such as: How can I best honor God by taking (even planning) time for rest? Why do I feel guilty when I take time to rest? How do I know *when* to rest? When would it be best to schedule rest for my typical day?

I should probably note here that many people (especially

some Christians and Jews) believe it is essential to set aside an entire day (Sabbath) each week for rest. Some include establishing guidelines about what will and will not be done. Indeed, one of the 10 Commandments is to "honor the Sabbath." Other people demonstrate this practice less stringently through weekly church attendance followed by a more "restful approach" to the remainder of their day. The intentional practice of planning an entire Sabbath day has never been a part of my life; however, I have often wondered if it should! (As I've asked God about such a practice, I have never felt that He was asking me to prioritize practicing a Sabbath day. But I may have just been resistant!)

Recreation is any activity in which a person engages (during non-work time) that produces enjoyment and is recognized as having a socially redeeming value. Recreational activities are designed to renew or recharge oneself intellectually and emotionally. Part of God's design for life is that we would engage in recreational activities.

Ecclesiastes 8: [15] So I commend the enjoyment of life, because there is nothing better for a person under the sun than to eat and drink and be glad. Then joy will accompany them in their toil all the days of the life God has given them under the sun.

Zechariah 8: [5] The city streets will be filled with boys and girls playing there.

The word "rest" is frequently used in scripture to denote engaging in a recreational activity. As with all the components, there is a wide variety of ways to engage in recreation. We often engage in recreational activities with others, which also becomes a form of Social Interaction. Consequently, our recreational choices are frequently influenced by the social and spiritual groups we participate in. As we consider Recreation as a component of the Natural Dimension, we should seek to discern the degree to which we are addressing this component in accordance with God's plan for us. It would be appropriate to reflect on questions such as: What type(s) of recreation would be most beneficial for me? Am I spending enough (or too much) time in this area of my life? Should I make any changes in this area?

Social Interactions are defined as exchanges between two or more individuals. Since Jesus identified loving "your neighbor as yourself" (Mark 12:31) as the second greatest commandment, it should be clear that God intends for us to interact with others. The phrase *"one another"* appears repeatedly throughout the Bible. In fact, 47 different verses in the New Testament specifically direct Christians to engage in meaningful interactions with others. Social Interactions can occur independently or with other components, such as Connecting with God, Work, Recreation, Rest, or Service. Social interactions are sometimes pleasant and, at different times, unpleasant or even confrontational. God often uses our Social Interactions to teach us truths and challenge our ongoing transformation. This is especially true when we combine Social Interactions with Connecting with God. Many churches encourage their members to participate in small groups (often called Care Groups or Bible Study Groups). Social interactions within this context enable us to develop deep friendships and grow spiritually as group members care for one another. Care and Bible Study Groups have significantly contributed to my spiritual growth.

One's temperament (which I will discuss in more detail in Essential Question #3) can significantly influence how much attention one devotes to Social Interactions. For example, those who are more of an introvert are likely to spend less time engaged in social interactions (or at least experience less pleasure from such engagement). In comparison, those who are more extroverted will likely spend more time engaging in social interactions. When we consider Social Interactions as a component of the Natural Dimension, we want to discern the degree to which we are addressing this component in accordance with God's plan for us. It would be appropriate to reflect on questions such as: Do I spend enough (or too much) time engaging in Social Interactions? Are there specific individuals with whom I should spend more (or less) time interacting? Are there any particular truths (about myself or life in general) that You are trying to teach me through my interactions with any specific individual(s)? Which relationship(s) (if any) require more attention? What changes would you like me to make in this area of my life?

Service is simply engaging in activities to benefit others (or some agency). In the Old Testament, God made it clear to Abraham that God's people are called to serve others: "I will make you into a great nation, and I will bless you; I will make your name great, and you will *be a blessing.*" (Genesis 12:2). As we will see in Essential Questions #3 and #4, Service is an area of activity that helps us discover a great deal about ourselves, produces a great deal of satisfaction, and ultimately is one of the ways through which we find a great deal of personal fulfillment.

One of the motivations God places within our hearts is for our lives to *matter.* Deep within us is the need to contribute positively to the world – to make a difference. Each act of Service is an expression of that inner drive. In fact, you will likely feel particularly *unfulfilled* if you are not engaged in some service experience. The more your service matches the person God created you to be, the more fulfillment you will experience. As with the other components listed above, the goal is not to find something to do in the Service area so you can "check the box" as having been completed. Instead, our goal is to discern how God is leading us to serve the needs of others. Our goal – *at all times* – should be to do our best to be a *follower of God* and not the master of our own destiny.

> **Proverbs 3:** [5] Trust in the LORD with all your heart and lean
> not on your own understanding; [6] in all your ways submit
> to him, and he will make your paths straight.

Notice that this verse does **not** say that we are to *suspend* our understanding; we are just *not* supposed to allow our understanding to be what ultimately determines our actions. We are called to always follow God's leadership to the best of our ability. As we consider Service as a component of the Natural Dimension, we desire to discern the degree to which we are addressing this component in accordance with God's plan for our lives. It would be appropriate to reflect on questions such as: Am I serving in the way(s) You desire for me? Am I devoting too much (or too little) time to serving the needs of others? What are you trying to teach me through my serving activities? What (if any) adjustments do you desire me to make in this area of my life?

You might wonder whether diet and exercise should be included in some way in this discussion. Since these topics appear infrequently in scripture, I do not believe they qualify as a primary component of the Natural Dimension. However, recognizing that we must maintain some degree of physical health to prolong and enjoy life, we must consider diet and exercise in planning and living our lives. For many people, activities that support a healthy physical lifestyle can be designed to address one or more of the components, such as Recreation and Social Interactions.

I also wondered if I should have designated *participation in a faith community or church* (or even a small group) as a separate component of the Natural Dimension, since this <u>IS</u> an integral part of one's spiritual journey.

Hebrews 10: [24] And let us consider how we may spur one another on toward love and good deeds, [25] not giving up *meeting together*, as some are in the habit of doing, but encouraging one another ...

Romans 12: [4] For just as each of us has one body with many members, and these members do not all have the same function, [5] so in Christ *we, though many, form one body* [the Church], and each member belongs to all the others.

I Corinthians 12: [13] For we were all baptized by one Spirit so as to *form one body* [the Church] – whether Jews or Gentiles, slave or free – and we were all given the one Spirit to drink. [14] Even so the body is not made up of one part but of many.

While the Church (and our engagement within it) is an integral part of God's Plan for our lives and advancing His purposes, *participation in a faith community will become a natural outcome as one seeks to know and follow God* and becomes more familiar with biblical writings. Additionally, participation in a faith community combines the already existing components of Connecting with God, Social Interactions, and Service. For these reasons, I have chosen not to make participation in a faith community a separate component of the Natural Dimension.

When considering how these six components might find expression in your life, each component does not need to be given equal value. For example, while spending significant, regular time Connecting with God will always pay huge dividends, you may only need to engage in Recreational activities on an occasional basis. Also, the degree to which each component is addressed in your life is a highly personal and individual matter – you need God to show you the *mix* that is right for you at any given point in your life. However, *all six components must find expression in your life to experience emotional, spiritual, intellectual, and physical equilibrium.* While there may be brief periods when you can't include activities in all six components, maintaining such an imbalanced lifestyle will inevitably result in unnecessary problems if allowed to continue over an extended period. However, an imbalance is sometimes necessary during extremely busy or tumultuous times. It should also be noted that several of these components can be addressed in a singular activity. For example, if you were to join a bowling league, you could simultaneously address Rest, Recreation, and Social Interaction. It is also essential to understand that you **_do not earn_** God's blessings by arranging your life around the six components. Inclusion of the components is just the way God designed life to be lived!

To close this part of the discussion, I would like to point out it is a highly beneficial personal discipline to periodically (perhaps quarterly or annually) set aside an extended period of time for reflection – maybe a day or more – to examine how you are addressing each of the six components in your life. Failure to reflect on how you are addressing these six components may result in unnecessary disappointment, disequilibrium, and a lack of personal fulfillment. The usual busyness of life often results in our lives becoming *unbalanced*. One of my devotionals includes the monthly reading of the following poem by Alister Maclean, which nicely addresses the need for regular review of our life practices.

As the rain hides the stars,
as the autumn mist hides the hills,
happenings of my lot
hide the shining of Thy face from me.
Yet, if I may hold Thy hand
in the darkness,
it is enough;

since I know that,
though I may stumble in my going,
Thou dost not fall.

Summary

Two perspectives are involved in the search for answers to Essential Question #2: "How has God Designed Life to be Lived?" The first perspective (just discussed) is that we must establish a lifestyle that appropriately encompasses the Six Components of the Natural Dimension. We must understand that a proper "balance" of activities within and among these components is necessary for experiencing a life of harmony, stability, and peace. Whenever we find these qualities lacking, we must pause and ask God to show us where we might need to adjust one or more of these components.

The second (and more significant) perspective for finding answers to this Essential Question is that God has established a seemingly infinite number of *principles* that impact every area of our lives – including personal relationships, finances, our emotional, spiritual, and psychological well-being, as well as many more. To find answers that address this second perspective (involving both the Spiritual and Natural Dimensions), we must develop the habit of asking God, "What does **this** (experience, problem, challenge, conflict, etc.) teach me about how You Designed Life to be Lived?" Finding answers to these questions – and aligning our lives accordingly – will lead to an ever-increasing sense of stability and peace, contributing to the development of a sense of meaning, purpose, and fulfillment.

The idea of a *home* might serve as a practical illustration for understanding the significance of these two very different perspectives. To establish a home, one must be concerned about the building (house or apartment) and all the contents placed inside, as well as all the people and activities that occur within the building on a regular basis. The *physical structure and furnishings* provide a sense of separation, protection, and stability from outside forces and events – a place for us to find rest and be settled. Balancing your life among the six Components of the Natural Dimension will produce a sense of calm, rest, and stability. This is the first perspective mentioned above. Once established, however, adjustments to these components are only required occasionally, just as we only occasionally make changes to our physical house and its contents.

Everything else that pertains to making a house a *home* – the people and all the experiences and interactions occurring inside the house – is the second perspective, and these issues are what make life most enjoyable, meaningful, purposeful, and fulfilling. When you seek answers to Essential Question #2: "How has God Designed Life to be Lived?" you will spend almost all of your time looking for answers from this second perspective – learning more about how we can live our lives better. As you develop a deeper understanding of God's ways for living out each day – and integrate them into your life – your "house" becomes a "home".

Essential Questions #1 and #2 seek to understand foundational truths of life that will never change – because God never changes. (**Malachi 3:** [6] "I the LORD do not change.") However, examining Essential Questions #3 and #4 will differ slightly. Some aspects of our personal lives will remain unchanged, while others will change (hopefully, for the better) considerably over time. When we consider these questions about ourselves – "Who am I?" and "What is God Calling Me to Do?" – the answers we discover about our Natural Self and our circumstances will frequently change. However, some of the answers we discover related to our Spiritual Self and God's ultimate plans for our lives will remain constant. For example, the "Who Am I?" question can be seeking to understand the present state of my beliefs, attitudes, and feelings (which will change over time), or it can be searching for answers about my God-given personal abilities and attributes (which remain unchanged). Therefore, Essential Questions #3 and #4 must be examined and explored from both perspectives.

The journey to discover meaningful answers for the remaining two Essential Questions will simultaneously be the most challenging and personally rewarding questions you will ever pursue. Successfully answering these questions will uncover your destiny and release the significance you have always known exists deep within you!

Chapter 8
Essential Question #3: Who Am I?

Who among us hasn't struggled with the question of personal identity? While I'm sure the search begins very early in life, the question: "Who Am I?" becomes a major focal point of our lives in early adolescence and plagues us until we find adequate answers – and, regrettably, many people never do! The purpose of Essential Question #3 is to help you discover and release your *essential nature* – the significance and exceptionality that resides within you – the person God created you to be – which will ultimately lead to the most significant amount of happiness and personal fulfillment possible. I am incredibly excited to help you understand and process this pivotal question!

Before unpacking Essential Question #3, I think it is important to understand some crucial aspects of humankind and how God planned for us to interact with Him. To gain a deeper understanding of ourselves, we need to consider our identity in contrast to the identity of our Creator. The following discussion will take us "into the weeds" a bit, but these concepts and terms will be used later to examine how we can find meaningful answers to Essential Question #3: "Who Am I?".

Spiritual and Natural Dimensions

The Bible reveals that God is an eternal Spirit and exists within the Spiritual Dimension. However, humankind exists in the Natural Dimension, and we must learn how to bridge these two dimensions to experience a meaningful relationship with Him.

> **John 4:** [24] "God is spirit, and his worshipers must worship in the Spirit and in truth."

> **Colossians 1:** [15] The Son is the image of the invisible God, the firstborn over all creation. [16] For in him all things were created: things in heaven and on earth, visible and invisible, whether thrones or powers or rulers or authorities; all things have been created through him and for him.

> **1 Corinthians 2:** [13] This is what we speak, not in words taught by human wisdom but in words taught by the Spirit, explaining spiritual realities with Spirit-taught words. [14] The person without the Spirit does not accept the things that come from the Spirit of God but considers them foolishness, and cannot understand them because they are discerned only through the Spirit.

The Bible also indicates that angels are spirits (Hebrews 1:13-14) and that evil spirits exist (Romans 8:37-39). By extension, it seems reasonable to assume that everything in the Spiritual Dimension has a *spiritual* composition, just as all things in the Natural Dimension are composed of matter. That which is spiritual in nature is not detectable by our natural five senses. This difference in *essence* between the Spiritual and the Natural Dimensions presents some unique challenges for us as we attempt to know and follow God.

When God initiated creation, He created the Natural Dimension and everything it contains. Men and women, as created beings, exist in the Natural Dimension. However, while humankind has been a *natural being* since creation, each person also *possesses a spirit*. It was the *spirit* of Adam and Eve that died at the time of the Fall in the Garden of Eden.

> **Genesis 2:** [17] but you must not eat from the tree of the knowledge of good and evil, for when you eat from it you will certainly die.

We know that their spirit died because Adam and Eve continued to live in their natural bodies after the Fall. Additionally, the spirit within a person comes to life when one is "born again."

> **John 3:** [5] Jesus answered, "Very truly I tell you, no one can enter the kingdom of God unless they are born of water and the Spirit. [6] Flesh gives birth to flesh, but the Spirit gives birth to spirit. [7] You should not be surprised at my saying, 'You must be born again.'"

It is essential to understand that *the Spiritual Dimension tran-scends the Natural Dimension* (Figure 8-1).

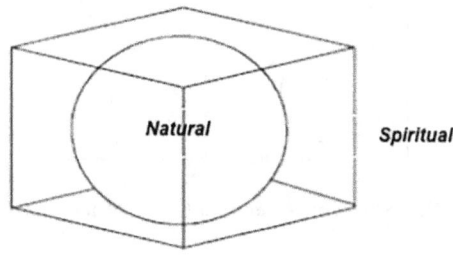

Figure 8-1: Spiritual Dimension Transcends the Natural

Isaiah 55: [8] "For my thoughts are not your thoughts, neither are your ways my ways," declares the Lord. [9] "As the heavens are higher than the earth, so are my ways higher than your ways and my thoughts than your thoughts."

Because He is supernatural and omnipotent, God can enter the Natural Dimension at any time and in any way He desires. We grow spiritually, emotionally, and intellectually as our understanding extends beyond the Natural Dimension into the Spiritual Dimension. When our bodies die, certain aspects of our natural being transition into the Spiritual Dimension.

Philippians 3: [21] ... will transform our lowly bodies so that they will be like his glorious body.

Scripture tells us that God created humankind in His own "image" (Genesis 1:27). As God is a "triune" being (Father, Son, and Holy Spirit), so is humankind (Spirit, Soul, and Body). (Figure 8-2)

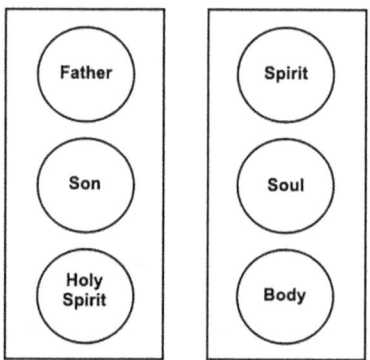

Figure 8-2: Triune Nature of God and Humankind

1 Thessalonians 5: [23] May God himself, the God of peace, sanctify you through and through. May your whole spirit, soul, and body be kept blameless at the coming of our Lord Jesus Christ.

Our *spirit* is the most significant aspect of our being because it is the conduit through which we interact with God. That is, God, as a Spirit, interacts with our spirit. In turn, our interactions with God occur through our spirit. As our spirit grows and matures, so does our relationship with God, thus helping us fulfill The Greatest Commandment (Matthew 22).

Proverbs 20: [27] The human spirit is the lamp of the LORD that sheds light on one's inmost being.

John 4: [24] "God is spirit, and his worshipers must worship in the Spirit and in truth."

Our *soul* is the most complex aspect of our identity and will be discussed in detail below. Our *body* influences our lives in many ways. However, to understand Essential Question #3, it is important to recognize that many unfiltered motivations and "drives" (one element of Stage 1 thinking) emanate from our physical being (body) and must be identified and considered as we make decisions about how to live. Understanding and synthesizing the influences of the spirit, soul, and body is a significant part of finding meaningful answers to Essential Question #3.

Through many passages, the Bible indicates our *soul* is also comprised of three parts: Mind, Will, and Emotions (Figure 8-3). Since knowledge is contained within one's mind, **Proverbs 2:10** establishes that the *mind* is a component of the soul of humanity ("For wisdom will enter your heart, and *knowledge will be pleasant to your soul*."). The following verses from the Book of Job (7:15 – So that my *soul would choose...* and 6:7 – My *soul refuses...*) verify that the *will* of humankind is also a component of the soul. Since we experience *emotions* such as love, hatred, and joy, many verses establish that one's *feelings* are contained within the soul.

Isaiah 61: [10] I delight greatly in the LORD; my *soul rejoices* in my God. (NASB)

Song of Songs 1: [7] Tell me, O you whom my *soul loves* (NASB)

2 Samuel 5: [8] David said on that day, "Whoever would strike the Jebusites, let him reach the lame and the blind, who are *hated by David's soul*... (NASB)

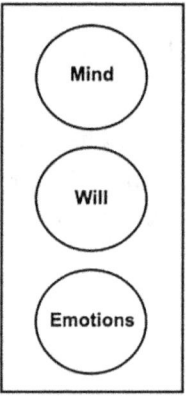

Figure 8-3: Soul of Humankind

Using the discussion above as a foundation, let us look more deeply at how our "triune" essential nature (Spirit, Soul, and Body) influences our approach to finding meaningful answers to Essential Question #3: "Who Am I?".

Shortly after God created Adam and Eve, they ignored the only constraint God placed on them (Genesis 2:17; 3:1-7 – God never desired His Creation to have knowledge of evil, and disregarding this one constraint resulted in the death of their spirit.).

Because of their sin (disregarding God's will), they were expelled from the Garden of Eden (Genesis 2 and 3). From that point on, the lives of all people have been influenced by the presence of sin in themselves, others, and the world at large. Being created in the image of God speaks to our *Divine Self*. The ways in which the influence of sin corrupts our Divine Self speaks to our *Natural Self*. Finding meaningful answers to the question, "Who Am I?" will require examining our identity from both perspectives.

Natural Self and Divine Self

Your *Natural Self* consists primarily of your mind, will, and emotions at any given time. At this very moment, your Natural Self is your current, imperfect mental/emotional framework and how your beliefs and feelings influence the choices you make each day (plus those aspects of your body that might influence those choices). Your Natural (imperfect) Self is the result of how your own sin has infected your life, and how the sins of others (and the corrupted world at large) have impacted your life. The presence of sin has impacted our lives in the same way that a virus infects a computer, corrupting the Divine Nature God originally designed for humankind and the world. Because thoughts, beliefs, and behavior patterns change over time, your Natural Self is in a regular state of flux.

Your *Divine Self is the person God created you to be* and includes every aspect of your being – Spirit, Soul, and Body, as well as your Mind, Will, and Emotions – without any corruption from sin. When you are born again, your Divine Self comes to life instantly within your spirit. **Your Divine Self is both unique and unchanging.**

2 Corinthians 5: [17] Therefore, if anyone is in Christ, the new creation has come: The old has gone, the new is here!

[18] All this is from God, who reconciled us to himself through Christ and gave us the ministry of reconciliation.

Because of Jesus' sacrificial life, death, resurrection, and ascension, when God looks at you, He sees your **Divine Self**, spotless and blameless.

Psalm 103: [12] as far as the east is from the west, so far has he removed our transgressions from us.

God also envisions you living at the fullness of your potential when He looks at you.

Galatians 2: [20] I have been crucified with Christ and I no longer live, but Christ lives in me. The life I now live in the body, I live by faith in the Son of God, who loved me and gave himself for me.

You need to understand that *God is not angry with you, and He is not disappointed in you*. As our perfect Heavenly Father, God looks at us like a parent looks at their very young children – recognizing their amazing potential and longing to see their potential fully developed and released. God's view of us and all of His plans for us are based on His perfect love for us and motivated by His desire for us to experience the "full life" that Jesus came to make possible.

John 10: [10] The thief comes only to steal and kill and destroy; I have come that they may have life, and have it to the full.

Understanding Spiritual Growth

From the moment you are born again, there is an ongoing battle between your Natural and Divine selves.

> **Galatians 5:** [17] For the flesh desires what is contrary to the Spirit, and the Spirit what is contrary to the flesh. They conflict with each other, so that you are not to do whatever you want.

What occurs within you as you seek to know and follow God – allowing the truths you discover to transform your mental and emotional framework – is what scripture identifies as "the renewing of your mind."

> **Romans 12:** [2] Do not conform to the pattern of this world, but be transformed by the renewing of your mind. Then you will be able to test and approve what God's will is – his good, pleasing, and perfect will.

Conforming "to the pattern of this world" refers to the ways in which your mental and emotional framework (Natural Self) has developed as you have created your own set of personal beliefs about how life "works" – of which much is false, or at least not entirely true. As you replace these "inaccurate" beliefs within your mental framework with truth, your Divine Self gains more significant influence in your life, and your Natural Self is expressed to a lesser extent (i.e., "transformed"). The progression of "spiritual growth" is captured in Figure 8-4.

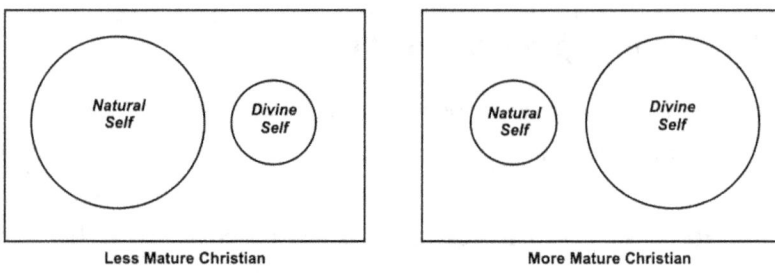

Figure 8-4: Relationship Between Natural Self, Divine Self and Spiritual Maturity

A soundboard comes to mind when I ponder the extreme complexity of the Natural (and Divine) Self (some professionals have identified over 600 personality traits). Technicians use soundboards to adjust the "sound quality" produced by the various instruments and singers' voices during a musical performance. Soundboards contain dozens of dials, slides, and switches that the technician adjusts to modify the overall quality of the musical sound an audience receives. In the same way, our Natural and Divine Selves include a wide variety of physical, intellectual, behavioral, and emotional characteristics. Some of these characteristics are "either-or" (e.g., male or female), other characteristics are a matter of "degree" (e.g., how much of a "planner" you are), while still other characteristics are a matter of "location" on a scale of opposing orientations (e.g., where you would be located on the introvert-extrovert scale). God established a unique combination of "settings" for us when we were each "created."

Jeremiah 1: [5] "Before I formed you in the womb I knew you, before you were born I set you apart ..."

To experience "growth" toward our Divine Self, some of these characteristics will remain fixed, while others are designed (by God) to stay within a ***predetermined range***. (**NOTE:** This "predetermined range" is established by God and is unique to each person. Also, it is vital to understand that living "outside" of your unique "predetermined range" for any aspect of your Divine Self will have "unpleasant" consequences.) For example, I will always be a male, but my tendency to plan events in my life (as opposed to being spontaneous) should remain within a specific range. If I "under-plan" or "over-plan," I will begin to feel anxious to some degree, but planning within my "God-assigned range" will result in "peace of mind." (Additionally, if I "over-plan" – which is my imperfect tendency – I will drive my wife crazy!) *Living according to God's design for life means discovering God's unique "settings" for you and aligning your life accordingly.* While we will never reach "perfection" on this side of eternity, God's plan for your life includes ongoing transformation toward His unique "settings" for you – your Divine Self.

Many benefits derive from understanding the current "condition" of our Natural Self and God's unique "design" of our Divine Self. The first (and maybe most significant) benefit is that we can stop comparing ourselves to others! Understanding that God created us to be unique individuals with a unique life plan will free us from comparing ourselves to others. There will always be some people who appear to us as "better" in some ways and "worse" than us in other ways. But life is not a competition; there is not one "ideal" we should all seek to attain. God calls each of us to a unique set of characteristics; He challenges us to become our best self – our Divine Self. We need to understand and accept – even celebrate – who we *are* and who God *created us to be.*

A second benefit of understanding the dynamics involved between our Natural and Divine Selves is that it can help us better understand and accept others – especially the people who are closest and most important to us. I mentioned earlier that my "over-planning" tendencies can create tension in my relationship with my wife. Still, my ability to understand and accept my wife's

Natural and Divine Selves also dramatically benefits our relationship – because our differences are something God frequently uses to challenge my ongoing transformation.

Here's one example. While my wife and I share many values and interests, I prefer a high level of planning and order, and my wife prefers to act with greater creativity and spontaneity. So ... there is a cup in one of our kitchen cabinets where we "normally" store a pair of scissors. Virtually every time I use the scissors, I put them back in the cup. My wife, however, often leaves the scissors on the counter (or somewhere else) after using them. Her tendency to do this was because the use of those scissors was a minor aspect of a more significant task she was focused on completing, and the completion of that task was what captured her attention. We used to have arguments about stuff like this. But as God helped me better understand my wife's Natural and Divine Selves (as well as my own), I accepted that finding the scissors on the counter (or in the refrigerator!) would become a regular part of our lives! Whether God might be challenging my wife to develop the habit of returning the scissors to the cup is between her and God (and she probably returns the scissors to the cup on many occasions that I know nothing about!). But God's challenge *to me* was to be mindful of my wife's many positive attributes, which I appreciate and admire, and to keep quiet and put the scissors back in the cup myself! (I won't get into the challenges we faced with doing laundry!)

Additional benefits derived from understanding our Natural Self and Divine Self include a better understanding of conflicts we experience with others, how to best avoid or overcome conflicts, and how to improve damaged relationships. A further benefit of gaining insights is the additional insights into Essential Question #2: How has God Designed Life to be Lived?

Like Essential Question #2, our struggle to answer Essential Question #3 involves a dual focus. On the one hand, **we need to** understand our current Natural Self, but we also need to gain an improved understanding of our Divine Self. Spiritual growth occurs as we gain a deeper understanding of our Natural and Divine Selves and pursue God's guidance and power in the transformation process (Figure 8-4). So, Essential Question #3 has two parts: I must not only seek answers to the question, "Who Am I?" but also consider the question, "Who Does God Want Me to Become?". I believe that the *process of open-ended questioning* is the gateway to growth in our understanding and transformation.

The questions you should consider throughout your day that would provide insights into your Natural and Divine selves and aid you in your journey of spiritual growth include: "What caused me to respond like *that*?" "Why does *that bother* me so much?" "Is there a better way for me to handle challenges like *that*?" "Why do I feel *this* way?" "What would a more mature response look like?" "Why is *this* so easy for me?" "Why do I enjoy *this* so much?" "Why *don't* I like *that*?" "Should I do more things like that even though I don't want to?" *As we examine our inclinations, motivations, and patterns of thinking and acting in a wide range of experiences each day, we gain insight into both our Natural and Divine Selves.* While it can often take a long time to find answers and then God's insights into how we can change, this dynamic of seeking answers to open-ended questions is an integral part of the spiritual growth process.

Two goals are accomplished by asking questions like those suggested above. First, we begin to understand aspects of our Natural Self that require transformation. Recognition of our shortcomings helps us remain humble and provides fodder for prayer and reflection as we seek God's guidance and support on our spiritual journey. Second, questions like those suggested above help us better understand our Divine Self because these are the attributes we wish to see magnified in our lives. *The recognition of, and growth toward, your Divine Self will result in the most significant amount of meaning, purpose, and fulfillment in your life.*

I think it's important to point out here that every aspect of our Natural Self that requires transformation — including feelings, attitudes, beliefs, understandings, habits, etc. - was developed at points in our past (sometimes even when we were very young children). Our lack of understanding and maturity at that time "caused" us to process past experiences in ways that resulted in a "faulty" Natural Self. That is, we developed "wrong" or "unhealthy" attitudes, beliefs, patterns of thinking, etc., because we lacked the understanding and wisdom (maybe even support and protection) necessary for growing and developing in the way God intended. And we will continue to make similar "errors" unless God intervenes and helps us transform our Natural Self.

The process God typically utilizes to affect the transformation of our imperfect Natural Self is to challenge us to "re-live" (to some degree) many of our past experiences – both intellectually and emotionally – thereby enabling us to modify our Natural Selves by replacing falsehoods or errors we embraced in the past with a better understanding of truth. *This process of "re-living past experiences" is essential to our spiritual, intellectual, and emotional growth.* However, transforming some aspects of our Natural Self can be a challenging and lengthy process. We must develop the capacity to "wrestle" or "argue" with God – bringing our *true self* with all its anger, anxieties, fears, confusion, and pain to the surface – and allowing Him to sort it all out and bring healing, comfort, and acceptance, as well as a new (better) understanding of those past experiences.

Psalm 51: [6] Behold, You desire truth in the innermost being, And in the hidden part You will make me know wisdom. (NASB)

James 1: [2] Consider it pure joy, my brothers and sisters, whenever you face trials of many kinds, [3] because you know that the testing of your faith produces perseverance. [4] Let perseverance finish its work so that you may be mature and complete, not lacking anything.

Romans 8: [18] I consider that our present sufferings are not worth comparing with the glory that will be revealed in us. [19] For the creation waits in eager expectation for the children of God to be revealed. [20] For the creation was subjected to frustration, not by its own choice, but by the will of the one who subjected it, in hope [21] that the creation itself will be liberated from its bondage to decay and brought into the freedom and glory of the children of God.

It is essential to understand that the transformation of our Natural Self is not accomplished *exclusively* in isolation. The expectation is *not* for us to lock ourselves inside a closet to wrestle with God alone and reappear as a fully transformed person. Some individual battles might be won in isolation, but our overall transformation often occurs through our conversations and interactions with others. For example, I have experienced transformation myself and seen the transformation of others through involvement in Bible Study or Care groups over many years. Additionally, many people experience great success interacting with a mature Christian counselor or therapist in dealing with the transformation of their Natural Self. The assistance of mature Christians or trained professionals can often facilitate transformation more efficiently and effectively than in isolation. However, whether accomplished alone, in groups, or with the assistance of a counselor, therapist, or trusted friend, you must be willing to allow God to bring about all the transformation He desires. **Fully surrendering to God is the only way to experience the "full life" God has planned for you.**

In addition to using reflective questioning to explore the attributes of your Natural Self and Divine Self, many man-made diagnostic assessments can be extremely helpful. The **Myers-Briggs Type Indicator**, the **DiSC Assessment, StrengthsFinder**, and **Spiritual Gift Assessments** are all instruments I have found to be of great value in gaining insights and understanding of my Natural and Divine Selves. I *highly recommend* you utilize as many of these (or other) assessment instruments as possible. (Appendix D includes a summary of how these instruments have helped me answer the question: "Who Am I?") While each of these instruments is man-made (i.e., imperfect), they offer valuable insights into our Natural and Divine Selves. However, in each instance, you will need to compare the assessment results with your own life experiences, allowing God to guide you, to arrive at any conclusions regarding the validity of insights provided by each instrument.

Accepting & Celebrating Your Divine Self

It is vitally important for you to realize that **your Divine Self is unique.** God made you different (in some ways) than anyone who has ever lived. There is not one ideal person you should try to emulate. Even Jesus was (and is) a unique individual. While we would like to see many attributes of Jesus's life and character expressed in our lives, we are not trying to be *exactly like* Jesus. The same applies to other people. Some individuals may demonstrate specific habits, attitudes, or values you would like to become your own, but your goal should not be to imitate others. *Our responsibility – our primary aim – is to become the person God created us to be.* While *there is an ideal you*, there is *no ideal person you should seek to emulate.*

It is imperative that you learn to accept and celebrate the unique individual God created you to be! Among the biggest hindrances in life are feelings of inadequacy and insignificance. "Voices" inside your head, and the many times you are criticized or dismissed by others, can undermine your ability to realize your full potential and calling. But God views you differently from how you view yourself. He sees your true abilities and strengths, and the significance you will experience by realizing your full potential.

God sees how your unique Divine Self can serve His purposes and fulfill your longing for meaning, purpose, and significance. He sees the many ways He has planned for you to contribute to His redemptive plan by unleashing your unique gifting and calling. God desires to show you your true value and potential. He wants you to fully accept and celebrate who He has created you to be, and He longs to guide and empower you in your journey to know and follow Him.

Jeremiah 33: [3] "Call to me and I will answer you and tell you great and unsearchable things you do not know."

Psalm 32: [8] "I will instruct you and teach you in the way you should go; I will counsel you with my loving eye on you."

Before closing this discussion of Essential Question #3: "Who Am I?", it is important to note that we need to understand one more part of our identity: *"the heart."* As I researched the original biblical languages used for the words translated as heart, soul, and spirit in both the Old and New Testaments, I believe *the heart is the synthesis of one's spirit, soul, and body. Our heart is the center of who we are at any given time,* and *it is from the heart that we are called to live*.

Proverbs 4: [23] Keep your heart with all vigilance, for from it flow the springs of life.

Luke 6: [45] "A good man brings good things out of the good stored up in his heart, and an evil man brings evil things out of the evil stored up in his heart. For the mouth speaks what the heart is full of."

Proverbs 21: [2] All deeds are right in the sight of the doer, but the Lord weighs the heart.

Proverbs 23: [7] For as he thinketh in his heart, so *is* he. (KJV)

We must live from our heart – the contents of which only God Himself can know, reveal, and change. Our heart is the source through which God energizes and propels us to fulfill our unique calling. From the depths of our hearts, we discover the courage, wisdom, and strength we need to live our lives with confidence, energy, and power. It is also within our hearts where the battles for all our significant breakthroughs are fought and won. *Your heart is where you will find the real you.* And the work it takes for the real you to be discovered, developed, and released is what the journey to know and follow God – The Great Adventure – is all about. We must learn to *wrestle with God* – to question, argue, pray, and plead – to experience the transformation He desires within our hearts.

Jeremiah 4: [3] This is what the LORD says...: "Break up your unplowed ground and do not sow among thorns. [4] Circumcise yourselves to the LORD, circumcise your hearts."

Luke 8: [15] "But the seed on good soil stands for those with a noble and good heart, who hear the word, retain it, and by persevering produce a crop."

While the Bible challenges us to grow in wisdom and understanding, the knowledge we gain does not solely produce the changes that result in our transformation. We are indeed involved in the process of spiritual growth, but *it is the Spirit of God at work within us that accomplishes the most significant changes.*

Zechariah 4: [6] 'Not by might nor by power, but by my Spirit,' says the Lord Almighty.

The transformation process is certainly mysterious, but what God ultimately changes within us is our heart – **and *only God can change our hearts*.** As you seek to know and follow God, your most significant challenge is to press into Him until He supernaturally produces changes within your heart. That is God's promise to us, and as He brings about our transformation, we grow ever closer to Him and experience an ever-burgeoning sense of meaning, purpose, and fulfillment in our lives.

Ezekiel 36: [25] I will sprinkle clean water on you, and you will be clean; I will cleanse you from all your impurities and from all your idols. [26] I will give you a new heart and put a new spirit in you; I will remove from you your heart of stone and give you a heart of flesh. [27] And I will put my Spirit in you and move you to follow my decrees and be careful to keep my laws.

As you grow in awareness of your Natural Self and Divine Self and press in to know and follow God, He will continue transforming your heart. Through that process – the ongoing transformation of your Natural Self toward your Divine Self – the significance that lies within you will emerge. And that sense of significance will be revealed and released as you discover and live out God's unique call on your life. It is absolutely critical to pursue an ever-deepening understanding of your Divine Self and wrestle with God to see your Divine Self gain increased prominence in your life. Your Divine Self is the person God created you to be. And all of this is accomplished as you seek deeper, more meaningful answers to Essential Question #3: "Who Am I?"

You are a truly unique individual. Only you possess your set of abilities, strengths, sensitivities, and motivations. Only you possess your insights, concerns, and interests in seeing God's justice prevail in the world. Therefore, **only you can accomplish what God has designed for your life, and only you can advance God's unique purposes for your life.** You may not realize it, but you are essential to God's redemptive plan for the world. If you fail to discover and release your Divine Self and surrender to how God desires to deploy you, an essential part of God's redemptive plan will remain undone. **Finding and living out your Divine Self and calling will release your destiny.** You must discover the person God created you to be and, with His guidance and ongoing support, allow that person to live freely, powerfully, and joyfully.

In the next chapter, we will explore how God's process for releasing your Divine Self unfolds as you seek answers to Essential Question #4: "What is God Calling Me to Do?" It isn't until you find answers to this final Essential Question that you can indeed follow God because you can't be a follower unless you can discern where the Leader is leading you!

Chapter 9

Essential Question #4: What is God Calling Me to Do?

The concise answer to Essential Question #4 is this: *God is calling you to know and follow Him*. The entirety of the Christian life is built on the principle that God desires good things for you and will provide those good things as you strive to follow His guidance. The key rhythm we need to cultivate is to actively <u>seek</u> God's will, patiently <u>*wait*</u> to discern His guidance accurately, and then earnestly strive to *surrender to* what He asks us to do. As we adhere to this simple 3-step pattern of seeking, waiting (for an answer), and surrendering, God will transform our mental framework – broadening and deepening our understanding of who He is, how He has designed life to be lived, and who we are – thereby transforming the way we live our lives.

> **Romans 12:** [1] Therefore, I urge you, brothers and sisters, in view of God's mercy, to offer your bodies as a living sacrifice, holy and pleasing to God – this is your true and proper worship. [2] Do not conform to the pattern of this world, but be transformed by the renewing of your mind. Then you

will be able to test and approve what God's will is – his good, pleasing and perfect will.

James 1: [17] Every good and perfect gift is from above, coming down from the Father of the heavenly lights, who does not change like shifting shadows.

The more you delve into Essential Questions #1-3, the more you'll realize the depth of transformation required in your life. Instead of striving to change yourself, a task that can never fully align with God's purposes, it's crucial to place your trust in God's plan for your growth and transformation. *The purpose of life is to know God and follow His guidance, becoming the person He created you to be, and doing the good works He has ordained for you.*

The journey of following Him will always yield superior results than crafting and pursuing your own plans, providing a sense of reassurance and security in your spiritual journey. For example, if you sense that God is challenging you to deal with expressions of anger in your life, and *your plan* is to try very hard to control your angry outbursts, you may experience some reasonably good results. However, your "success" in managing your anger on your own power will likely lead to unhealthy feelings of pride. Following your own plan would have altered the balance between two vices – less anger but more pride.

However, if you followed God's guidance (instead of your own plan), He would likely guide you on a path with multiple steps. First, He would lead you to understand that you have little power to control your angry thoughts. This would lead to the development of humility. Next, over a period of time, God would deliver you from the pattern of destructive thoughts and actions, replacing them with increased compassion and love. The result of following God's plan would be not just eliminating destructive instances of angry outbursts, but also growth in your character in multiple ways, illuminating a path of transformation you could never have envisioned on your own.

> **Proverbs 3:** [5] Trust in the Lord with all your heart and lean not on your own understanding; [6] in all your ways submit to him, and he will make your paths straight.

> **Isaiah 55:** [8] "For my thoughts are not your thoughts, neither are your ways my ways," declares the Lord. [9] "As the heavens are higher than the earth, so are my ways higher than your ways and my thoughts than your thoughts.

Our lives are so flawed, and our understanding of God and His ways so limited (imperfect Natural Self) that we could never chart an effective plan for our own transformation in any area of our lives. We need God's wisdom, guidance, and strength. That is why we must develop the habit of seeking God and following His leadership rather than relying on our own reasoning. As we grow in our understanding of who God is, how He has designed life to be lived, and who we are (Essential Questions #1-3), we will increasingly grow in our capacity to discern what God is indeed asking us to do (Essential Question #4).

This is one of life's great paradoxes: **God calls us to accept full responsibility for our own lives _and_ fully surrender to His leadership.**

> **Romans 14:** [12] So then, each of us will give an account of ourselves to God.

> **Galatians 6:** [5] For each one should carry their own load.

> **James 4:** [7] Submit yourselves therefore to God. (ESV)

Matthew 16: [24] Then Jesus said to his disciples, "Whoever wants to be my disciple must deny themselves and take up their cross and follow me.

The tension between these dual responsibilities is similar to that of a captain of a military ship, who is simultaneously responsible for the vessel and crew under their care, while also being responsible for fully surrendering to the leadership of their superiors. In the same way, the focus of Essential Question #4 is on your personal responsibility for every aspect of your life while continually seeking to discern and follow God's leadership. In short, God wants you to take full responsibility for who you are, what you say and do, and your goals in life, but all of this *only* as God directs you. I know that might seem like a heavy burden, but everything in your life is under the gentle care of God's mercy and grace.

Hebrews 4: [16] Let us then approach God's throne of grace with confidence so that we may receive mercy and find grace to help us in our time of need.

To better understand how we can honor these dual responsibilities simultaneously, let us examine our lives from four different perspectives: Moment-by-Moment Surrender, the 6 Components of the Natural Dimension (Chapter 7), Personal Gospel Message, and Personal Life Calling.

I. Moment-by-Moment Surrender

Our consciousness continually vacillates between thoughts of the distant past, near past, present, near future, and beyond. We often spend time reflecting on some aspects of the past to gain an understanding that enables us to make wise choices in the present, which, in turn, will produce positive outcomes in the future. At other times, we reflect on past experiences that have caused hurt, confusion, disappointment, loss, or failure, seeking healing and a better understanding of God's purposes for allowing these difficult experiences. As we focus on our present circumstances, many questions often resonate within our hearts and minds: "What am I supposed to do?" "How should I respond to this?" "How can I make wise choices today that will have long-term benefits?" "In what ways should I be planning for the future?"

We instinctively realize that the quality of our life (now and in the future) is at stake in the choices we make moment by moment each day. Other than waiting for God's divine intervention, the process you use to make decisions is one of the most significant influences on the outcomes you experience in life. If you believe God is real and desires good outcomes for your life, the wisest course of action is to solicit God's input in making the decisions that will most impact your life. "What is God calling me to do?" "How can I make the right decisions for my life today?" How you answer Essential Question #4 will profoundly impact every area of your life. These observations should make it clear that Essential Question #4 may be the most crucial question of all.

Essential Question #4: "What is God Calling Me to Do?" addresses the essence of what it means to follow God – to do what God specifically directs you to do. Because God is always purposeful in what He does, *every answer you discover to this Essential Question throughout your spiritual journey is pregnant with the most profound sense of meaning and purpose anyone could ever hope to find.* Like the previous Essential Question ("Who Am I?"), understanding God's purposes for what He calls you to do must be viewed from two different viewpoints.

First, God desires to provide direction for our lives through experiences that help us develop godly character attributes. That is, God will often *direct* our lives in ways that provide opportunities for us to grow.

> **Proverbs 16:** [9] In their hearts, humans plan their course, but the LORD establishes their steps.

> **Romans 5:** [3] We also glory in our sufferings, because we know that suffering produces perseverance; [4] perseverance, character; and character, hope.

In addition to **directing** us into experiences that help us develop character, God sometimes **allows** experiences to occur that can achieve His character-growing purposes in our lives. That is, sometimes the challenges we face result from actions initiated by others but used by God to advance His Kingdom purposes in our lives.

> **Romans 8:** [28] And we know that *in all things* God works for the good of those who love him, who have been called according to his purpose. [29] For those God foreknew he also predestined to be conformed to the image of his Son, that he might be the firstborn among many brothers and sisters.

God's *directives* and *interventions* in our lives that encourage character growth are manifestations of His work *IN* each of us. But God also desires to advance His Kingdom purposes *THROUGH* each of us. So, the second way God directs our lives is for us to accomplish the unique "call" He has placed on our lives – fulfilling our destiny.

Jeremiah 29: [11] "For I know the plans I have for you,"
declares the Lord, "plans to prosper you and not to harm
you, plans to give you hope and a future."

Ephesians 4: [1] As a prisoner for the Lord, then, I urge you
to live a life worthy of the calling you have received.

So, sometimes God intervenes in our lives in ways designed to
help us develop godly character, while at other times, His purpose
is to accomplish "good works" that He has "assigned" to us.

Ephesians 2: [10] For we are God's handiwork, created in
Christ Jesus to do good works, which God prepared in
advance for us to do.

Often, God directs our lives in ways that accomplish both
objectives simultaneously. However, the only way you will ever
find meaningful and timely answers to the question, "What is God
Calling Me to Do?" is by asking – and then waiting until He
responds.

John 15: [5] "I am the vine; you are the branches. If you
remain in me and I in you, you will bear much fruit; apart
from me you can do nothing. ... [7] If you remain in me and
my words remain in you, ask whatever you wish, and it will
be done for you. [8] This is to my Father's glory, that you bear
much fruit, showing yourselves to be my disciples.

People often interpret Jesus' directive to "remain in me, and
my words remain in you" as meaning that we must devote significant time to reading, understanding, digesting, and even memorizing scripture. Indeed, that is a valid takeaway from this passage.

However, I think a broader and equally valid interpretation is that Jesus' reference to His "words" also means the ways He desires to "speak" to us personally on a moment-by-moment basis as we seek His guidance. The most significant growth and fulfillment will occur as we continually connect and interact with Jesus – receiving His guidance, wisdom, strength, support, and other manifestations of His grace.

Philippians 2: [13] "For God is working in you, giving you the desire and the power to do what pleases him". (NLT)

When God "speaks" to us or directs our attention to a specific topic, the directions or insights we receive might be related to issues from 1) the distant past, 2) the recent past, 3) the present, 4) the near future, or 5) the distant future. In each of these cases, God's intention and motivation is always to reveal some truth that can aid in the transformation of our thoughts, attitudes, and actions. (In Chapter 8, we characterized this as the transformation of our Natural Self toward our Divine Self.) Let's examine a few brief examples to help clarify these thoughts.

Many of our attitudes, beliefs, and habits (our current mental framework) were established during childhood or adolescence. To bring about meaningful transformation in our lives, God will sometimes direct our attention to experiences from our distant past and provide us with new insights into those experiences, thereby modifying our thinking and understanding. The insights we receive from these reflections will result in some degree of transformation ("renewing our mind"). Our attitudes, beliefs, and habits can also develop from our day-to-day experiences. For example, God might direct our thinking toward experiences from the recent past (like a conflict with a co-worker) to provide insights that, when acted upon, will accomplish additional transformation. *Every time God directs our thinking to experiences from our past (dis-*

tant or recent), He intends to deepen our understanding of one or more of the four Essential Questions.

However, we live our lives forward, not backward. Therefore, God will also direct our attention toward issues related to the present and future. God desires to direct our present actions – what we will or will not do day-by-day – as well as in the days, weeks, and years ahead. The Holy Spirit will often direct our attention back and forth between past and present experiences as we consider how to respond to the challenges we face each day. As God brings memories to mind, our responsibility is to ask God to clarify how He wants us to respond to those issues.

For example, suppose God brings a painful memory from the past to mind. In that case, He may desire to "walk" you through that experience again to bring about a deeper understanding of the experience that will aid you in dealing with a present situation. In addition to thinking about issues from the past, present, and near future, God will sometimes direct your attention to matters related to the distant future. For example, during your teenage years, God's plan is for you to develop an understanding of the opposite sex. He will not only *direct* you regarding whom you should date now and what you can learn from those experiences, but also aid you in discerning what kind of person you should select as a spouse in the future.

At its most basic level, God's design for your life is for you to grow in your capacity to **know,** **follow,** and **trust** Him. As you grow in these three capacities, your life will align more fully with God's will and plan. To grow in the **_knowledge_** of God means to gain insights into His character and His ways of thinking, feeling, and acting. To grow in your capacity to **_follow_** God means to increasingly seek to understand and obey what He desires of you (thereby decreasing the emphasis placed on your own desires or plans). Growing your capacity to **_trust_** God means you increasingly wait for God to "move" rather than attempting to control things by your own power. *Growth in these three foundational capacities – knowing, following, and trusting God – is the heartbeat of spiritual growth.* At any given time throughout your day, God desires to intervene in your life in ways that will develop one or more of these three capacities. Let me provide an example.

As I attempt to capture my thoughts in writing this portion of this chapter, we are in the 11th month of the Coronavirus pandemic of 2020. Because my wife and I are in the high-risk category, we have spent almost all of our time at home. As an introvert, I have no problem accepting the confinement; I actually enjoy it most of the time! Also, my temperament makes it relatively easy for me to establish and maintain personal disciplines. So, the confinement should help me with the writing of this book. In fact, during the first four months of the pandemic, I spent several hours writing almost every day. But then, almost instantaneously, the motivation to write disappeared. I was convinced that God had called me to write this book. I had already written portions of every chapter and could have easily written more in each chapter (so I knew I *could* finish the book). But the motivation to continue writing had disappeared. Instead of *taking personal control* of the situation and disciplining myself to continue writing each day, I directed my attention to God to discern how I *should* respond to the loss of motivation. I wanted to understand and follow God's will.

Several questions surfaced in my heart and mind. "Should I use my ability to discipline myself and continue to write each day?" "Should I wait for the motivation to return?" "Is this 'the enemy' trying to prevent me from obeying God's will for my life?" or "Is this You, God, interrupting or redirecting my daily disciplines?" "Has this 'call' to write a book been a prideful motivation, or did I correctly discern Your call to write?" Many questions like these arose within me over the days and weeks that followed.

At first, God didn't respond directly to my questions; I just "sensed" He was asking me to *wait* for some "answer" before making any decisions. Over the several months before I began writing again, I grew in my capacity to know, follow, and trust God. The growth, however, wasn't linear. That is, I didn't first grow in knowledge, second in my capacity to follow, and then deepen my trust in Him. Instead, the capacities in all three areas occurred seemingly randomly. But over the entire time, my knowledge of God "deepened" as I surrendered to the possibility that God might be calling me to abandon the writing project entirely. My capacity to follow God grew as I surrendered my daily activities to His leadership. My trust in God grew as I surrendered to the understanding that His ways are different than mine, and He will always act in ways that will bless, protect, and guide me further into His will for my life.

Then, almost instantaneously, the motivation to write returned. The writing hiatus – about six months – was meant by God to help me grow in my capacity to know, follow, and trust Him. It also allowed me to bring fresh insights into every chapter. When you find yourself in a situation where your mind is flooded with questions, pause, and ask God to help you understand how He desires you to respond. *Periods of waiting for God to respond are an essential part of the process of learning how to follow Him.*

As I mentioned earlier, we face the paradox of dual responsibilities. First, we are personally responsible for our thoughts, words, attitudes, and actions. Second, we are responsible for following God's leadership. When we feel personally accountable for accomplishing some task or goal, our natural inclination is to create and implement an *action plan*. However, when we think God is responsible for something, our natural inclination will generally be to *wait* for God to act or to direct us in some way. Both inclinations are appropriate (although waiting can be tough) and are often intertwined in our daily experiences. *However, even in situations where we are responsible for engaging in some endeavor, we still need to create space for God to intervene in any way He desires.* Sometimes, God directs us on a path to achieve a goal, and sometimes, God intervenes supernaturally to accomplish the same end.

When you believe God is directing you toward accomplishing a particular goal in the days or years ahead, His plan is *not* for you to rely *exclusively* on your own personal abilities and resources. Instead, God's plan is for you to **intentionally direct your attention to following Him** so He can direct your life – and the plan to reach the goal – in ways that will best accomplish His purposes. So, you are *not* supposed to give primary attention to achieving God's goals for your life using your own wisdom and power. Instead, *your primary attention needs to be directed toward knowing, following, and trusting God* in and through the experiences as they unfold.

> **Proverbs 3:** [5] Trust in the Lord with all your heart and lean
> not on your own understanding; [6] in all your ways submit
> to him, and he will make your paths straight.

However, that does not mean God never wants us to engage in thoughtful planning. Sometimes, God **does** want us to think in a planful way.

> **Proverbs 21:** [5] The plans of the diligent lead to profit as
> surely as haste leads to poverty.

Our challenge, however, will **always** be to create "space" for God to intervene or to direct our thinking or actions at any time and in any way He chooses. *Our greatest challenge is to discern when we are to take control and when we need to wait and let God take control.* It might be helpful to understand it this way: we are responsible for the *inputs* (our actions), but God is responsible for the *outcomes*.

We may not realize it, but we spend a significant amount of

time thinking each day. Often, our thinking is directed toward completing various tasks and responsibilities from our daily to-do list. However, when not functioning on "auto-pilot," we frequently spend a lot of time thinking in seemingly random ways, drifting from one topic to another and shifting our attention between the past, present, and future. Since God has ordained that our transformation is based upon the "renewing of our minds" (Romans 12:2), it is imperative that some of your time is spent thinking in *intentional* ways – directed explicitly toward the ways God desires to lead and guide you. *The primary vehicle for spiritual, emotional, intellectual, and psychological transformation is to develop the habit of inviting God into all of our conscious thinking.*

God's Purposes for Your Life

While God's interventions may often be "hidden" or seem to occur randomly, God is planful in how He works in our lives.

> **Philippians 2:** [13] for it is God who works in you to will and to act to fulfill his good purpose.

One of our challenges is to discern how God desires to use our daily situations. That is, what is God trying to accomplish through any particular event or experience? At any given point in time, God will be "working in you" to achieve one or more of the following six purposes:

1. Teaching you something about who He is (Essential Question #1).
2. Teaching you general principles about how He has designed life to be lived (Essential Question #2).
3. Teaching you something about who you are (Essential Question #3).

4. Allowing or designing circumstances to draw you closer to Him and others.

5. Allowing or designing circumstances to develop your character and habits.

6. Directing your life in a new direction or toward a new objective (Essential Question #4).

Understanding these six purposes – and discerning God's intentions for any particular circumstance – will add meaning and purpose to everything in your life. That is why we must develop the capacity to discern the connection between our daily experiences and God's purposes. This will require an understanding of the ways we think each day.

Our conscious thoughts vacillate among four different modes: reflective thinking, planning, acting, and reacting. When we reflect, we examine past experiences and current circumstances to make sense of some aspects of our lives. Reflective thinking aims to move us forward with greater confidence, clarity, and purpose. Motivated to improve our life circumstances, reflective thinking naturally leads to planning. When we plan, we create a set of objectives (including action steps) designed to accomplish a predetermined goal (which likely arose from our reflective thinking). Our daily actions derive quite naturally from times of reflection and planning. Reacting (or responsive behavior) occurs as situations interrupt the "flow" of our planned day.

As we recognize how our day-to-day experiences advance God's purposes in and through our lives, we will experience increased meaning and purpose in what we do each day. But making those connections requires divine revelation. As you develop the practice of initiating moment-by-moment connections with God, combined with planned experiences for connecting with Him, you will more readily see God's six purposes being developed in your life and experience an ever-increasing sense of meaning, purpose, and fulfillment. Let's examine two primary ways we can create "space" in our lives to provide for those kinds of "connections" with God: Daily Challenges and Opportunities, and Rhythms of Life.

Daily Challenges and Opportunities

You can only focus on one issue at any particular moment. However, most of us spend much of our day running on "auto-pilot" – functioning out of habit and ritual. We generally think and act in predictable ways. However, there are times each day when this seemingly "preprogrammed" thinking and acting is interrupted. Sometimes, the interruption presents as a "problem" that demands your attention, such as a co-worker asking a question. At other times, the interruption is just a thought or idea that "pops" into your mind. Regardless of how an interruption occurs, as we develop the habit of directing our attention toward God, to discern how He wants us to respond to the "interruption," He will direct us in ways that will advance one or more of His six purposes for our life. So, our primary challenge is to direct our consciousness – *as often as possible* – toward seeking God's input into our lives.

The primary way we direct our consciousness toward God is by intentionally *inviting* God into our experiences. Just speak to God within your mind. Your "words" might be: "God, help me make sense of this." "Show me what You want me to see about this situation." "How should I respond?" "Is there anything I'm supposed to do?" The more you develop the habit of inviting God into your moment-by-moment thinking, the more you will grow, and the more you will see God's purposes for your life unfold. One way I developed this habit during my teaching career was by placing a scripture card on my computer monitor at school. Each time I viewed that card, it reminded me to invite God into my day.

I also placed a small placard with the initials F.R.O.G. on a cabinet at the back of my classroom. Viewing those initials, which stood for **F**ully **R**ely **O**n **G**od, reminded me to invite God into my thoughts and actions.

As you develop the habit of directing your attention toward seeking God, moment-by-moment and day-by-day, He will direct your life in ways that benefit you most. All you need to do is practice turning your attention to Him; He does all the "heavy lifting." That is why I frequently direct your attention to the singular idea of following God, as this mindset causes you to seek His input as the starting point for every decision and concern in your life.

Moment-by-moment interactions with God will automatically occur as we step out of "auto-pilot living" and develop the habit of directing our conscious thinking toward Him. However, if we are not careful, this reflection, planning, acting, and reacting pattern will only focus on managing our current life circumstances. To fully achieve God's purposes for our lives – and to optimize the meaning, purpose, and fulfillment God desires for us – we must allow God to direct our thinking in new ways. Changing our focus from day-to-day thinking to reflecting, planning, and acting in ways that will bring about God's plan for our lives will require us to connect with God during periods directed solely for that purpose. We will need to *manage* our current day-to-day patterns of living and allow God to help us create sufficient "space" within which He can speak into our lives in significant ways.

II. Rhythms of Life – 6 Components of the Natural Dimension

You will spend your time on either planned or unplanned activities. At almost any time, one can switch to the other. The unplanned moment-by-moment connections with God have been discussed above. The following discussion explores how you can connect with God in intentional and meaningful ways.

In Chapter 7 (Essential Question #2: How Has God Designed Life to be Lived?) I identified 6 Components of the Natural Dimension and stated that it is normally God's plan for our lives to include activities in each of these areas:

1. **Connecting with God** – doing anything *with* God.
2. **Work** – activities that *must* be done for survival or orderly living.
3. **Rest** – *disengaging* from activities with any other identified purpose.
4. **Recreation** – experiences or activities that are *enjoyable*.
5. **Social Interactions** – experiences or activities done *with others.*
6. **Service** – activities done with the intent *to serve the needs of others.*

In most circumstances, your life should include one or more activities in each of these six areas. Part of your responsibility is to examine how each component will find expression in your life. Most people habitually practice the same pattern of behaviors in each component for extended periods – sometimes even years! However, part of your responsibility is to ask God if He desires you to modify any of your actions. At any given time, God may direct your attention to one of these areas and encourage you to make modifications. While these kinds of planful interactions with God can occur at any time, the area that most directly influences spiritual growth and transformation is setting aside time to connect with God daily.

Connecting With God

While our overall goal is to develop the habit of connecting with God as often as possible throughout each day, it is essential to cultivate our ability to connect with Him in *planned and intentional ways*. While many people can connect with God through activities like walking, running, listening to music, or other forms of exercise or relaxation, times spent without distractions are often of the *most significant value*. I have found the following five activities most effective in connecting with God meaningfully.

1. Scripture Readings
2. Devotional Readings
3. Silence and Solitude
4. General Reading or Writing
5. Worship

Now that I'm retired, my typical day begins with the first three practices. Currently, I read from five different devotional books, follow a "read through the Bible" yearly plan, and then spend some time in silence and solitude where I have no "agenda" other than connecting with God. My time of solitude will include times of seemingly random thought, interrupted by times of prayer. I allow my mind to "wander" and only interrupt my thinking if I sense I've lost my connection with God. The total time spent on the first two activities is usually 45-60 minutes daily. The time I spend in silence and solitude can vary greatly. Frequently, silence and solitude lead to a time of writing to capture what I have been thinking about. In that case, my writing time can expand quite a bit. Sometimes, God leads me into additional times of silence and solitude as I try to attend to the Holy Spirit's promptings. Reading times vary from day to day and depend significantly on my wife's daily activities. *In general, I strive each day to discern how God might guide my ongoing activities.* However, I still spend a considerable amount of time each day just lost in my thoughts, asking God to guide me toward accomplishing His purposes.

As I write these words, we are confined mainly by COVID-19 restrictions, so I spend minimal time engaged in work, recreation, social interactions, or service. However, I expect that will change. When it does, my "plans" for connecting with God might change significantly. I should also note that my approach to connecting with God may not be suitable for every person's lifestyle or temperament. Many people find it more effective to schedule these practices at different times in their day. For example, some people find it most helpful to carve out time in the middle of their workday, before or after dinner, or before going to bed. Many people also build multiple shorter periods spread throughout their day to connect with God.

It's also important to know that my present daily schedule is not something I established all at once. Instead, each component (as well as the overall "flow" of my day) unfolded over many years. The more I learned about God, His ways, and myself, the more my scheduled activities developed in productive ways. For many years, I struggled to faithfully set aside time to connect with God in meaningful ways. And even during those times that I was faithful, that time didn't always seem to be particularly beneficial. I often felt like I was "checking off boxes" of being obedient to God rather than feeling like I was actually connecting with Him.

But God used my entire journey to help deepen my under-standing of all four Essential Questions. Over time, my "success" at being faithful to connect with God increased, as did the depth of my "connections" and their *effectiveness* in bringing about noticeable transformation. I attribute my ability to grow in faith-fulness to my "connections" with God and the outpouring of His grace. As I persistently asked God for the capacity to be more faithful, He responded by changing my heart – increasing my desire to connect with Him – which translated into the strength and determination I needed to adjust my behavior patterns. I believe *persistently seeking God* is the most essential ingredient to spiritual growth.

> **Matthew 7:** [7] Ask, and it will be given to you; seek, and you will find; knock, and the door will be opened to you. [8] For everyone who asks receives; he who seeks finds; and to the one who knocks, the door will be opened.

I took the time to describe part of my journey in connecting with God, so that you would not feel the need to establish the "ideal" plan all at once. Instead, if you sense God is calling you to change how you connect with Him, try to discern what God is leading you to do "next." Ongoing transformation is always about what God asks you to do, one step at a time. Just remember it's the journey that counts, and mostly the journey of deepening your relationship with God.

> **Galatians 5:** [25] Since we live by the Spirit, let us keep in step with the Spirit.

> **Psalms 119:** [133] Direct my footsteps according to your word.

Each time you connect with God – whether during planned time or amid your busy day – God will always direct your mind in a way that is designed to advance one or more of His six purposes for your life. If you genuinely attempt to follow God's guidance rather than trying to change yourself in ways you think will be beneficial, the pathway God chooses will often not be one you would have chosen for yourself. Your natural tendency will be to focus on what you believe is the area(s) of growth that *seems* (to you) most important to change. However, God often works in very different ways that may appear to you as less important.

> Isaiah 55: [8] "For my thoughts are not your thoughts,
> neither are your ways my ways," declares the LORD. [9] "As
> the heavens are higher than the earth, so are my ways
> higher than your ways and my thoughts than your
> thoughts.

I wrote earlier that God desires to accomplish His purposes both **IN** and **THROUGH** us. As you see the connections between your daily experiences and how God is accomplishing His purposes **IN** you, meaning and purpose will increase significantly. My experience, however, has been that as I see God's purposes being advanced **THROUGH** me, I have experienced the most significant degree of fulfillment. While God may direct your thoughts in many ways throughout your day as He advances His purposes in your life, two areas of thought will significantly influence the degree of fulfillment you experience. Both areas fall under the category of Service: 1) Your Personal Gospel Message and 2) Your Personal Life Calling.

When I first introduced the Essential Questions in Chapter 6, I explained that each question functions as a *container*. That is, as we connect with God, He will frequently give us insights that fall into one or more of the four Essential Question containers. As each of these four containers fills with increased understanding, our lives become more aligned with God's will, and we experience ever-deepening levels of meaning, purpose, and fulfillment. Similarly, your Personal Gospel Message and Personal Life Calling also function as *containers*. As your understandings and experiences increase in these two *containers*, you will become more effective in advancing God's purposes **THROUGH** you and experience enhanced levels of fulfillment.

III. Personal Gospel Message

> **Mark 16:** [15] [Jesus] said to them, "Go into all the world and preach the gospel to all creation."

When I first began attending church services after becoming born again, one of the themes present in many of the messages I heard preached was each believer's responsibility to "preach the Gospel." Indeed, no one can be born again without first hearing the Gospel, so believers' call to "preach the Gospel" made perfect sense. However, I felt intimidated by the idea of personally communicating the Gospel message to others. I felt like I didn't have a deep enough understanding of the Gospel to offer the gift of salvation to anyone on my own.

The intimidation turned into guilt as I continued to be instructed about my responsibility and then failed to share the Gospel message with people I encountered. I wanted to share what Jesus had done for me and the "new" life I was discovering, but I never understood how to effectively connect my experiences to "preaching the gospel." The frustration and guilt surfaced each time I heard a preacher remind me of this God-given responsibility. However, as I grew in my understanding of God and His ways, a deeper understanding of my responsibility to "preach the Gospel" emerged.

When preachers teach about believers' responsibility to share the Gospel, they often use the words "witness" and "testimony" (both biblical terms). These words are commonly associated with courtroom proceedings, where an attorney attempts to prove a case before a judge and jury. I want you to recognize that it's not the responsibility of the witness to prove the case; their role is to provide a "testimony" of what they have personally "witnessed" or experienced. Your Personal Gospel Message has the same meaning. Your role in God's overall plan of calling people to become born again is to provide "testimony" when God provides the opportunity. So, it's not your duty to "lead people to Christ." **God is calling you to communicate to others only what you have personally experienced or learned in your spiritual journey as it relates to another person's needs.** *That is your Personal Gospel Message.*

For example, suppose a person you encounter is feeling a great deal of pressure fulfilling their personal responsibilities (e.g., as a mother), and you've learned how to express your fears and anxieties to God and have received His comfort, encouragement, direction, and strength. In that case, your "witness" or "testimony" is to describe your own experience in similar circumstances. If you feel bold enough, you might offer to pray for the person, or even pray on the spot. Your calling to "preach the Gospel" is only to be a true friend to another person (thus fulfilling the Second Greatest Commandment). You don't have to "prove" or "accomplish" anything. Just tell that portion of "your story" about how you have experienced God's Grace as it relates to the situation of a person with whom you interact. I once heard someone say, "A message spoken from your mind reaches a mind; a message spoken from your heart reaches a heart; but a message spoken from your life reaches a life." So, share your life experiences with God as He presents the opportunities for you to do so.

No one individual, other than Jesus Himself, can communicate the *entirety* of the Gospel message. Only Jesus is holy, strong, courageous, and wise enough to embody the fullness of truth, which is the Gospel message. Those who are called to follow Jesus and be used as vessels through which the Gospel message will be advanced are entrusted with only a portion of the whole Gospel message. Each messenger (or herald) must carefully discern the portion of the Gospel message God has revealed to them through their spiritual journey with Him.

This "Personal Gospel Message" is your primary calling and

"testimony" to the world. You must clarify this Personal Gospel Message through times of connecting with God and share your message with others as God creates those opportunities. However, while you pursue this calling, you must also recognize and honor the unique "Personal Gospel Message" God places on the hearts of others. Only as we each share our own "Personal Gospel Message" does the "full" Gospel message become preached to the world. While sharing your Personal Gospel Message is a primary call for every believer, you are also called to a unique set of "good works" to which God will direct you at various times and in multiple ways throughout your life.

> **Ephesians 2:** [10] "For we are God's handiwork, created in Christ Jesus to do good works, which God prepared in advance for us to do."

IV. Personal Life Calling

In the previous section, I explained that your Personal Gospel Message – **communicating how you have experienced God's grace working in you** – is a "calling" in your life. However, sharing your Personal Gospel Message is only one part of your calling. Your "full calling" is to become the person God created you to be, which includes sharing your Personal Gospel Message *plus* the variety of ways you will be led to serve God and others – your Personal Life Calling. In Chapter 8 (Essential Question #3: "Who Am I?"), I included my personal mission statement: "To help people better understand who God is, and how they might be blocking what He wants to accomplish in and through their lives." My Personal Calling, which has been expressed in various ways over the years, has always been enacted in ways consistent with my mission statement.

As you grow in your understanding of your Natural and Divine

Selves, you will be able to craft your own personal mission statement. However, your mission can be accomplished in various ways. The more you allow God to direct your life, the more you will understand your Personal Life Calling and the more you will experience meaning, purpose, and fulfillment. The only obstacles that can keep you from experiencing the "full life" (John 10:10) God has planned for you exist inside you. You will not fail to experience the "full life" because of prejudice, bigotry, hate, or any other stumbling blocks you might encounter in life. What will prevent you from experiencing the "full life" is fear of failure, feelings of inadequacy, procrastination, laziness, lack of direction, and any other false belief or flawed character attribute preventing you from moving forward. And all those internal issues can and will be overcome as you connect with God and follow His leadership.

How your Personal Life Calling unfolds (and might change) over time will be unique to you and is often related to your life situation. For example, your age or life stage might be a significant factor. If you are a teenager or young adult, your Personal Life Calling may be expressed in ways that will prepare you for (or lead you to) your career choice or employment. If you are married, the demands for caring for your marriage and family will likely modify how your Personal Life Calling finds expression throughout the many years of family and career building. If you are at or near retirement, how your Personal Life Calling finds expression may be influenced by your physical health and financial resources. However, regardless of your circumstances, the way your Personal Life Calling finds expression needs to be guided by God Himself and will *always involve serving the needs of others* in some way. But the benefit of living out your Personal Life Calling will always be the same – you will experience unprecedented levels of meaning, purpose, and personal fulfillment as you connect your planned and unplanned activities with God's plan for your life.

One additional – and highly significant – aspect of your Personal Life Calling is the impact God desires to accomplish **_THROUGH_** your life toward advancing His Kingdom Purposes. One of the major themes throughout the Bible is the impact of sin on the world and God's interventions to establish His Kingdom here on earth. The "Lord's Prayer" includes the words, "Your Kingdom come, Your will be done, on earth as is it in heaven" (Matthew 6:10). In Chapters 3 and 4 of the Gospel of Matthew, we learn about Jesus being baptized, and then "led by the Spirit into the wilderness to be tempted by the devil." In Matthew, Chapter 4, we read:

> [8] Again, the devil took him to a very high mountain and showed him all the kingdoms of the world and their splendor. [9] "All this I will give you," he said, "if you will bow down and worship me."

Also, the Book of Revelation presents insights into the final days on earth around the time of Jesus' second coming. Revelation 11:15 says:

> "The kingdom of the world has become the kingdom of our Lord and of his Messiah, and he will reign forever and ever."

These passages and many others help us understand that God desires to use His people, through their Personal Gospel Message and Personal Life Calling, to break Satan's power over the "kingdoms of this world" and establish God's Kingdom here on earth. "Kingdoms of this world" can be understood as areas that greatly influence the culture of a society. In America, these areas of influence would include government, education, the arts, the family, the church, science, technology, and the media. Satan's influence has been like a cancer and has increasingly brought about decay and destruction in each of these earthly "kingdoms". As God's people mature, they will increasingly act as "salt" and "light" to inject godly principles and values within each arena.

> **Matthew 5:** [13] "You are the salt of the earth. But if the salt loses its saltiness, how can it be made salty again? It is no longer good for anything, except to be thrown out and trampled underfoot. [14] "You are the light of the world. A town built on a hill cannot be hidden. [15] Neither do people light a lamp and put it under a bowl. Instead, they put it on its stand, and it gives light to everyone in the house. [16] In the same way, let your light shine before others, that they may see your good deeds and glorify your Father in heaven.

(In the book, "Invading Babylon: The 7 Mountain Mandate", Lance Wallnau and Bill Johnson do an excellent job of describing these earthly "kingdoms" as well as how God intends to use His people to break Satan's power in these realms.)

There are three ways mature Christians can influence the "kingdoms of this world." First is their impact on the culture of the environments within which they function. The values Christians demonstrate as they live their lives in front of others, along with their integrity and compassion, have a profound influence on those around them. Your ability to maintain stability, peace, humility, strength, and confidence as you confront challenges gives regular "witness" to the reality and power of God's work in a believer.

The second way mature Christians influence the worldly kingdoms within which they function is by sharing their Personal Gospel Message. As you develop relationships with others, God will provide opportunities for you to share how your relationship with Jesus has impacted your life. As others recognize how the power of God's Presence brings meaning, purpose, and fulfillment to your life and produces incredible levels of strength and peace, God will use your "message" to draw them to Himself.

The third way mature Christians impact the "worldly kingdoms" within which they work is by influencing the entire realm's operational functions. Mature Christians bring integrity, creativity, excellence, and wisdom that change how a "worldly kingdom" operates. Whether you're an accountant, dishwasher, mother, or policeman, how you fulfill your "professional" duties influences how others behave. And as you "advance" in performing your duties, your sphere of influence will broaden. As more worldly kingdoms are managed and directed by mature Christians, the entirety of those domains becomes influenced by Christians. Over time, as more and more Christians discover and live out their Personal Life Message and Calling, "the kingdoms of this world" increasingly become "kingdoms of our Lord".

Many Christians believe God's "call" on their life must be somehow closely related to the Church, like being a pastor or missionary. The reality, however, is that *God's "call" extends to every area of life, including* the Church. So, your Personal Life Calling may be as an educator, a firefighter, a small group leader, a stockbroker, a musician, a politician, an usher or greeter, a mother or father, or any other way God might direct you to serve. *Any way God specifically gifts and leads you to invest prayer and effort, will be part of your Personal Life Calling.* God's ultimate goal (for working *through* you) is for you to advance a culture of godly values, wisdom, excellence, and integrity into one or more of the "earthly kingdoms" to advance His Kingdom purposes "on earth as it is in heaven."

Your Personal Life Calling will use your most significant interests, insights, abilities, passions, and strengths. You are a uniquely gifted person. No one God has created has your unique gifts, abilities, interests, strengths, and weaknesses. God has created you to contribute to the world uniquely through your life. As you allow God to clarify and grow your Personal Gospel Message and Personal Life Calling, you will become more closely aligned with the person God created you to be and experience ever-increasing levels of meaning, purpose, and fulfillment. (Appendix E contains an overview of my Personal Life Calling.)

It is vitally *essential* for you to know you have all the resources necessary for experiencing the "full life" present within you. However, "lies" or misunderstandings in your mental or emotional framework hindering your progress must be replaced with the truths that lead to success and fulfillment. The Apostle Paul discussed this "renewing your mind" process in Romans 12:1-2 (see chapter opening).

In Chapter 11, I will enumerate several "lies" or misunderstandings of God and His ways that, if allowed to direct your thinking and actions, will undermine God's working in and through you. However, the most significant "lie" that prevents most people from fully living out their Personal Life Calling relates to feelings of inadequacy. You will frequently "hear" the following "lies" being spoken in your mind as you press into God to fulfill your Personal Life Calling: "You're not good (or smart, or holy, or strong, or responsible, etc.) enough to do this!" "Why would God choose *you* when so many other people are better suited for this responsibility?" "What makes you think God would pick you?" "You're so full of yourself!"

There are an infinite number of ways the devil will attempt to undermine God's working in and through you by stirring up feelings of inadequacy and fear within you. Your response must be the same as that of the Apostle Paul. After enumerating some of his own challenges, he writes the following truth that he discovered as central to fulfilling God's call on his life:

Philippians 4: [13] "I can do all things through Him who strengthens me." (NASB)

The Apostle Paul discovered an essential truth about how God works in and through us. Our faith and trust in God's power, promises, and faithfulness enable us to overcome every obstacle and challenge. Jesus said that the "truth will set us free," and those truths are found in pursuing Him.

John 8: [32] "Then you will know the truth, and the truth will set you free."

John 14: [6] Jesus answered, "I am the way and the truth and the life.

We experience the "full life" Jesus came to provide for us as we walk in relationship with Him and allow the Holy Spirit to renew our minds. We embrace many falsehoods – about God, ourselves, and how God designed life to be lived – that can keep us from accomplishing all God wants us to be and do. Only the Voice and Presence of God Himself can speak the words, deliver the healing, and provide the power and motivation each of us needs to overcome the obstacles within us and reveal the truths that set us free.

While we must discover many truths, it's not **_WHAT_** you know, but **_WHO_** you know that makes the difference. Only by walking closely with God can one discover essential truths. And only God can direct you in the ways that will accomplish all His good purposes in and through your life. We must find the best ways to truly "connect" with Him and then build those practices into our daily lives. Only in Him, with Him, and through Him will we discover and walk in all His ways.

Psalm 32: [8] I will instruct you and teach you in the way you should go; I will counsel you with my loving eye on you.

Acts 17: [28] For in him we live and move and have our being.

There are three significant reasons for accomplishing the tasks God assigns to us. The first seems somewhat selfish: to experience God's blessings. However, that's not entirely selfish because God desires to bless us. He wants us to experience all the "good things" He has planned for us to enjoy. However, it is also true that seeking God's blessings can often devolve into an inappropriate level of selfishness, which can lead to a series of experiences that are not pleasing to God. But it is always true that our lives will continually be enriched as we seek to know, follow, and surrender to God's leadership.

The second reason we need to accomplish the tasks God has assigned us relates to how God's purposes are usually achieved. God can do anything independently, but typically, God chooses to work with and through people. Many of God's purposes will not be accomplished until some person responds to a divine directive. By our collective disobedience, we can postpone the release of many of God's Kingdom purposes. That's why Jesus taught His followers to pray, "Thy Kingdom come, Thy will be done on earth as it is in Heaven." The tasks God assigns you are essential to His overall plans for the world. What you choose to do (or not do) matters significantly to God's redemptive plan for humankind. Your life matters to God.

The third reason it's essential to accomplish the tasks God assigns you is the most important of all: so that God receives the glory.

Matthew 5: [16] Let your light shine before others, that they may see your good deeds and glorify your Father in heaven.

Bringing glory to God is essential for advancing His purposes on earth and is an important ingredient in experiencing His blessings. As the focus of your attention for accomplishing a given task is directed toward honoring and obeying God, the degree of "blessings" you experience will increase significantly. For example, I experience great inner satisfaction and fulfillment whenever I have the opportunity to help others grow in their understanding of God and His ways. And I experience the same satisfaction and fulfillment whether I speak with an individual or a large group. However, suppose my "teaching" is done pridefully, drawing attention to *me*. In that case, I will not experience the same satisfaction and fulfillment as I would if my focus were directed toward honoring God.

God primarily reaches people through other people. So, if accomplishing any task directs people's attention toward God, then His Kingdom purposes are more fully advanced. One of God's primary objectives in our transformation is to help us grow in humility. The more we recognize our utter dependence on God, the more we grow in humility, and the more God will receive the glory as we accomplish the tasks He assigns us.

As I bring this chapter to a close, I want to point out that the "answers" you discover to Essential Questions #1-3 often appear in isolation. However, sometimes, an answer you receive for one question directly impacts your understanding of other Essential Questions. In either case, each time you receive an answer to Essential Questions #1-3, it will *always* enable you to improve your ability to discern Essential Question #4. In other words, *as you discover more about who God is, how God designed life to be lived, and who you are, the knowledge gained will improve your ability to discern what God is calling you to do.*

Essential Question #4: What is God Calling Me to Do?

In Chapters 6-9, we examined each Essential Question in detail and discovered how an increased understanding of these Essential Questions leads to increased meaning, purpose, and fulfillment in our lives. In Chapter 10, the final chapter in Part 2, we will see how an improved understanding of all four Essential Questions develops in daily life and how God weaves together our ongoing discoveries, making us into the unique person He created us to become.

Chapter 10
The Essential Questions in Context

God expresses many of His purposes and plans for our lives through the multitude of promises He makes in the Bible that apply to all those who follow Him. Allow the following verses to energize your faith and speak to your heart and mind.

Jeremiah 29: [11] For I know the plans I have for you," declares the LORD, "plans to prosper you and not to harm you, plans to give you hope and a future.

Psalms 32: [8] I will instruct you and teach you in the way you should go; I will counsel you with my loving eye on you.

Deuteronomy 31: [8] "The LORD himself goes before you and will be with you; he will never leave you nor forsake you. Do not be afraid; do not be discouraged."

John 16: [33] "I have told you these things, so that in me you may have peace. In this world you will have trouble. But take heart! I have overcome the world."

Isaiah 41: [10] "So do not fear, for I am with you; do not be dismayed, for I am your God. I will strengthen you and help you; I will uphold you with my righteous right hand."

Isaiah 40: [31] ... those who hope in the LORD will renew their strength. They will soar on wings like eagles; they will run and not grow weary, they will walk and not be faint.

Philippians 2: [13] For it is God who works in you to will and to act in order to fulfill his good purpose.

Perhaps the most powerful and comprehensive of God's promises is expressed by Jesus Himself in the Gospel of John:

John 10: [10] "The thief comes only to steal and kill and destroy; I have come that [you] may have life, and have it to the full."

This last verse resonates in your heart because the "full" life that God has planned for you corresponds perfectly with the dream already present in your heart, reassuring you that your life is meant to have meaning and purpose and be characterized by a deep sense of personal fulfillment. However, God's plans and purposes for your life don't "magically" emerge as you passively sit and wait! The "full" life you desire unfolds as you actively seek to follow God and increasingly become the unique person He has created you to be.

The Great Adventure requires your active involvement in the process. While God has the power to make instantaneous, super-natural changes in any area of your life, because of His deep-seated desire to experience an intimate personal relationship with you, God will typically bring about changes in your life gradually (and often, over a lengthy period) as you endeavor to walk closely with Him. That is why you need to develop the practice of connecting with God as often and as deeply as possible. At any given time, God is available to "interact" with you in one or more of the following ways to effect the transformations that will result in the unfolding of the "full" life He has planned for you.

1. Replacing a falsehood with a corresponding truth
2. Deepening your understanding of a truth you already embrace
3. Revealing some aspect of your Natural or Divine Self
4. Challenging you to "release" some aspect of your Divine Self
5. Deepening or clarifying your Personal Gospel Message
6. Deepening, clarifying, or redirecting your Personal Life Calling
7. Challenging you to take a specific action step – sometimes in an entirely new direction, and often moving you out of your comfort zone
8. Supplying a needed "resource" such as strength, courage, comfort, provision, etc.

Whether God directs your thinking toward the past, present, or future, His goal is always to further your development toward becoming the person He created you to be.

Romans 8: [28] And we know that *in all things* God works for the good of those who love him, who have been called according to his purpose. [29] For those God foreknew he also predestined to be conformed to the image of his Son, that he might be the firstborn among many brothers and sisters.

Among the most significant challenges you will face will be those requiring a "change of heart," such as becoming more compassionate or desiring to please God more than yourself. We have some degree of control over our thoughts, attitudes, and actions, but only God can change our hearts – and He promises to do so!

> **Ezekiel 36:** [26] "I will give you a new heart and put a new spirit in you; I will remove from you your heart of stone and give you a heart of flesh."

While God can do anything instantaneously, those "heart changes" typically occur gradually over an extended period of time. As God challenges us in our pursuit of further transformation, He uses our desire for growth to draw us to Himself. As our relationship with God deepens, He releases more and more grace into our lives, enabling the desired changes to occur. While some people think they are not "good enough" even to approach God, the opposite is true. Dallas Willard is quoted as saying, "The greatest saints are not those who need less grace, but those who consume the most grace, who indeed are most in need of grace – those who are saturated by grace in every dimension of their being. Grace to them is like breath." The more we recognize our need for God and spend time interacting with Him, the more He will accomplish in and through our lives.

The Great Commandment and The Lord's Prayer are two of Scripture's most significant passages regarding advancing God's purposes. A deep understanding of these two passages is instrumental in our search for meaning, purpose, and fulfillment. They also relate directly to the work God desires to accomplish in and through our lives. Let's examine these two passages individually.

The Great Commandment

> Matthew 22: [36] "Teacher, which is the greatest commandment in the Law?" [37] Jesus replied: "'Love the Lord your God with all your heart and with all your soul and with all your mind.' [38] This is the first and greatest commandment. [39] And the second is like it: 'Love your neighbor as yourself.' [40] All the Law and the Prophets hang on these two commandments."

Jesus was asked by one of the "spiritual leaders" of His day to identify the "greatest" commandment. The Jewish leaders who questioned Jesus had developed a religious system containing 613 commandments that, they said, must all be done to please God. By asking Jesus to identify the greatest commandment, they intended to find a way to embarrass and discredit Him publicly. Instead, Jesus turned the tables and embarrassed them by reducing the 613 commandments to just two!

In Chapter 9, we discussed God's six purposes for your life. Each purpose ties directly to developing a greater love for God and others. As God leads you to discover answers to any of the four Essential Questions or helps you further develop your Personal Life Message and Personal Life Calling, He is simultaneously increasing your capacity to fulfill The Great Commandment. And, as you increasingly live out The Great Commandment, you are increasingly becoming the person God created you to be.

But we can only express genuine love (to God and others) from our hearts, which is why God promises to change our hearts. One of the ways God accomplishes this "change of heart" is by allowing us to be put in circumstances that require us to demonstrate love toward Him or others. As we can express genuine love freely, we experience a deep sense of fulfillment. However, as we fail to respond with genuine love, we are convicted of our shortcomings and challenged to cry out to God even more for deeper transparency, humility, and transformation. And as we reach out to God in these ways, He responds by impacting our lives in one or more of the eight ways listed above.

In the minds of the Jewish leaders who questioned Jesus, the primary focus of life was to obey a massive set of laws to avoid God's wrath and earn His blessings. The error of this legalistic mindset is addressed in **2 Corinthians 3:6 (CEV),**

> "*He makes us worthy* to be the servants of his new agreement that comes *from the Holy Spirit* and **not from a written Law**. After all, the Law brings death, but the Spirit brings life."

Jesus came with an entirely different message than was being taught by the religious leaders of His day. Instead of focusing on not violating any of the 613 commandments, Jesus's message was to repent for one's sins and surrender to a loving God who desires to bless His people greatly. Instead of viewing commandments as behaviors that must be addressed (done or not done) to avoid punishment or suffering, I believe God's intent for stating "laws" such as the 10 Commandments (and other biblical practices) was to help His people understand the *principles* He designed for living (Essential Question #2) which will produce optimal outcomes in their lives. So, rather than trying to avoid breaking a commandment, we should focus on seeing how closely we can attain the ideals of the principles God has established.

To clarify this idea, consider a "commandment" (or biblical principle) as a large circle with a dot at the center. (*Figure 10-1*) The area within the circle represents all the behaviors and attitudes consistent with the commandment, while the dot at the center represents the ideal or "spirit" of the commandment. The outer edge of the circle is the "letter of the law" – the boundary that must not be violated. Instead of focusing our attention on the edge of the circle and thinking the commandments are strict boundaries that must never be crossed, God intends for us to focus on trying to reach the "dot" (the ideal) at the center of the circle.

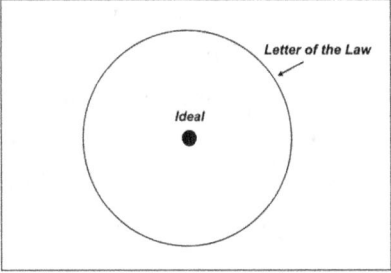

Figure 10-1: Understanding Commandments

I believe God's Design for Life (Essential Question #2) includes all of the laws, commandments, and life principles revealed throughout Scripture, which define the ideals we should seek to incorporate into our lives. And, as we strive to attain these ideals – crying out to God for the strength and grace to do so – He responds by transforming our hearts and souls. Following such a plan helps us to become the person God created us to be and thereby experience the "full life" God has planned for us.

You have probably heard people talk about the "God-sized hole" that exists within each of our hearts. The idea is we remain "empty" to some degree until our hearts find rest through a vibrant relationship with God. Jesus' command to love God with every part of our being merely recognizes the fundamental importance of establishing and maintaining a vibrant personal relationship with our Creator. So, the "God-sized hole" in our hearts is a built-in motivation to fulfill The Greatest Commandment.

Similarly, the second greatest commandment, to "love your neighbor as yourself," matches an inner need that many people fail to recognize as also existing within their hearts – the need to establish and maintain meaningful relationships with others. The two "great" commandments are statements Jesus made that match the two deepest desires God has placed in the hearts of the people He created. **The Great Commandment, then, is both an expression of the deepest needs God built into our hearts and an expression of the work He desires to accomplish within each of us.** I believe it saddens God greatly when we allow ourselves to be distracted by so many empty pursuits and fail to pursue developing deeper relationships with Him and the people He has placed in our lives.

The Lord's Prayer

Matthew 6: [9] "This, then, is how you should pray: "'Our Father in heaven, hallowed be your name, [10] your kingdom come, your will be done, on earth as it is in heaven. [11] Give us today our daily bread. [12] And forgive us our debts, as we also have forgiven our debtors. [13] And lead us not into temptation, but deliver us from the evil one.

At its most fundamental level, prayer is a "connection" between us and God. To experience the transformation God desires to accomplish in our lives, we must connect with Him. That is why scripture so frequently mentions the importance of prayer in the life of a believer. The apostles must have undoubtedly been aware of the importance of prayer in Jesus' life, which motivated them to learn how to pray. That very question the apostles posed to Jesus led to the inclusion of The Lord's Prayer in Scripture. If this, according to Jesus, is how we are supposed to pray, then it behooves us to consider the implications of the prayer's full meaning. Many authors have written entire books examining The Lord's Prayer, but I want to mention a few thoughts related to the Four Essential Questions.

The entire focus of The Lord's Prayer is the request for God to move in our lives in ways that advance the personal transformations God desires to accomplish **IN** us, as well as to cause God's Kingdom purposes to be advanced **THROUGH** us. It should be clear that the first request, "Your kingdom come, your will be done, on earth as it is in heaven," is Jesus's affirmation that God desires to use each of us to advance His "Kingdom" purposes here on earth. One of the most critical focuses in your requests from God should be asking Him to help you understand and accomplish the unique "assignments" He has ordained for your life. Living out those "assignments" – whether internal or external – is a significant pathway for experiencing fulfillment in your life and advancing God's Kingdom purposes on earth.

Ephesians 2: [10] For we are God's handiwork, created in Christ Jesus to do good works, which God prepared in advance for us to do.

Philippians 2: [13] for it is God who works in you to will and to act in order to fulfill his good purpose.

While our mind will vacillate between thinking about the past, present, and future as we walk through each day, we can only "act" in the present. So, anytime God uses a circumstance to capture your attention, it encourages you to connect with Him (i.e., pray). Each time you connect with God, it is an opportunity to further "fill" one or more of the "containers" that will help produce additional meaning, purpose, and fulfillment in your life. At the end of each "connection" with God, you should ask, "What am I supposed to do *now*?" God's answer will either encourage you to think more deeply about something, because additional "processing" is necessary, or to act in some specific way.

If God asks you to spend more time thinking about something, continue to reflect on the question or issue. (Most deep transformations occur over an extended period.) If God asks you to perform a particular task, then complete the task to the best of your ability. I mentioned earlier that the pathway for every Christian is the same three-step process: 1) ask God what He wants you to do; 2) wait for Him to respond; and 3) obey Him to the best of your ability. The Christian journey is really that simple. (However, I must also admit that following that *simple* 3-step plan is often very challenging!)

The Need for Balanced Growth

It is important to understand that the four Essential Questions are equally important. While we may place more emphasis on one question for a while, a balanced spiritual maturity only occurs as we discover answers to all four Essential Questions. An imbalanced growth in one or more of the Essential Questions will likely cause a person to embrace faulty beliefs, which will, in turn, cause them to wander off God's will for their life.

For example, an overemphasis on Question #1, "Who is God?" might result in an overly theological perspective placing too little emphasis on serving others or causing one to be overly critical of those with different beliefs. Some believers place too much focus on Question #2, "How has God Designed Life to be Lived?" and become overly legalistic, practicing a set of religious activities instead of developing an intimate relationship with God. Not surprisingly, non-believers frequently place primary attention on Question #3, "Who Am I?" and can become quite narcissistic. An overemphasis on Question #4, "What is God Calling Me to Do," might result in an overemphasis on "good works" and too little emphasis on one's relationship with God or personal character transformation. Because our Natural Self tends to desire to take control, our primary focus must always be on surrendering to God's leadership. Only as we seek to both know and follow God will He alert us when an imbalance occurs and redirect our attention as needed.

Before moving on, I'd like to explain how knowledge and understanding added to all four "containers" have benefited me. It was only during the 18-24 months preceding the writing of this book that I recognized the significance of the four Essential Questions. Since then, I have found myself returning to these questions more frequently. In the months since this has become my practice, I have learned more about God, His ways, myself, and God's call on my life than I have in the preceding ten years. So, while I was convinced of the validity of the premise of this book before I began writing, I am even more assured the longer I see the benefits of continuing to focus on finding more profound answers to the four Essential Questions.

However, the focus of one's life should not be primarily directed toward finding answers to the four Essential Questions. Instead, the focus of life must always be on the singular devotion to know and follow God! The benefit of these "containers" is recognizing their value as "repositories" for collecting and organizing truths as you seek to make sense of all God is teaching you. As these "containers" become increasingly filled – and you see how they work together – you will supernaturally experience more significant meaning, purpose, and fulfillment from your daily endeavors. Additionally, you will increasingly become the person God created you to be and fulfill God's Kingdom-building purposes for your life!

The journey of seeking and processing answers to the Essential Questions is not only a rewarding experience, but each discovery has beneficial outcomes. One of the benefits of discoveries in the four Essential Questions is the identification of life principles that can serve our Level 2 Thinking (see Chapter 5). These principles can function in two ways. First, life principles can guide our responses to events throughout the day. For example, when a student misbehaved in my classroom, understanding the principle that "all people are worthy of being treated with dignity and respect" would help prevent me from criticizing the student or trying to embarrass them in an attempt to change their behavior. The second way life principles can help guide daily living is through their influence on self-evaluation and planning our lives. For example, knowing that "Connecting with God" is an essential component of a God-directed life, I regularly plan my daily schedule to include quality time for this purpose.

A second benefit of our discoveries in any of the Essential Questions is that we can use what we learn to understand other Essential Questions better. For example, as I became aware of the truth that God had designed "components" that should find expression in each of our lives (Essential Question #2), that understanding caused me to wonder about how God's organized, planful nature interacts with His compassionate nature (Essential Question #1). This awareness then challenged me to consider how God might want to "interrupt" my planned daily activities to meet someone else's immediate needs (Essential Questions #3 and #4).

A third benefit of finding answers to the Essential Questions is that they provide insights into our Personal Life Message and Personal Life Calling. Turning our attention to God and receiving whatever He "imparts" in response to our current needs will always benefit multiple areas of our lives. For example, as God increases my confidence in His faithfulness to fulfill a given promise, it simultaneously increases my confidence in God's faithfulness to respond to my needs in other areas of my life. That is why we need to develop the habit of regularly connecting with God and seeking His input for every aspect of our lives. God is, indeed, the source of "every good and perfect gift" (James 1:17).

In the Introduction, I stated, "God has placed a dream in each of our hearts that our lives are meant to have meaning and purpose and should be characterized by a deep sense of personal fulfillment." There is another sort of "dream" within each of our hearts that is actually a little intimidating to consider. As individuals, we all know we are worthy of being treated with dignity and respect. Beyond that understanding, however, is the awareness that a measure of particular "significance" (or even greatness) resides deep within us, seeking both affirmation and expression. In our hearts, we know that we really *are* "special" – we can make a significant difference in the world. That is what God intends to bring to fruition in your life. Discovering and living out your Personal Life Message and Personal Life Calling is instrumental in finding expression for your true significance and experiencing the "full" life!

> **2 Corinthians 4:** [7] But we have this treasure in earthen vessels, so that the surpassing greatness of the power will be of God and not from ourselves. (NASB)

> **Daniel 7:** [27] Then the sovereignty, power, and greatness of all the kingdoms under heaven will be handed over to the holy people of the Most High.

However, admitting to knowing we have tremendous potential within us also puts us at risk. We are often challenged by questions such as, "What if I can't live up to that promise?" "What if I cannot muster the strength, courage, and determination necessary to live up to my potential fully?" The fear of failure is real! And that's why God addresses fear on so many occasions.

Deuteronomy 31: [6] "Be strong and courageous. Do not be afraid or terrified because of them, for the Lord your God goes with you; he will never leave you nor forsake you."

Joshua 1: [9] "Have I not commanded you? Be strong and courageous. Do not be afraid; do not be discouraged, for the LORD your God will be with you wherever you go."

Isaiah 41: [13] "'For I am the Lord, your God, who takes hold of your right hand and says to you, 'Do not fear; I will help you. [14] Do not be afraid, for I myself will help you,' declares the Lord, your Redeemer, the Holy One of Israel."

2 Timothy 1: [7] For the Spirit God gave us does not make us timid, but gives us power, love and self-discipline.

The challenge ahead of you – The Great Adventure – is to embark on the journey of knowing and following God! That includes understanding His will for your life and then endeavoring to complete the tasks He calls you to do. From God's perspective, the purpose of your journey is to help you experience the "fullest" life possible. That is your basic calling, and following that call will ultimately lead to fulfilling your God-given destiny. The only question is whether you are willing to seek to know and follow God. In the closing chapters, I will guide you to direct your ways to accomplish this basic calling.

God is calling you to walk with Him day by day, moment by moment, and experience by experience.

Micah 6: [8] He has shown you, O mortal, what is good. And what does the LORD require of you? To act justly and to love mercy and to walk humbly with your God.

Isaiah 48: [17] This is what the Lord says – your Redeemer, the Holy One of Israel: "I am the Lord your God, who teaches you what is best for you, who directs you in the way you should go.

As you discover and practice walking closely with God, He will show you what is good, right, just, and true. God will continue to reveal Himself to you in greater and greater depth, teach you His ways, help you better understand who He created you to be, guide you in the choices you need to make, and provide the resources you need to accomplish all He directs you to do. God accomplishes all these objectives – and more – as He directs your thoughts toward past, present, and future events. You are responsible for turning your attention to God and allowing Him to modify your understandings and actions according to His plans and timing. This is the journey of life – The Great Adventure! As you surrender to God's leadership and walk closely with Him, you will experience a burgeoning sense of meaning, purpose, and fulfillment.

Summary

In Chapter 6, I introduced the Essential Questions as "containers" into which knowledge and understanding increase as you connect with God through both scheduled and unscheduled interactions. (See Figure 10-2)

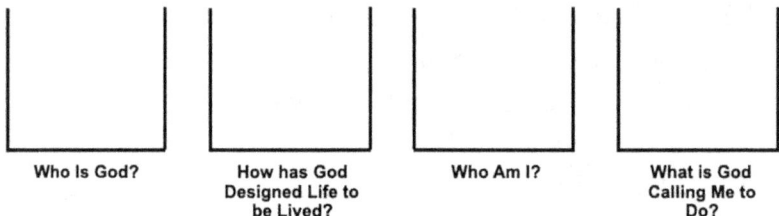

| Who Is God? | How has God Designed Life to be Lived? | Who Am I? | What is God Calling Me to Do? |

Figure 10-2: Essential Questions

In Chapter 9, I introduced the concepts of your Personal Gospel Message and Personal Life Calling as special ways God works in and through your life. I would also like you to consider these two topics as "containers" for storing knowledge and understanding. (See Figure 10-3) Each time you connect with God meaningfully, there is a potential for increasing the contents in one or more of these six "containers." As knowledge and understanding increase, you will experience ongoing spiritual growth.

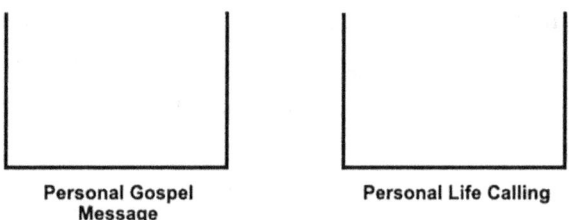

| Personal Gospel Message | Personal Life Calling |

Figure 10-3: Additional Containers of Knowledge & Understanding

In Chapter 8, I introduced the idea of your Natural Self and Divine Self. As you experience ongoing spiritual growth and maturation, your Natural Self will have a decreasing influence on your life, and your Divine Self will have an increased influence on how you think and act.

__Your primary responsibility__ is to increasingly connect with God and then process His interactions with you in a way that adds to one or more of the six "containers" mentioned above. *You are not "responsible" for your growth; God is! Your responsibility is to direct your life in ways that connect you with God as often and as deeply as possible.* Your interactions with God will always result in ongoing spiritual growth. (See Figure 10-4)

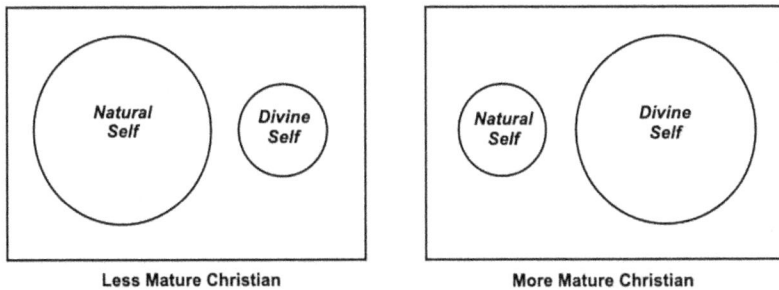

Less Mature Christian   **More Mature Christian**

Figure 10-4: Relationship Between Natural Self, Divine Self and Spiritual Maturity

The four Essential Questions, as well as your Personal Gospel Message and Personal Life Calling, serve as focal points for collecting and organizing the truths God reveals to you. As you spend time prayerfully reflecting on these truths, God will synthesize your learnings and instill wisdom and understanding that will significantly enhance your life. In Part 3 (Chapters 11 and 12), we will revisit the previously presented main ideas and suggest a pathway for applying the many ideas presented throughout the book.

Part Three

Planning Daily Activities

You've selected and paid for your cruise, researched the ship's amenities, and considered possible excursions at each port you will visit. But as your cruise date approaches and the excitement for the upcoming adventure increases, there are still a few practical tasks to address. These include completing the online check-in process, printing boarding passes and luggage tags, packing for the trip, and remembering to bring your passport! In the same way, there are a few more ideas to consider before embarking on The Great Adventure!

In Part 3, I will address two critical topics. First, it is essential to realize that some aspects of your mental framework – your foundational beliefs, understandings, and propensities – can significantly undermine your life journey. In Chapter 11 (Things We Get Wrong), I will present several core misunderstandings that, if present in your mental framework, will significantly interfere with your spiritual growth. These are fundamental biblical principles that must be understood and embraced. Secondly, in Chapter 12, I aim to review the main ideas presented throughout the book and help you develop an initial plan to implement in your journey to know and follow God.

Chapter 11
Things We Get Wrong

As I was growing up, my father participated in a bowling league. The first time I went with him to watch, I was immediately drawn to participate. I wanted to try rolling the ball down the lane and knocking down all the pins! However, when my dad allowed me to try, my ball rolled into the gutter! And once the ball fell into the gutter, there was no chance the ball would ever knock down even a single pin! Sometimes, in our attempt to know and follow God, some of our thoughts (mental framework) fall into a "gutter;" we latch onto ideas that prevent us from rightly understanding who God is and how He has designed life to be lived. Additionally, these wrong ways of thinking will cause us to embrace faulty ideas of who we are and what God calls us to do.

When my children were young, I took them to a bowling outing sponsored by the children's ministry of our home church. To my surprise and delight, the bowling alley had placed inflated pouches in all the gutters. These pouches prevented the bowling ball from ever falling into the gutter. Problem solved. The ball would always strike at least some pins! This chapter presents some of the ways our faulty mental framework can "fall into a gutter," thereby causing us to think and act in ways that will prevent us from fully realizing all God desires for our lives. The following ideas will serve as "inflated pouches" and prevent you from thinking and acting in ways that hinder the outpouring of God's blessings.

God has built into our hearts and minds the desire to make sense of our lives and to search for meaning and purpose. Additionally, we live in a society that values rationality and logic. These two tendencies motivate us to use our reasoning capacities to make sense of our life experiences. However, many of our natural reasoning patterns are contrary to the ways God has designed life to be lived. This contrast between our ways and God's ways should humble us and open our hearts to learning.

> Isaiah 55: [8] "For my thoughts are not your thoughts, neither are your ways my ways," declares the LORD. [9] "As the heavens are higher than the earth, so are my ways higher than your ways and my thoughts than your thoughts."

Suppose our foundational understandings (conceptual framework) about God and His ways are faulty, each time we confront a related biblical truth. In that case, we will likely generate "applications" of those truths that are not entirely valid. Consider the following example. Suppose my conceptual framework leads me to believe God wants me to be a strong, confident person who sets challenging goals for myself and uses my gifts and abilities to make those goals a reality. In that case, if I read Philippians 4:13 ("I can do all things through Christ who strengthens me."), my application might be that, as a Christian, I should boldly and confidently pursue my goals in life, using this "promise" to generate the motivation and strength I need to succeed. However, suppose instead, my mental framework leads me to believe God wants me to be a humble person and not rely entirely on my own strength and abilities, but to depend on Him (Proverbs 3:5-6 – "Trust in the Lord with all your heart and lean not on your own understanding: in all your ways submit to him, and he will make your paths straight."). In that case, when I read the same Philippians verse, the application would likely be to boldly and confidently **trust** God to empower me to stand firm in any situation He calls me to pursue and **wait** for God to bring about the outcome He desires. This second perspective is more biblically sound.

I do indeed possess gifts and abilities. However, if I depend entirely on "my own understanding" and skills – which is *not* God's intent – I will likely use some of my "talents" in ways that will not fully honor God or advance His purposes. Additionally, if I believe that I have accomplished my goals because of my own abilities and perseverance, I will likely become prideful – and that's not a good thing! With this understanding of how a faulty mental framework can lead to misunderstandings and misapplications of biblical truths, I would like to examine several ways our conceptual frameworks may need to be **modified.** It is essential to understand that many truths God wants to teach us are counterintuitive. That is, the truths that define the workings of God's Kingdom are often much different than what we would naturally assume.

A Proper Focus

John 14: [6] Jesus answered, "I am the way and the truth and the life. No one comes to the Father except through me.

The main objective of life is to follow God's leadership to the best of our ability. Everything of value and worth flows from God Himself (James 1:17 – Every good and perfect gift is from above ...). His plans for us are always designed to move us closer to experiencing the "full life" Jesus came to provide (John 10:10). Consequently, all of our plans and actions must flow from our desire to know God and surrender to His leadership. Any activity or thought leading in a different direction is not a pathway God has called us to follow. Because God is sovereign and desires to rule and reign in our lives (so He can release the fullness of His blessings in and through us), **we must focus on <u>identifying and following the <u>*right path*</u></u> rather than trying to <u>produce the *right outcomes*</u>**.

We must understand and follow what God is calling us to <u>***do***</u> rather than what God is calling us to <u>***accomplish***</u>. This is HUGE! God always calls us to surrender to His will – this is ALWAYS the bottom line. God will never call you to disobey Him to accomplish something for Him. Our focus must be directed toward following the correct process. **We are responsible for following God; God is responsible for the results!** Whenever you consider what you should do, you must examine the degree to which your actions draw you (and others) closer to God. That is the ultimate measure of the "correctness" of one's beliefs and actions.

Examining Core Beliefs

As humans, we have the innate drive to have our own way prevail. Pleasure-seeking and self-will behaviors are core to our Natural Self. Therefore, we must always be aware that our motivations might be at least partially designed to please ourselves rather than God. Consequently, we must become aware of the likelihood that our imperfect Natural Self has infected our mental framework. There is a good chance some of your most foundational beliefs about life might be misguided. A large part of the process of our transformation is the modification of false beliefs (Romans 12:2 – "... be transformed by the renewing of your mind."). Toward the purpose of "renewing your mind," the following ideas are designed for you to examine some of your own core beliefs about how life works. For each idea presented, examine your approach to life to better understand how your current mental framework influences your thoughts and actions. Then, ask God to give you insights into how your mental framework might need to be modified. The following list of ideas is not meant to be exhaustive; these are just some of the critical misconceptions I have seen God modify in my mental framework.

Inside-Out vs Outside-In

You will never find *lasting* meaning, purpose, and fulfillment through personal recognition or accumulating possessions or wealth. Neither is the "full life" experienced from setting and achieving lofty goals using your own strength and abilities. Indeed, some benefits are realized by such pursuits, but the "fruit" of self-generated accomplishments always fades, and we find ourselves looking once again for something more.

> **Ecclesiastes 1: [14]** I have seen all the works which have been done under the sun, and behold, all is futility and striving after wind. (NASB)

You will not experience a growing sense of meaning, purpose, and fulfillment by making your life look different on the "outside". Instead, the "full life" emerges within you – automatically – as your life aligns with God's unique plans for you. And your life will only align with God's plans as you better understand and follow God. *All the critical changes God desires to make in your life begin on the "inside" of you – in your heart and mind.* As you seek to grow on the "inside," you will be searching for ways to think, feel, and act differently. As these inner changes occur, your outward life will begin to change – as a direct result of surrendering to the directives God has given, or by the "resources" (such as hope and peace) God has supernaturally provided.

So, if your current focus is "outside-in" – setting goals to change your life on the "outside" to produce a better quality of life "inside" – your orientation is backward. For example, you will not experience breakthroughs in life because you can muster up the strength to persevere in accomplishing your goals. Instead, you will experience breakthroughs because God provides the strength, patience, and wisdom within you as you pursue the path of surrendering to His leadership over an extended period of time. That is the difference between an inside-out versus an outside-in perspective for living.

Isaiah 41: [10] So do not fear, for I am with you; do not be dismayed, for I am your God. I will strengthen and help you; I will uphold you with my righteous right hand.

Building Character vs Eradicating Sin

This is an example of an "inside-out" rather than an "outside-in" orientation, but worthy of special recognition. The Bible contains hundreds of verses that inform us of God's ways and remind us of our shortcomings and failures.

Romans 3: [23] for all have sinned and fall short of the glory of God.

Relying on "our own understanding," we would likely believe we are responsible for changing our ways to align our lives with the truths contained in scripture. However, anyone who has tried to muster the strength to obey all of God's commandments will recognize the futility of such an approach. We fail to completely eradicate sin from our lives because that is not the way God designed life to be lived. Again, God accomplishes transformation from the "inside-out" rather than the "outside-in." As God builds character within our lives and changes our hearts, the outgrowth of those changes removes our motivations and tendencies to sin.

> **2 Peter 1:** [3] His divine power has given us everything we need for a godly life through our knowledge of him who called us by his own glory and goodness. [4] Through these he has given us his very great and precious promises, so that through them you may participate in the divine nature, having escaped the corruption in the world caused by evil desires.

> **Galatians 5:22-23 (MSG)** – But what happens when we live God's way? He brings gifts into our lives, much the same way that fruit appears in an orchard – things like affection for others, exuberance about life, and serenity. We develop a willingness to stick with things, a sense of compassion in the heart, and a conviction that a basic holiness permeates things and people. We find ourselves involved in loyal commitments, not needing to force our way in life, able to marshal and direct our energies wisely.

These passages (as well as many others throughout Scripture) teach us that as we press into God, He supplies the resources necessary for living lives that are pleasing to Him. We don't utilize our own power for living; we rely on God's provisions to transform our lives. Our challenge is to connect with God regularly and deeply. And He even provides the resources we need to seek Him!

Humbly Acknowledging Our Weaknesses vs Being Strong

We tend to think vulnerability – recognizing and admitting our shortcomings and constant need for God's provision for every area of our lives – is a sign of weakness. However, learning how to rest confidently in a state of humility and vulnerability is actually the most powerful posture one can accomplish. The Apostle Paul reveals this truth in 2 Corinthians, Chapter 12.

> [9] But he said to me, "My grace is sufficient for you, for my power is made perfect in weakness." Therefore I will boast all the more gladly about my weaknesses, so that Christ's power may rest on me. [10] That is why, for Christ's sake, I delight in weaknesses, in insults, in hardships, in persecutions, in difficulties. For when I am weak, then I am strong."

This is an integral part of how God designed life to be lived. Many – if not all – of our life experiences are intended by God to help us discover how we can "abide" in Him and experience the strength, confidence, and power that results from being effectively connected to God.

> John 15: [4] "Abide in me, and I in you. As the branch cannot bear fruit by itself, unless it abides in the vine, neither can you, unless you abide in me. [5] I am the vine; you are the branches. Whoever abides in me and I in him, he it is that bears much fruit, for apart from me you can do nothing." (ESV)

Jesus said the "Greatest Commandment" is to love God "with all your heart, soul, mind and strength" (Mark 12:30). This goal is not accomplished by filling your mind with a set of truths that you diligently follow in your own strength to produce the "full" life. Instead, the goal is that the truths you discover lead you to seek God with increased regularity and intensity so He can personally walk with you throughout each day, teaching, guiding, and empowering you in all your ways. The result of your growing relationship with God is a renewed heart and the provision of resources necessary for fully surrendering to His leadership. The outcome of this pattern of seeking God and receiving the power needed to follow Him leads to an increasing sense of meaning, purpose, and fulfillment.

Conviction vs Guilt

If you were to consider what a fully transformed life should look like and then compare that image to your current status, I suspect you would see many differences. Our culture leads us to believe that the proper way to bring about change in our lives is to identify goals, develop a strategy to reach those goals, and then implement that strategy. That process of change seems so logical. But that's not how God brings about change in our lives; He merely challenges us to follow Him. As you connect with God and are reminded of your sinful ways, the proper response is not to be consumed by guilt. Instead, the appropriate response is conviction. The difference between guilt and conviction is very significant. Guilt leads to anxiety, insecurity, and fear; conviction leads to humility, security, surrender, and peace.

Feelings of guilt include the recognition of one's offense accompanied by an obligation to pay a penalty. On the other hand, conviction is only the recognition of having committed a transgression without the need to pay a penalty. God intends for Christians only to experience conviction for their sins. When we experience conviction, the proper response is to acknowledge our sins and then thank God that all of our sins are fully forgiven because of the redemptive work of Jesus accomplished through His life, death, resurrection, and ascension. Jesus received the punishment for all of your sins, for all time, on Himself as He sacrificed His life on the cross. By being born again, we receive complete forgiveness and adoption into God's family with all the benefits of being a child of God!

> Romans 8: [1] Therefore, there is now no condemnation for those who are in Christ Jesus, [2] because through Christ Jesus the law of the Spirit who gives life has set you free from the law of sin and death.

God's purpose for revealing sin in our lives is only to humble us, remind us of our fully forgiven status before Him, and generate feelings of love, peace, and security within us. However, because God greatly desires us to experience the "full" life that comes from fully following Him, He will regularly work to bring our lives more fully into alignment with His ways.

God eliminates sinful patterns in our lives by first building within us a deep desire to experience freedom in a particular area. It is not just the feeling of conviction that signals God's desire to effect change in our lives. The sense of conviction must also be accompanied by a strong belief that God desires to bring about freedom *at this time*. Because we sin in many ways, God only works in a limited number of areas at a time. *The presence of a deep desire for freedom in any particular area of sin in our lives (e.g., patterns of anger or lust) is the primary signal that God desires to bring about changes in that area.* Other areas of sinful patterns will become the focus of transformation later. The way God brings about freedom from sin in any area of our lives is discussed further in the next section.

Areas of Focus vs Goals

It is a good practice to regularly spend time before God, just reflecting on your life. These times of reflection will reveal that much of your life – thoughts, actions, attitudes, and desires – falls far short of being pleasing to God. In our Natural Self, our "take-away" from a revelation of our sinfulness is to create a list of changes we need to make ("outside-in" reasoning). As previously mentioned, our culture leads us to believe that the proper way to bring about change in our lives is to identify goals, develop a strategy to reach those goals, and then implement our strategy by working hard to achieve the identified goals. This same process is to be repeated for all our other goals. However, God's way of bringing about change in our lives is for us to follow His leadership and guidance – and _not_ try to change ourselves.

In the previous section, I mentioned that when conviction of one's sin is accompanied by a strong desire to experience freedom, *the intense desire for change signals God's desire to bring about transformation in that area of one's life at present*. However, this awareness does not mean you are supposed to engage in the goal-setting and accomplishment routine. God doesn't want you to take control; He wants you to surrender that area of your life to Him.

Our sinful patterns often include other aspects of our Natural Self. For example, if we have the sinful pattern of being overly critical of others, we might think we must stop speaking in critical or cynical ways. However, you will not experience freedom over your critical nature unless God helps you become more humble and develop greater compassion for others. Our list of goals that need to be accomplished to experience freedom from any area of sin will always fall short of all that God knows needs to be addressed. As I previously noted, when conviction of one's sin is accompanied by a strong desire to experience freedom, the intense desire for change signals God's desire to bring about transformation in that area of one's life at the present time. However, this awareness does not mean you are supposed to engage in the goal-setting and accomplishment routine.

Proverbs 14: [12] There is a way that seems right to a man, but its end is the way to death. (ESV)

Proverbs 3: [5] Trust in the LORD with all your heart and lean not on your own understanding; [6] in all your ways submit to him, and he will make your paths straight.

Works, Grace, and Acts of Service

In Chapter 7, where we examined Essential Question #2, "How has God Designed Life to be Lived?" I explained that God doesn't punish us when we break one of His rules for living. The guidelines God established for living are the kinds of actions, thoughts, attitudes, and motivations leading to the best possible life outcomes. If we violate any of those guidelines, God doesn't automatically *punish* us; He doesn't plan events or circumstances designed to make us suffer for our failure to live in perfect alignment with His commands. Instead, the adverse outcomes we experience when we violate one of God's standards are the natural consequences of living outside the principles God has established for life.

For example, if I interact with people disrespectfully, I will likely experience conflicts in my relationships with those people. The discord in my relationships is not a *punishment* from God; it is just a natural consequence of not treating people with dignity and respect, which is one of God's principles for relationships. So, our actions in life do matter, just not in direct correlation with rewards and punishments. Let's look more closely at how our actions influence the outcomes we experience.

There are hundreds, if not thousands, of Bible verses that seem to correlate obedience to God's commands with experiencing His blessings. Here are just a few:

Deuteronomy 28: [1] If you fully obey the LORD your God and carefully follow all his commands I give you today, the LORD your God will set you high above all the nations on earth. [2] All these blessings will come on you and accompany you if you obey the LORD your God.

Isaiah 1: [19] "If you are willing and obedient, you will eat the good things of the land; [20] but if you resist and rebel, you will be devoured by the sword." For the mouth of the LORD has spoken.

Luke 11: [28] "Blessed rather are those who hear the word of God and obey it."

In contrast to these passages, many verses suggest that experiencing God's blessings is *not* connected to our obedience to God's commands.

Romans 3: [20] Therefore no one will be declared righteous in God's sight by the works of the law; rather, through the law we become conscious of our sin. [21] But now apart from the law the righteousness of God has been made known, to which the Law and the Prophets testify. [22] This righteousness is given through faith in Jesus Christ to all who believe. ... [24] and all are justified freely by his grace through the redemption that came by Christ Jesus.

Ephesians 2: [8] For it is by grace you have been saved, through faith – and this is not from yourselves, it is the gift of God – [9] not by works, so that no one can boast.

So, some passages show a connection between our actions and God's blessings, and some suggest otherwise. How can we understand these seemingly contradictory assertions in God's Word? The key is understanding God's Grace and the difference between works and acts of service.

Grace is an outpouring of some "blessing" from God. Sometimes, grace is manifested in great and miraculous ways, such as receiving healing from a terminal illness. However, grace is also manifested in less dramatic ways, such as God moving on your boss's heart to give you a raise, or feelings of satisfaction and fulfillment as you complete tasks throughout the day. The critical point to understand is that *grace is a blessing God provides that is not tied to specific behaviors.* Instead, God supplies grace when He knows it's necessary to help us move forward. In contrast, God will likely withhold grace when we move in ways that are not God's will for our lives.

"Works" is a term typically ascribed to actions one takes motivated to "earn" God's blessings. The whole point of grace is that it is freely given by God and NOT directly connected to our actions (as suggested by the Romans and Ephesians passages above). God doesn't want us to obey His commands because we desire to earn His approval. God wants us to follow His leadership because of our love for Him and our desire to please Him – disconnected from the motivation of a reward. Loving, unselfish adherence to God's principles for living can only be generated by the transformation of our hearts. And God transforms our hearts as we seek to know and follow Him.

The transformation of our hearts that God accomplishes motivates us to engage in acts of loving service toward God and others. *Acts of service, then, are manifestations of a transformed heart.* As we respond to God's promptings to engage in acts of service, our lives become more aligned with God's ways, and we experience more of His blessings. Therefore, our primary goal must be to seek to know and follow God because that is what initiates the transformation process.

Surrender vs Obedience

Since seeking to know and follow God fuels our transformation, you might be inclined to think you are *responsible for obeying* God's command to do so. However, because God desires that you love Him (The Great Commandment), His focus is not on your obedience; God desires you to *surrender* to His leadership! Obedience requires harnessing the inner strength necessary to accomplish a task one is not really motivated to do. Surrender, however, is yielding one's ego and heart to God. Surrender is an admission of our inability to obey fully, recognizing we lack the necessary resources. It is our surrender to God that moves Him to extend grace. In our weakness, we properly seek God and surrender to Him.

> **Psalm 27:** [4] One thing I ask from the LORD, this only do I
> seek: that I may dwell in the house of the LORD all the
> days of my life, to gaze on the beauty of the LORD and to
> seek him in his temple.

God doesn't ask us to obey Him in our strength; He invites us to surrender – in our weakness – to His desires already placed within our hearts. The proper response to God is not to create a list of things you are supposed to do and then try to bring your actions into compliance. Instead, God desires that you pay attention to the desire for greater surrender already present in your heart and seek Him for the wisdom and strength you need to understand and surrender to His leadership. This is another example of how God works from the "inside-out" rather than the "outside-in." God has placed within you a deep desire to change your life significantly. Take time to identify those desires already present deep within you. Then, seek God's grace and yield yourself to Him as much as possible. Yield to what He asks you to do in this state of surrender. God is not looking for your obedience; He is looking for your surrender.

> Jeremiah 10: [23] I know, O Lord, that the way of man is not in himself, that it is not in man who walks to direct his steps. (ESV)

> Hebrews 4: [16] Let us then approach God's throne of grace with confidence, so that we may receive mercy and find grace to help us in our time of need.

Being vs. Doing

In many of the points above, the primary focus was on the relationship between our actions and God's responses. This connection between our behaviors and God's blessings might lead you to think that your "status" with God is also related to your actions. That is not the case! God assures us that His love never changes, that He is always ready to receive us whenever we seek Him, and that He is always pursuing us to follow Him.

> Jeremiah 31: [3] The Lord appeared to us in the past, saying: "I have loved you with an everlasting love; I have drawn you with unfailing kindness."

> Isaiah 54: [10] "Though the mountains be shaken and the hills be removed, Yet my unfailing love for you will not be

shaken nor my covenant of peace be removed," says the LORD, who has compassion on you.

Jeremiah 29: [12] Then you will call on me and come and pray to me, and I will listen to you. [13] You will seek me and find me when you seek me with all your heart. [14] I will be found by you," declares the LORD.

Moreover, God's love and commitment to us are not only unchanging, but God's view of us also never changes. If you are a Christian, God sees you as "complete" in Christ. When God looks at you, He sees your Divine Self fully realized.

Psalms 103: [11] For as high as the heavens are above the earth, so great is his love for those who fear him; [12] as far as the east is from the west, so far has he removed our transgressions from us.

Hebrews 10: [10] And by that will, we have been made holy through the sacrifice of the body of Jesus Christ once for all.

2 Corinthians 5: [21] God made him who had no sin to be sin for us, so that in him we might become the righteousness of God.

To be a Christian is to be "in Him," and to be "in Him" is to "become the righteousness of God." That means each time God looks at you, He sees the "righteousness" of Jesus. God doesn't see your sins and shortcomings. When God looks at you, He sees the fully mature person He has created you to be. As a loving Father, God always blesses you for everything you do right and encourages you to continue growing and prospering in all you do.

Colossians 1: [21] Once you were alienated from God and were enemies in your minds because of your evil behavior. [22] But now he has reconciled you by Christ's physical body through death to present you holy in his sight, without blemish and free from accusation.

Whenever you are embarrassed about your ongoing sinful actions and motivations and apprehensive about seeking God's help, remember that His lovingkindness is everlasting and that He greatly desires to meet with you and bless you.

Being Used by God vs Using God

When I first came to faith, my motivation was totally selfish. I wanted a more successful and fulfilling life, and I thought acknowledging God might be the missing piece to the "puzzle" of life I was trying to solve. As I walked forward in response to the altar call, I remember feeling that "life" instantaneously made sense! If God created all of life, He must have also created all the "rules" that govern everything He created. With that understanding, it made perfect sense to follow God to experience success in life. However, as I began attending church, listening to television evangelists, and reading the Bible, I was confronted with some challenging truths.

John 12: [25] Anyone who loves their life will lose it, while anyone who hates their life in this world will keep it for eternal life.

Matthew 16: [24] Then Jesus said to his disciples, "Whoever wants to be my disciple must deny themselves and take up their cross and follow me. [25] For whoever wants to save their life will lose it, but whoever loses their life for me will find it.

Luke 14: [33] In the same way, those of you who do not give up everything you have cannot be my disciples.

The teachings I received, based on passages such as these, made me wonder if I had signed up for the right deal! It took several years of seeking to know and follow God before I was able to reconcile my desire for a better life with the Biblical challenges of dying to my self-centeredness. I gradually learned that by fully seeking God and surrendering to Him to the best of my ability, He would make the changes within my heart necessary for empowering me to die to purely selfish motivations willingly. I also discovered God desired to bless His children's lives and to use them to bless others.

Matthew 23: [12] For those who exalt themselves will be humbled, and those who humble themselves will be exalted.

Proverbs 22: [4] Humility is the fear of the Lord; its wages are riches and honor and life.

Genesis 12: [2] "I will make you into a great nation, and I will bless you; I will make your name great, and you will be a blessing. [3] I will bless those who bless you, and whoever curses you I will curse; and all peoples on earth will be blessed through you."

2 Corinthians 9: [8] And God is able to bless you abundantly, so that in all things at all times, having all that you need, you will abound in every good work.

Never forget that God Himself placed the dream in your heart for experiencing a life of meaning, purpose, and fulfillment. And God uses our inner motivation to realize our dreams to draw us to Himself, change our hearts and minds, and move us forward to advance His Kingdom's purposes through all He calls us to do. Don't be overwhelmed with guilt because of your selfish desires. Instead, recognize any conviction about selfishness as a mechanism God uses to draw you to Himself for further transformation, and as confirmation that He desires more good things for you.

Surrender 1st, Understanding 2nd

God created us to be rational creatures. It is our nature to be inquisitive and seek to understand our experiences, making sense of the world around us and our place within it. As children, we discover that a cause-and-effect relationship exists in many of our life experiences. A young child, for example, learns early in life that crying often brings someone to attend to their needs. From childhood, we begin to identify desirable outcomes and search for ways to achieve them. God even encourages us to develop an understanding of Him and how He has designed life to be lived.

> **Proverbs 4:** [5] Get wisdom, get understanding; do not forget my words or turn away from them.

> **Jeremiah 33:** [3] Call to me and I will answer you and tell you great and unsearchable things you do not know.

God desires us to learn and practice His ways to experience a richer, more meaningful, and more fulfilling life. But God doesn't want us to be limited by only acting in ways that make sense to us. Sometimes, He wants us to follow Him in ways that don't immediately make sense – they might even seem ridiculous. For example, it makes "sense" that if we save or invest money, we will have more money to spend in the future. However, God challenges us to give our money to others freely and promises that our giving will increase our prosperity.

Proverbs 11: ²⁵ A generous person will prosper; whoever refreshes others will be refreshed.

Luke 6: ³⁸ "Give, and it will be given to you. A good measure, pressed down, shaken together and running over, will be poured into your lap. For with the measure you use, it will be measured to you."

In many instances, God directs us to behave in counterintuitive ways. That's what a life of faith is all about. And living by faith – believing God will always lead us in ways that benefit us – always pleases Him.

Hebrews 11: ⁶ Without faith it is impossible to please God, because anyone who comes to him must believe that he exists and that he rewards those who earnestly seek him.

Indeed, this "living by faith" pattern is essential for our ongoing transformation.

As we saw earlier (Romans 12:2), the transformation we greatly need occurs by "the renewing of our mind". *This means we literally need to think differently to be transformed.* If we are limited to what we already "know," there can be no further transformation of our mind. Only as we are challenged to live in ways "outside" our current level of understanding do we discover new truths, and our minds are transformed. God will often lead you in ways that do not make immediate sense. That is, God may lead you in ways you cannot understand. In those instances, it is necessary for you to "live by faith." Hence, our surrender to God's direction often comes first, and then understanding follows.

As I mentioned at the beginning of this chapter, the counterintuitive points listed above are meant to protect us from thinking and acting in ways contrary to God's ways. If we live contrary to God's ways, we will experience less than God's best and may become frustrated by the lack of sufficient "progress" in our spiritual journey. When you experience a persistent state of frustration, that should signal that the path you have been pursuing might be based on a misunderstanding of God's ways. Also, we must never forget that the *journey* matters most and not the *"destination"* – the achievement of any particular goal or outcome. We often become so goal-oriented that we forget the importance of the journey itself. We make this error due to our lack of understanding that life is, first and foremost, designed to be lived in fellowship with God. And we experience fellowship with Him as we regularly interact with Him throughout our life journey.

This chapter presented several counterintuitive biblical principles. However, this list is not to be understood as comprehensive. God will teach you many other surprising truths as you seek to know and follow Him. And each "revelation" will keep your thinking "out of the gutter" and redirect your life in amazing and productive ways. In the final chapter, I want to summarize many of the essential truths presented throughout the book and suggest a "template" to help you plan the "next steps" for your journey.

Chapter 12
Your Journey

God's deepest desire is for us to experience and enjoy a profoundly intimate relationship with Him. This is the essence of what Jesus communicated when He was asked, "What is the Greatest Commandment?" and He responded, "Love the Lord your God with all your heart and with all your soul and with all your mind and with all your strength." (Mark 12:30). A large part of loving God involves the practice of spending time with Him – connecting with Him at a profoundly personal level.

The fact that loving God is the "greatest commandment" means loving Him is the most essential aspect of life. God wants you to experience a "full life" (John 10:10), and loving God is the most significant element. However, you cannot really love someone unless you "know" that person deeply. Genuine love also involves accepting, respecting, and appreciating who that person is at the deepest part of their being – including their motivations, feelings, and actions. Genuine love also involves deep trust and allegiance, allowing us to walk in unity and harmony with that person.

To love God fully involves trusting that He is good, always acts in your best interest, and that His plans are always trustworthy. God's desire and hope is that your own desire to love Him would motivate you to seek to know and follow Him to such an extent that you develop greater confidence in Him than you do in yourself. God also desires that your motivation to follow and please Him would become your highest priority. Because genuine love can only be given freely, God gives you the free will to follow your heart's desires. And, since God knows the most extraordinary life possible is one fully surrendered to His leadership, He regularly reaches out to you to woo you into seeking Him so that you would come to fully know Him and grow to love Him deeply. *Your most important responsibility in life is to respond to God's promptings to connect with Him.* And the purpose of connecting with God is to increase your capacity to know, love, and follow Him. Everything in life that is good derives from our pursuit of God.

James 1: [17] Every good and perfect gift is from above, coming down from the Father of the heavenly lights, who does not change like shifting shadows.

John 6: [44] "No one can come to me unless the Father who sent me draws them, and I will raise them up at the last day."

James 4: [8] Come near to God and he will come near to you.

Jeremiah 29: [13] "You will seek me and find me when you seek me with all your heart."

Hebrews 11: [6] And without faith it is impossible to please God, because anyone who comes to him must believe that he exists and that he rewards those who earnestly seek him.

Jesus's statement in John 10:10 communicates that one of *His primary purposes* for coming to earth was to make it possible for each of us to experience a "full" life – a life characterized by meaning, purpose, and a profound sense of personal fulfillment. You must embrace one fundamental principle to experience the "full" life Jesus came to provide: *you must understand, accept, and follow God's unique design for your life to the best of your ability.* While there are many similarities in God's plans for all people, His plans for your life will be unique in many ways.

Since God created everything, He has the right to decide how everything He has created should function. When you consider the incredible detail, beauty, complexity, and diversity in all God has created, it is easy to understand that He created us to be unique beings. If you fail to understand and accept the truth of God's unique plan for your life, you will frequently experience unnecessary suffering and loss. Therefore, in addition to seeking to love God with all your heart, soul, mind, and strength, *you must make the primary focus of your life to seek to know and follow God's unique plan for your life.*

Any step to the left or right of God's design for your life will be a step that falls short of experiencing the most desirable outcomes possible. Only as we follow God's personalized directions for living will our lives be directed optimally. Once again, **if you fail to understand and accept this foundational axiom of life – the necessity of following God's unique plans for your life – you will continue to be frustrated and disappointed by the outcomes you experience.** This does not mean, however, that accepting this truth will result in a life without disappointments, frustrations, and sometimes even profound loss.

You will, in fact, experience many challenging and disappointing situations. But those seemingly "negative" experiences are either natural outcomes of living in a world infected by sin or part of God's unique plan for your life. However, when your life is wholeheartedly directed toward knowing and following God, you have the promise that every disappointing and frustrating experience will contribute to your ultimate success.

> Romans 8: [28] And we know that in all things God works for the good of those who love him, who have been called according to his purpose. [29] For those God foreknew he also predestined to be conformed to the image of his Son, that he might be the firstborn among many brothers and sisters.

In this final chapter, I will highlight some of the most important points mentioned throughout the book and present several Life Principles that will contribute to the most significant amount of transformation and blessing possible. I truly desire that the Holy Spirit would guide you in ways that would provide the most direct, efficient, and productive outcomes in your life. And I know that kind of guidance must come directly from God to you. My prayer and hope are that these final thoughts will enable your connections with God to occur with ever-increasing frequency and effectiveness, and you will discover how to maximize your capacity to know and follow Him. With these thoughts in mind, I will share several Life Principles for your consideration. My encouragement to you is to:

- Prayerfully consider the significance of each principle.
- Ask God to firmly establish each principle in your heart and mind (allowing the Holy Spirit to apply each principle in any way He desires).
- Ask God to assist you in understanding how you should respond to the challenge(s) presented by the principle. (This must be your own *unique* response rather than attempting to duplicate someone else's

response. You must *personally* receive directions from God. **WAIT** until you do! There will be many similarities in practices among believers, but your life will contain many unique elements.)

- Periodically review each life principle, asking God to show you if (and how) He might desire you to modify how you are living your life.

Life Principle #1: Establish and Maintain an Ever-Growing Practice of Connecting with God.

Acts 17: [24] "The God who made the world and everything in it is the Lord of heaven and earth and does not live in temples built by human hands. [25] And he is not served by human hands, as if he needed anything. Rather, he himself gives everyone life and breath and everything else. [26] From one man he made all the nations, that they should inhabit the whole earth; and he marked out their appointed times in history and the boundaries of their lands. [27] God did this so that they would seek him and perhaps reach out for him and find him, though he is not far from any one of us. [28] *'For in him we live and move and have our being.'*

Everything good, productive, and beneficial for your ongoing personal development and transformation will come from following God's unique plan for your life. The more regularly and effectively you connect with God, the more closely you can follow His plan for your life. That is why your personal connections with God must become your highest priority in life. However, even the motivation to connect with God cannot be fulfilled exclusively by your own best efforts. We are always "limited" by our current capacity for seeking Him. Only as God increases the motivation to pursue Him – within your heart – will you be able to connect with Him with greater frequency and intensity. **We need God to grow us so we can seek and connect with Him more fully.** We can only begin connecting with God from whatever point we find ourselves, and then allow God to change us as we continue to give our best efforts.

The first step in this process is to discover how you, personally, best connect with God. For some people, reading the Bible is the best way to connect with Him. For others, connecting with God occurs most readily as they encounter His creation, perhaps through a hike in the mountains, by sitting on a quiet pier over-looking a body of water, or by simply sitting in a comfortable chair on their patio, enjoying a cup of coffee and silently viewing their garden. For still others, listening to worship music best enables them to connect with God. *You must discover the settings and experiences that best enable you to connect your thoughts and heart to God.* The experience of connecting with God will result in a sense of "renewal" as if you were starting life afresh.

> **Lamentations 3:** [22] The steadfast love of the LORD never ceases; his mercies never come to an end; [23] they are new every morning; great is your faithfulness. (ESV)

The "renewal" we experience from connecting with God brings increased hope, confidence, and a sense of well-being. This renewal can also include feeling comforted or bringing a greater understanding and focus to what you should pursue as a "next step." Sometimes, the renewal you experience will be the sense that you have connected with something *tangible* or discovered an essential part of yourself. God manifests His grace in many ways, but when we connect with Him effectively, we walk away from the experience changed in some significant way. You will not always be able to connect with God deeply; our personal shortcomings often get in the way. But over time, if you are faithful to keep trying, you will see your capacity to connect with God effectively expand, and your connections with Him will deepen.

For many, in the earlier stages of our spiritual journey, our connections with God will likely occur through activities that free our mind of "distractions" (e.g., walking or listening to worship music) and from being "fed" by external resources such as listening to preaching or reading the bible or other devotional materials. During these times of connecting with God, it will be normal for us to "bring to Him" our cares and concerns. And during these times of "prayerful reflection," we will receive the "resources" we need to know and follow His plan for our lives. At some point, however, I believe God will bring each person to the realization that practicing solitude and silence is the most effective way to connect and interact with Him on a level that transforms us profoundly.

As I explained earlier, practicing silence and solitude includes being in a place without distractions (to your physical senses) and without any predetermined personal agenda. Approach God with no plan other than to spend time with Him and follow whatever "plan" He has for the experience. This type of connection with God is not a time for you to bring any particular questions to Him (although He may bring some to your attention), and this is not a time for you to present a "problem" you want Him to "solve" for you. Your questions and desires are extremely important, but finding answers to your questions (your agenda) is not the primary purpose of practicing solitude and silence. The purpose of a time of solitude and silence is merely to present yourself to God and say, "Here am I, Lord, speak and deal with Your servant as You desire."

Don't try to "force yourself" to practice silence and solitude. Allow the desire for this spiritual discipline to grow within you. I believe God will "call" you to such a practice, and He will do so when He knows it will be most productive and beneficial for you. I'll address the topics of humility and pride below, but the practice of connecting with God (in any form) is not a "test" of our spirituality. God's primary intention for calling us to connect with Him is to empower us to know and follow Him and His plans for our lives. God's plans for our lives will unfold as we allow Him to set the agenda and the timing for our ongoing spiritual growth.

Life Principle #2: Develop a God-First Orientation.

> Isaiah 55: [8] "For my thoughts are not your thoughts, neither are your ways my ways," declares the Lord. [9] "As the heavens are higher than the earth, so are my ways higher than your ways and my thoughts than your thoughts."

> Matthew 6: [33] "But seek first his kingdom and his righteousness, and all these things will be given to you as well."

It is part of our Natural Self to be self-directed rather than God-directed. We are instinctively selfish creatures motivated to seek a life of pleasure and ease. When we take the time to plan our way intentionally, our natural inclination is to plan for a future that we believe will bring the most significant amount of comfort and happiness. But what *we think* is in our best interest is often short-sighted – if not downright wrong and harmful. We need to discern what *God thinks* (rather knows) is best for us.

> Proverbs 14: [12] There is a way that appears to be right, but in the end it leads to death.

God brings about transformation within us and empowers us

226

to know and follow Him by first helping us understand He is the ultimate source from which we experience a life of meaning, purpose, joy, and fulfillment. To experience the "full life," our "plans" must focus on the goals and objectives God develops within us rather than deciding for ourselves what is in our own best interest. Once we recognize that a life focused on knowing and following God must be our primary objective, He redirects our focus from achieving our own goals and desires to understanding and following His unique plan for our lives. We must develop a God-first orientation to change from being self-directed to being God-directed. As this shift in our conscious thinking occurs, we will operate more from our Divine Self than from our Natural Self.

A God-first orientation means seeking God's input before taking major actions or making significant decisions. We often react instinctively to situations in our daily lives rather than seeking God's guidance on how to **_respond_** to our circumstances. This change is essential because our reactions are almost always self-serving in some way and focused on our desires, which are often quite different than God's will. A God-first orientation would resist the temptation to react immediately and, instead, direct our attention to God in search of His guidance. A God-first orientation may never be fully accomplished, but it should remain one of our chief goals. Unless our actions, activities, and plans align with God's plan for our lives, we will miss out on an outpouring of God's grace. Consequently, it would be wise for us to periodically assess our progress toward developing a God-first orientation.

Life Principle #3: Actively Engage in a Vibrant Faith Community.

Much of the emphasis of this book has been placed on your personal responsibility to seek God to establish, maintain, and grow a personal, intimate relationship with Him. Through your relationship with God, He will guide you into understanding and fulfilling your unique calling. By following God's leadership throughout your life journey, your life will be characterized by an ever-deepening sense of meaning, purpose, and fulfillment. In a nutshell, that is the premise of this book. And I believe Scripture fully supports this argument. However, one might get the impression from this assertion that God designed Christian life to be a decidedly individual pursuit. It is not.

While you *do* have a great deal of personal responsibility, God's design for the Christian life involves a great deal of engagement with others. (Remember, the "Second" Greatest Commandment is to "love your neighbor as yourself.") And most of the involvement with others is designed by God to assist you in your transformation. Sometimes, engagement with others involves God using you to invest in the development of others, and sometimes, your engagement with others will be designed for them to invest in your development. Frequently, these emphases occur concurrently.

Proverbs 27: [17] As iron sharpens iron, so one person sharpens another.

Hebrews 10: [24] And let us consider how we may spur one another on toward love and good deeds, [25] not giving up meeting together, as some are in the habit of doing, but encouraging one another—and all the more as you see the Day approaching.

When Jesus was challenged to identify *"The* Greatest Commandment", He indicated there were actually two! The first involved each person's responsibility to establish a loving, personal relationship with God, and the second was to develop loving, personal relationships with others. In fact, Jesus explained, "All the Law and the Prophets hang on these two command- ments." (Matthew 22:36-40). The loving "relationships with others" Jesus mentioned involve many different types of relationships. However, the relationships that matter most to establishing and maintaining a vibrant, healthy, personal relationship with God occur most often within the context of a vibrant faith community – typically, but not exclusively, within the context of a local church.

If you have not already done so, you should locate, attend, and support a local faith community. Usually, that will be a local church, but sometimes, joining a faith community begins with an individual or a small group. The Bible contains hundreds of verses stressing the importance of receiving guidance and support within a spiritual community. The New Testament alone contains approximately 60 "one another" commands. For example: "Love one another." (1 Peter 1:22), "Be devoted to one another." (Romans 12:10), and "Serve one another." (Galatians 5:13). While I could write an entire book about the importance of the local church – as literally thousands have – let me say *that being an active participant in a vibrant faith community is one of the most essential components of a healthy, Christian life.* It is difficult to capture what constitutes a "healthy" faith community briefly, but I encourage you to look for a place where:

- people appear to have warm, loving relationships with one another,
- the music challenges you to love, worship, and surrender to God,
- the people who are worshiping seem to engage with sincerity,
- the spoken messages communicate that God is loving, kind, and inviting you to know and follow Him,

- you feel personally motivated to be open and honest with your thoughts and feelings,
- Scripture is used in a way that helps you understand it's okay not to have your life completely "together" but *draws* you to God for the wisdom and strength needed to grow.

While there is much more that could be said about the importance of being an active member of a vibrant faith community, the point here is to stress the necessity of belonging to such a community to avoid the perils – and lack of growth – that often follow from being too isolated in one's spiritual journey.

Life Principle #4: Cultivate Authenticity, Vulnerability, Humility, and Surrender.

Psalm 51: [6] You desire truth in the innermost being, and in the hidden part You will make me know wisdom. (NASB)

1 Peter 5: [5] In the same way, you who are younger, submit yourselves to your elders. All of you, clothe yourselves with humility toward one another, because "God opposes the proud but shows favor to the humble." [6] Humble yourselves, therefore, under God's mighty hand, that he may lift you up in due time.

James 5: [16] Therefore confess your sins to each other and pray for each other.

Proverbs 23: [26] My son, give me your heart and let your eyes delight in my ways.

One of the inclinations of our Natural Self is to become a person of courage, strength, conviction, and confidence. Those are undoubtedly desirable and generally beneficial traits. However, when these traits are derived from our own efforts, they often produce undesirable outcomes such as pride and arrogance. God desires us to demonstrate courage, strength, conviction, confidence, and many other desirable character attributes. But they must be manifestations of the work of the Holy Spirit in and through us to advance God's purposes. *God's pathway for achieving courage, strength, conviction, confidence, and many other desirable character attributes is not through our own power but by growing in authenticity, vulnerability, humility, and surrender.*

Growing in *authenticity* means increasingly presenting your true self to others rather than the self you want them to see. Growing in *vulnerability* means increasingly revealing to others (when appropriate) areas of your life where you fall short of God's standards. Growing in *humility* means increasingly developing an awareness of your shortcomings and a growing appreciation for the many people whose influence has contributed to your spiritual and character strengths. Growing in your capacity to *surrender* means you are developing an ever-increasing capacity to yield to God's will rather than your own, and your desire to please God is also growing in intensity. Ideally, all four of these capacities should be growing throughout the entirety of your spiritual journey. However, since we all fall short, and the absence of growth in these character attributes can lead to serious personal failures, we must periodically assess how these attributes are developing in our lives.

Because pride is a sin that often challenges us, we are prone to assessing our own level of spiritual maturity and comparing ourselves to others. If Satan is a "0" and Jesus is a "10" on the scale of spiritual maturity, it doesn't matter where our current "level" of maturity might be measured. Regardless of our "level" of spiritual maturity, we will always need God's mercy and grace and the "salvation" only faith in Jesus can provide. However, what does matter is the *"direction"* in which our heart is "moving" along the maturity scale.

When I pause to examine the direction in which my life is moving, I always want to be growing closer to Jesus – becoming more focused on discerning His will and pleasing Him. If I am not, if my attention is becoming more self-focused rather than God-focused, I must seek God and ask for His mercy and grace to make whatever changes or adjustments are needed to redirect my life toward following God to the best of my ability. Practicing authenticity, vulnerability, humility, and surrender will keep us moving in the right direction.

If we are not diligent in examining our lives and making adjustments when needed, we put ourselves at risk of making potentially disastrous mistakes. Much like a person "in recovery" from a severe addiction, every Christian is capable of "backsliding" – even in very, very serious ways! There is no "standing still" regarding your spirituality; you either move towards Jesus or away from Him. That is why it is important to regularly ask God to examine your heart and reaffirm that you are directing your life in ways that please Him.

Hebrews 12: [1] Therefore, since we are surrounded by such a great cloud of witnesses, let us throw off everything that hinders and the sin that so easily entangles. And let us run with perseverance the race marked out for us, [2] fixing our eyes on Jesus, the pioneer and perfecter of faith.

Life Principle #5: Embrace the Cyclical Pattern of Transformation

While God has the power to bring about instantaneous change of any kind in our lives, He typically brings about transformation gradually, often over an extended period. That is, our personal transformation will unfold progressively as we continue to follow God to the best of our ability. Figure 12.1 outlines the general pattern through which transformation typically develops.

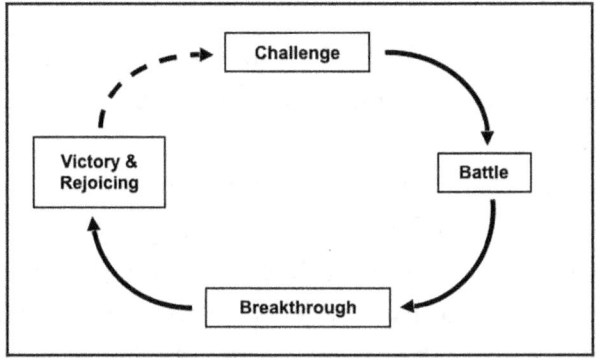

Figure 12.1: Transformation Cycle

Changes will occur in every dimension of our lives throughout our spiritual journey, generally following a discernible pattern. First, we will be presented with a **challenge** of some sort. Sometimes, the challenge will be in the Natural Dimension (e.g., financial pressures or relational conflicts). At other times, the challenge will be in the Spiritual Dimension (e.g., a sin pattern). Challenges often have aspects that relate to both the Natural and Spiritual Dimensions. The challenges we face will often require intellectual, emotional, and spiritual growth to experience the transformation God desires to bring about. It is essential to remember that God always has a righteous purpose for every challenge He allows in our lives.

Romans 8: [28] And we know that in all things God works for the good of those who love him, who have been called according to his purpose. [29] For those God foreknew he also predestined to be conformed to the image of his Son, that he might be the firstborn among many brothers and sisters.

The challenge we encounter might be intended to teach us some particular truth, deliver us from some bondage, break an unhealthy practice or pattern in our life, or direct our life in some new way. The challenges we face often address multiple objectives God has established for our unique journey of deepening our relationship with Him and leading us to experience the "full life" He has planned for us.

The second stage of transformation is the **battle**. Once we are confronted with a challenge, the battle begins. Sometimes, the battle will be intense, and we will experience a great deal of anxiety, fear, or other forms of intellectual or emotional pressure. Extremely intense battles can even cause physiological challenges. However, most of our battles will only cause low levels of difficulty or discomfort – God moving us out of our "comfort zone". The battle should be understood as the period during which God has one or more specific transformational objectives that require personal growth on our part. Typically, the pressures you experience will seem to intensify until God's purposes have been accomplished to a significant degree. (We often repeat some battles as God accomplishes ever-deepening levels of transformation in our lives.)

The third stage of transformation is the **breakthrough**. The breakthrough occurs when the pressure dissipates and, typically, a significant insight, personal freedom, or victory is achieved. During the battle, God will work to change your mental, emotional, and spiritual frameworks and increase your understanding of one or more of the four Essential Questions. The breakthrough results in some modification of how you live your life. You then enter the final stage of transformation: **victory and celebration**, where you live a life more fully aligned with God's will. The more intense the battle, the more you will celebrate what God has accomplished in or through you!

There are two important principles to understand about this cyclical pattern of spiritual growth. First, because spiritual growth is intended to occur in an ongoing manner, this pattern will be repeated regularly throughout the entirety of our lives. That is why I included an arrow from "victory and celebration" back to "challenge." (I used a dashed arrow leading back to the challenge stage because sometimes a new challenge will be directly related to the previous challenge, while at other times the new challenge will seem entirely disconnected from the previous experience.)

The second principle related to this cyclical growth pattern is that you may experience multiple transformation cycles simultaneously. For example, you might find yourself in the breakthrough stage of one issue while simultaneously entering a new "battle" associated with an entirely unrelated issue. You also might experience multiple challenges and battles simultaneously, but never more than God knows you can handle.

1 **Corinthians 10:** [13] No temptation has overtaken you
except what is common to mankind. And God is faithful;
he will not let you be tempted beyond what you can bear.
But when you are tempted, he will also provide a way out
so that you can endure it.

It will be helpful for you to periodically "pull yourself away" from your daily concerns to evaluate your life holistically. Devote enough time to connect with God so He can enable you to view your life from His perspective. Allow God to show you some of the many "transformation cycles" you have already completed and where you are currently in the challenge(s) you face. This type of reflective analysis – which often occurs during times of solitude and silence – will renew and strengthen your faith and increase your capacity to persevere.

Life Principle #6: Establish Markers to Avoid Major "Failures."

Proverbs 4: [23] Above all else, guard your heart, for everything you do flows from it.

Haggai 1: [7] This is what the LORD Almighty says: "Give careful thought to your ways."

Our Natural Self seeks to control and direct our way so strongly that we are instinctively motivated to set long-range goals, craft appropriate plans, and then direct our lives along that path. However, life is *way* too complicated and unpredictable for us to be able to do that well. Some would argue that many individuals who have achieved outstanding accomplishments have lived according to the pattern of self-determination. My response to that assertion is that if we were to examine the lives of those individuals closely, we would likely find their lives also contained a great deal of disappointment, dysfunction, uncertainty, and loss. Outstanding achievements are rarely reflective of extraordinary lives. The truth is, we are fortunate if we can plan even one day well. That is why we are so delighted when we experience a "perfect" day! How shall we live, then, if we cannot successfully plan our lives by setting firm, long-range goals?

We are often best served by setting short-term goals, looking ahead perhaps 1-5 years, and then establishing intermediate goals to keep us engaged and moving toward those targets. However, as we live, we often discover our short-term goals must be modified – and sometimes even abandoned. Whenever a change of direction is warranted, one should feel free to do so. The real goal in life is a personal sense of meaning, purpose, and fulfillment. If our short- and long-range goals fail to move us toward accomplishing those important inner drives, they should be abandoned and replaced with new objectives.

Because life is so complex and confusing, and we are often personally inadequate in responding well to the many challenges that come our way, we need to be flexible enough to change direction when necessary. If we connect with God regularly, He will direct our attention to any "problem areas" connected to our pursuits. However, most of us will frequently experience periods where our connections with God fall short, and we fail to recognize God's promptings. Therefore, because of the complexities of planning and navigating our lives without the guidance we can so easily miss from God, it is essential to establish "markers" in our lives to keep us away from danger as we navigate our way, much like buoys at sea help sailors avoid harm on their journeys.

Jeremiah 31: [21] "Set up road signs; put up guideposts. Take note of the highway, the road that you take."

Proverbs 16: [17] The highway of the upright is to depart from evil; He who watches his way preserves his life. (NASB)

Oddly, when things are going well, we are often most prone to abandon quality connections with God. For example, when you experience a significant breakthrough (e.g., getting out of debt), you will enjoy a season of living in greater freedom and joy. Praise

God for those victories! However, while that particular battle might have been won, the war for our souls continues.

> **1 Peter 5:** [8] Be alert and of sober mind. Your enemy the devil prowls around like a roaring lion looking for someone to devour.

As long as God allows the devil to remain an influence here on earth, he will continually seek opportunities to attack you, as well as the people you love and the things you value. Sometimes, we fail to recognize when a new attack (or battle) has begun. The following suggested "markers" are areas where we should monitor our behaviors and experiences, looking for evidence that might alert us to potential danger. These alerts are intended to remind us to focus on walking in the center of God's will.

The idea is that when we recognize our "equilibrium" in any of these areas has been compromised – when we begin to feel things just aren't right – we intentionally press into God with greater intensity to receive His insights and counsel and help reestablish the sense of stability we seem to have lost. The loss of equilibrium in any of these areas can occur suddenly or develop gradually over a prolonged period. However, as soon as we become aware that we are experiencing disequilibrium, we must quickly turn to God for His assistance to prevent an unnecessary problem. God will help you identify the critical markers for you to monitor. The following have served as valuable markers for me.

- **Marker #1: Disharmony in the Six Components of the Natural Dimension**

In Chapter 7, I identified six God-ordained components of the Natural Dimension: 1) Connecting with God, 2) Work, 3) Rest, 4) Recreation, 5) Social Interactions, and 6) Service. These are areas of activity God has designed for us to establish and manage in our lives. During most periods in our lives, we will experience the most significant levels of emotional, spiritual, and intellectual health (equilibrium) when we are engaged in "God-directed" experiences in all six components. The type and frequency of activities we practice in these components often change throughout our lives. When God begins to direct us to modify our activity in one or more of these areas, we frequently fail to discern His promptings. That is why we need to monitor our activity in each component, especially if we feel like "something just isn't right" in our lives. If we fail to make the changes God desires and continue in the same pattern of behaviors, we open ourselves to the possibility of experiencing a personal "failure" or "loss" of some kind. In general, our failure to align our lives to God's ways "opens the door" for Satan to gain a foothold. While God always provides a way of escape, we can avoid these unnecessary difficulties by paying attention to God's promptings to modify our activities in one or more of the six components.

- **Marker #2: Abnormal or Alarming Emotional, Physical, or Mental Health Conditions**

One of the unpleasant consequences of living in a sin-infected world is the reality of our own imperfections. At different times, in various ways, and to varying degrees, we each experience physical and psychological challenges and display attitudes, actions, and emotions that demonstrate our imperfect Natural Self. While we must humbly accept the consequences of our lack of perfection, there will be times when any of these conditions occur with abnormal intensity. It is these abnormal conditions that can serve as markers.

Many of the common physical health challenges we experience can be alleviated by standard medical or pharmaceutical measures. However, physical health "markers" would involve an abnormal attack. Examples might include severe headaches or pains in other parts of your body, infections, or other infirmities that are not normal for you. The same is true for our emotional and mental health. Markers in these areas include abnormal levels of anxiety, anger, irritability, impatience, impulse control, depression, fear, and worry. If you become aware of any of these or other physical, emotional, or mental health challenges that are out of the ordinary, it should alert you to press into God with greater intentionality. Take time to connect with God deeply so He can show you how to respond to the challenge(s) you are facing. Addressing markers in these areas will often require the assistance of others, sometimes even the aid of professionals.

- **Marker #3: Unfulfilling Worship and Fellowship Experiences**

In Life Principle #3 above, I addressed the importance of active participation in a faith community. Here, I would like to examine two specific aspects in more detail: worship and fellowship. While the previous markers dealt with recognizing the *appearance* of an adverse condition, worship and fellowship markers deal with the awareness of the *absence* or *loss* of something good. Worship and fellowship markers, when they appear, are signals that God is calling you to modify how you connect with Him through these experiences.

God designed worship to be an intellectual, emotional, and spiritual expression of love, appreciation, adoration, and gratitude directed toward Him in recognition of who He is and all He has done. The more we know God, the deeper our worship will grow. Consequently, a deepening level of worship is an important indicator of spiritual growth. *You need to discover the conditions that help you worship in "spirit and truth" (John 4:24) and order your life in ways that allow worship to flow from your heart.* As long as your capacity to worship is strong (or increasing), you will grow spiritually. However, **the absence of the ability to worship can be evidence of a serious disconnection from God and warrants further investigation.** The same concern applies to fellowship with other believers.

Like worship, *fellowship is a God-ordained practice of interacting with other Christians for mutual edification and growth.* While social activities with other believers can be enjoyable and helpful, fellowship is a word used to describe a deeper connection with other believers (some refer to it as *experiencing community* with others). Fellowship occurs in an atmosphere where levels of honesty and authenticity allow relationships to deepen, and the focus of interactions places advancing God's Kingdom purposes as the highest priority. Fellowship doesn't automatically happen just because Christians meet.

Genuine fellowship only occurs when Christians gather to connect deeply with God and with one another. Similarly to worship, a deepening level of fellowship is a sign of spiritual growth, and **the absence of fellowship that is satisfying to your soul should signal that this area of your life needs to be evaluated more deeply.** Sometimes, the lack of fulfillment you experience signals that God is calling you to a deeper level of fellowship, and sometimes, the "loss" you experience in fellowship is due merely to the absence of meaningful involvement with other believers. In either case, a sensed lack of fulfillment in worship or fellowship should be viewed as a signal to connect with God more deeply, seeking His wisdom about the changes that need to be made.

As stated previously, the central premise of this book is our primary call to know and follow God. This call can only be fulfilled by the grace and direction we receive from Him. Throughout our entire spiritual journey, God will challenge us to connect with Him at increasingly deeper levels and with greater frequency. In response to that challenge, it will be necessary to modify how we connect with Him periodically. When you begin to recognize that your typical worship and fellowship experiences are not fully "satisfying," that awareness should drive you to press into God with greater intentionality to discern the changes He would like you to make. The need to make changes in the areas of worship and fellowship should not be understood as a failure. Instead, it often indicates you have moved to a new "stage" in your spiritual journey! All changes God initiates in our lives should be recognized as progress!

In addition to the markers listed above, God has often used financial pressure and relational conflicts as "markers" in my life. However, not all difficulties we experience in these or other markers are symptomatic of the need to modify our spiritual practices. Sometimes, God allows – even sends – challenges into our lives to test and strengthen our faith. It must be understood that "testing" does not imply a pass-fail analysis God uses to "judge" us. Instead, a "test" aims to help us better understand ourselves (Essential Question #3).

Since it's impossible to please God without faith (Hebrews 11:6), He is always guiding our spiritual journey in ways that can increase and strengthen our faith. The faith-building element of our spiritual journey sometimes involves challenges in the above-mentioned markers. The critical point is to identify the markers God will use in your life to alert you to the need to press into Him with greater intentionality. Markers protect us from potential danger, but seeking and following God produces meaning, purpose, and fulfillment.

Life Principle #7: Develop a Perseverance Mentality.

Isaiah 40: [31] Yet those who wait for the LORD will gain new strength; they will mount up with wings like eagles, they will run and not get tired, they will walk and not become weary. (NASB)

James 1: [12] Blessed is the one who perseveres under trial because, having stood the test, that person will receive the crown of life that the Lord has promised to those who love him.

One issue that has been most frustrating for me is *how long* it can take to achieve many breakthroughs! There have been some breakthroughs in my character development (patience, for example), which I have been pursuing for the *entirety* of my spiritual journey! I have seen improvement in these areas, but not the fullness of victory I know is possible. Becoming a fully devoted follower of Jesus is a lifelong journey and commitment. Many of the truths God desires to reveal and the transformation He desires to complete within us only come through the emotional, intellectual, and spiritual battles we face as we walk through the challenges and opportunities He brings (or allows).

What compounds the issue further is that *we often need to experience some challenges multiple times* before we achieve the fullness of transformation God desires for us. Because of the length and the frequency of the challenges we encounter, as well as their repetition, you will *often* experience feelings of frustration, impatience, and sometimes even despair. That is why you must regularly be reminded of the need to persevere. Thankfully, God will often bring to your awareness the *need* for perseverance. However, from the onset of any challenge, you must know that the breakthrough God wants you to experience may be very long in coming!

Starting Over

"If I knew then what I know now!" We have each repeated those words or felt that sentiment at least once. That feeling springs from an awareness that some critical aspects of our life would be significantly better if we had only started the endeavor (e.g., a relationship or job) differently. As a teacher, the tone of my classroom was very important to me. I desired a classroom environment that was both relaxed and welcoming for students, yet also conducive to learning. To create a relaxing and welcoming environment, students needed to feel some sense of *freedom* to choose how they would use their time in class each day. The classroom also needed to be mostly quiet and orderly to be conducive to learning. There was often a degree of tension between those two critical values. If I were too lax in setting boundaries for student behaviors at the beginning of the school year, the classroom would become too noisy and disorderly to be conducive to learning. However, if I were too strict, the classroom environment would not be relaxed and welcoming for students. How I began each school year greatly influenced the tone of my classroom. If I erred, it was usually due to giving students too much freedom. As a result, I sometimes found myself in a position midway through the school year where my classroom was too disorderly because I had misread the maturity level of my students at the beginning of the year. That's one instance when I would say, "If I knew then...".

I have also felt this way regarding relationships, finances, and other areas of my life. "If I had only started exercising in my 40s" ... "If I had only spent more time with my children when they were young" ... "If I had only been more patient" ... "If I had only saved or invested more wisely" ... We all recognize that in many areas of our lives, we find ourselves in a position that is less than optimal because of past decisions and actions. Some people get "stuck" and live a life full of regret and disappointment. But God desires to set us free from all our past mistakes.

Isaiah 43: [18] "Forget the former things; do not dwell on the past. [19] See, I am doing a new thing! Now it springs up; do you not perceive it? I am making a way in the wilderness and streams in the wasteland.

John 8: [31] "If you hold to my teaching, you are really my disciples. [32] Then you will know the truth, and the truth will set you free."

As a guaranteed benefit of our salvation, God has fully forgiven us for our past mistakes, no matter how awful they might have been.

Psalm 103: [10] "He does not treat us as our sins deserve or repay us according to our iniquities. [11] For as high as the heavens are above the earth, so great is his love for those who fear him; [12] as far as the east is from the west, so far has he removed our transgressions from us."

You must fully forgive yourself for all your failings to experience the freedom God desires for you and receive all the blessings God has in store for you!

In the Introduction of this book, I stated, "God has placed a dream in your heart that your life is meant to have meaning and purpose and should be characterized by a deep sense of personal fulfillment." If you have read this far, I know you desire greater meaning, purpose, and fulfillment. Now that you have been exposed to all the tools, it's time to begin anew.

Lamentations 3:[22] The steadfast love of the LORD never ceases; his mercies never come to an end; [23] they are new every morning; great is your faithfulness. (ESV)

God allows us to have a new beginning – a fresh start – absolutely any time we desire. He always welcomes us to start over – in **_every_ area of our lives**! He asks us to seek Him, discern His will, and follow through, all to the best of our current ability. As you reach the end of this book, I challenge you to do just that! Take time – maybe even schedule a personal retreat – to discern what God is asking you to do – how He wants you to begin anew – and follow through as best you can. God is in no hurry; take your time to discern His will for you.

The entirety of the challenge of the Christian life is to develop the habit of seeking to know and follow God. *The ongoing pursuit of a heart, fully surrendered to God, is what the Christian journey is all about.* Jesus said the greatest commandment was to "Love the Lord your God with all your heart and with all your soul and with all your mind and with all your strength." (Mark 12:30). To love God in that way requires a change of heart. And only God can change our hearts. So, seek Him. Seek Him with everything within you – and never stop seeking Him! And do your best to follow His guidance. That's all He asks of us. One of my favorite biblical promises is captured in the book of Jeremiah:

Jeremiah 29: [11] "For I know the plans I have for you," declares the LORD, "plans to prosper you and not to harm you, plans to give you hope and a future. [12] Then you will call on me and come and pray to me, and I will listen to you. [13] You will seek me and find me when you seek me with all your heart. [14] I will be found by you," declares the LORD, "and will bring you back from captivity."

Your Journey

I suspect the experience of reading this book will impact people in different ways. Some will be excited to have had their inner hopes and dreams validated. If that describes you, rejoice and thank God for His patience with you and His desire to fulfill your hopes and dreams. Some people may feel sad to realize they too quickly dismissed their dreams, or dismayed that they haven't expected more of themselves. If that describes you, know that God is neither angry with you nor is He disappointed in you. His plans for your future are even more glorious than you can imagine. It's never too late to experience the fullness of God's blessings!

> Joel 2: [25] "I will repay you for the years the locusts have eaten ...[26] You will have plenty to eat, until you are full, and you will praise the name of the LORD your God, who has worked wonders for you.

> Job 8: [7] Your beginnings will seem humble, so prosperous will your future be.

Whatever your response to this book, please understand that God is the Author of the hopes and dreams present in your heart today. Don't give up! Those aspirations are not selfish, self-centered desires to be ignored and buried. Your hopes and dreams are to be eagerly pursued and will unfold as you surrender to God's leadership in your life! While the fulfillment of your dreams may look much different from what you imagine, the dreams themselves are a gift from God. Your inner dreams and desires are a promise of the life God desires for you. And He will bring your dreams to fruition if you follow Him to the best of your ability. The secret of life is really simple: seek God and follow His leadership. Your hopes and dreams will be fulfilled as you navigate the journey from where you are today to wherever God desires to take you.

While our hearts yearn for a life of meaning, purpose, and fulfillment, these outcomes must not be our chief aim. Instead, pursuing a heart that desires to know, follow, and please God must be our goal since a life aligned with God's purposes produces the life that will fulfill our heart's desires. Understand also that accomplishing all God desires for you brings great joy to God, just like parents are filled with joy as their children's lives are characterized by integrity, achievement, and happiness. Make it your chief goal, then, to ask God to give you a heart that increasingly seeks to know, follow, and please Him. Press into God, seeking a supernatural transformation of your heart.

> **Ezekiel 36:** [25] "I will sprinkle clean water on you, and you will be clean; I will cleanse you from all your impurities and from all your idols. [26] I will give you a new heart and put a new spirit in you; I will remove from you your heart of stone and give you a heart of flesh. [27] And I will put my Spirit in you and move you to follow my decrees and be careful to keep my laws. [28] Then you will live in the land I gave your ancestors; you will be my people, and I will be your God. [29] I will save you from all your uncleanness."

Final Thoughts

While there is always much we can learn from the past, and we will always have hopes and dreams for the future, we can only live in the present. *The most important thing you can ever do is what God desires in the present. And the only way you can know God's will is by asking Him.* If you repeatedly pay attention to God's priorities in your life, you will experience a deep sense of meaning and purpose throughout your day. Sometimes, you can run on autopilot for extended periods, feeling very good about your life. However, if you are not giving sufficient attention to God's priorities – or if His priorities for you have changed – you will begin to lose that sense of meaning and purpose. When that occurs (notice that I didn't say if, but when), you must view that as a "marker" to set aside quality time for reflection to discern where adjustments need to be made.

While the 7 Life Principles presented earlier in this chapter serve as a valuable source for deeper reflection, the following short Checklist is designed to assist you in determining where you might need to make immediate changes. Once you identify the area(s), you must engage in the four steps of Level 3 Reasoning (Appendix B) to determine precisely what adjustments God is challenging you to make. (Please Note: As you read the following questions, you will likely fall short in many ways. The goal of this Checklist is NOT to identify where you have room for improvement in your life. That list will always be very lengthy. Instead, the goal of reviewing this Checklist is to discern if God is asking you to make any specific adjustment(s) *now*.)

Checklist

- How well am I doing with setting aside time to connect with God?
- What is the *quality* of my connections with God?
- Am I making sufficient time to listen to God's voice?
- Do I need to give more attention to one of my significant relationships?
- Am I getting sufficient rest and exercise?
- Do I need to adjust my daily (weekly/monthly) routines?
- Do I need some wise counsel?

I have endeavored to capture the most salient points that God has taught me over the past 40+ years as I have sought to know and follow Him. While you might think personally possessing this body of knowledge is necessary for living a life that pleases God and is rich with meaning, purpose, and fulfillment, you would be mistaken. My purpose for sharing these insights is to demonstrate how reasonable and rational it is to *seek to know and follow God* and the utter foolishness of dismissing this central component of finding your way in life. It makes perfect sense to seek to know and follow God, the Author and Designer of everything we know as real!

I hope my writing has encouraged you to embrace this truth and the 3-step process God designed for us to know and follow Him: 1) do your best to seek Him; 2) discern what He is asking you to do next; and 3) follow through as best you are able. That's it. That is the "heartbeat" of the Christian life! Following this simple, 3-step process is the way to discover and unleash a life of profound meaning, purpose, and fulfillment. And those amazing outcomes emerge automatically as we seek to know and follow Him – much like fruit naturally grows on trees. There is honestly only one thing you must know: *God Himself is the source of all knowledge, understanding, and power necessary for experiencing a life of meaning, purpose, and fulfillment. And God is also greatly motivated to walk with you and provide anything and everything you will ever need to experience the "full" life He so eagerly desires for you.* The only requirement is to seek Him and follow His leadership to the best of your ability.

James 1: [17] Every good and perfect gift is from above, coming down from the Father of the heavenly lights, who does not change like shifting shadows.

Jeremiah 29: [13] "You will seek me and find me when you seek me with all your heart."

Closing Prayer of Commitment

Lord God, please help me discover how I can best connect with You. Draw me to Yourself. Help me understand how much You appreciate every effort I make to know, love, and follow You. Help me recognize that You view each effort I make as a free-will love offering. And that You receive each of my attempts to please and follow You with gladness and joy, as does a parent who appreciates and values simple drawings or other gifts from their young child. Oh God, help me understand Your love for me better, and may the awareness of Your love increase the desire of my heart to seek You even more, and follow You with greater focus and intentionality. Thank You for forgiving me for all the ways I have ignored and rebelled against You. I want to commit myself to You with all I have to offer. Please grant me the humility, grace, patience, and strength I need to follow You fully. Accomplish, I pray, all that You desire within and through me, as I seek to understand and follow Your will. Most especially, Lord God, help me to understand who You are, how You have designed life to be lived, who I am, and who You desire me to become, as well as all that You are asking me to do. I humbly ask these things in Jesus' Name, Amen.

Dear Reader,

If this book resonated with your spirit, please share your journey! Your reviews help others discover this resource and encourage me. Thank you for your support.

You can post your comment directly to my Amazon book page, to my website, or email me directly.

Thanks and Blessings,
Art Girard
art@artgirard.com

Appendices

Appendix A: "The God Thing"

Introduction

Everything written in this book is based on my best understanding of the truths I have discovered in the Bible. I will be challenging you to embark on a journey of discovery that I can confidently state will empower you to experience an ever-growing sense of meaning, purpose, and fulfillment. However, to achieve those benefits, you must genuinely accept biblical truths as being divinely inspired. Without that firm belief, you will be unwilling – or unable – to make the necessary changes to move forward. *The purpose of this chapter is to guide you through a series of personal reflections that might help you genuinely believe that God is real and that the Bible is, indeed, the inspired Word of God.*

The premise from which I am working is that because you have been created in God's image (Genesis 1:26-27), you possess all the "tools" you need to experience a truly meaningful, purposeful, and fulfilling life. If you find those attributes deficient, the problem is that you have not yet discovered which tools are most important and how to use them properly. (I'm still learning too!)

Appendix A: "The God Thing"

As you grow in understanding and direct your life accordingly, you will become more adept at using all the tools God has given you. Your *spirit* is the one tool you possess that is most important in life. Your spirit is the most significant part of your inner being because that is where God "connects" with you.

> **Proverbs 20:** [27] "The human spirit is the lamp of the LORD that sheds light on one's inmost being.

As you connect with God, He supplies the wisdom, understanding, courage, and strength you need to direct your life in ways that enable meaning, purpose, and fulfillment to emerge. (I talk more about your spirit – and how it fits into the rest of the human makeup in Chapter 8: "Who Am I?") For now, all you need to understand is that all the answers you need to move forward will come from within you. *God will personally communicate with you through your spirit* (Psalm 32:8 – "I will instruct you and teach you in the way you should go; I will counsel you with my loving eye on you.). And when He does, you need to accept it as true by "faith." Before going any further, let me address the issue of faith.

The Merriam-Webster dictionary defines faith as a "firm belief in something for which there is no proof." Similarly, the Oxford Dictionary defines faith as the "strong belief in the doctrines of a religion, based on spiritual conviction rather than proof." Notice that both definitions of faith include the *absence* of "proof." To "live by faith," then, is equivalent to saying that one is making decisions based upon "truths" or "principles" which ***have not* be proven**. That means, then, to NOT "live by faith" means one is living by "truths" or "principles" that ***have* been proven**. If that is accurate – and I believe it is – then *I would argue that <u>everyone lives by faith</u>!*

If you examine the goals you have pursued throughout your life, you will see that you have made almost every important life decision without *proof* that the outcomes you would experience would meet your expectations. For example, my primary goals throughout my adolescence and early adulthood were 1) to graduate from college and become a teacher, and 2) to get married and raise a family. These goals were based on the *belief* that they would help me experience a happy and fulfilling life. There was *no proof* that accomplishing those goals would guarantee the outcome of a happy, fulfilling life.

In fact, there is much evidence to *disprove* those beliefs. Visit any school, and you can easily find many people who earned a college education, became teachers, got married, and raised a family, who experienced anything but a happy, fulfilling life. Looking at the divorce rate among married, college-educated people with children is enough evidence to question placing faith in those goals! However, despite being aware of evidence to the contrary, I still had faith that those were worthwhile goals. And I have not been disappointed. *If you take the time to reflect on the important goals you have pursued, I believe you will discover that you have also been living by faith in many areas of your life.*

Reflection: Take a few minutes to process the last statement. Think about two or three important goals you have pursued – or are even pursuing now. Is there *proof* that accomplishing those goals will help produce a meaningful and fulfilling life? Or are you pursuing those goals with at least some degree of faith?

The question is not *if* you will live by faith. Instead, the question is: What will you use as a *foundation* for the decisions you will make that require faith? What I will be asking you to do in this chapter is to *reason your way* to a decision about the existence of God and the reliability of the Bible as the *primary* source of truth. And I'll ask you to make these decisions using the same processes you have used to make other important life decisions, which have also been based on faith.

You will not be able to *prove* the existence or non-existence of God. *You must decide by faith*, based upon the "evidence" you believe is most important. The question is: What do you **really believe is true** about the existence of God? That is the first decision that you must make. This is <u>the</u> *most critical decision* in all of life. If you conclude that your honest answer to the question of God's existence is to confidently state there is no God, you can stop reading now and go on doing whatever you want with your life. You are not likely to find any more significant meaning, purpose, or fulfillment than you are currently experiencing, but you can at least say you're living with integrity – making life decisions based on what you believe to be true. However, if you have never earnestly pondered the question of God's existence as an adult or are at least open to the possibility of God's existence, then I challenge you to read on.

"The God Thing"

If there is one truth about life everyone over the age of two understands, it is that there are consequences to our choices. As we mature and develop a greater understanding of how life "works," we grow in our capacity to predict the possible (or even likely) consequences of various choices. Most people then conduct a "cost-benefit analysis" before deciding how to act. If there is a God – if there is an "outside entity" that might be able to influence the outcomes we experience in life – then *we would be foolish* not to pursue a deeper understanding of how God's existence and influence might impact our lives.

In this chapter, I will walk you through a series of questions I believe everyone needs to consider. I'll also include my responses and the reasoning that informed my decisions. However, by faith, you must supply your own answers *to* each of these questions. It does not matter how long it takes you to decide, but the **journey** to your decisions must be *yours alone*. This is not a question about your parents' faith or any particular religion's beliefs. The issue is *your faith* – what you believe to be true about life and how you should direct your way.

Please note, however, that incomplete or inconsistent answers to the following questions will likely create confusion, uncertainty, and inner conflict, undermining your ability to move forward confidently. As I stated, everything I have written in this book is based on a Biblical worldview. That is, I genuinely believe God is real; He is the Author and Creator of life, the Bible (in its original languages) is the inspired Word of God, and the truths the Bible contains are meant to inform how we live our lives. If you *cannot fully agree* with these statements, you must conscientiously work through the following questions.

I will also share a few additional thoughts before you start your journey. First, the following questions are questions that *I needed to answer*. Your questions may be slightly different. God leads us in the ways He knows are necessary for us to build a solid foundation for our relationship with Him. If you need to find answers to a different set of questions – which *will* become part of your journey at some point – make sure you are asking the *right* question. How will you know? If you pay attention to the thoughts that come to mind – and the feelings you experience in your "gut" – when you are actively pursuing the *wrong* question, you'll begin to feel uncomfortable about the question you have been pondering, and a "better question" will come to mind. (That is one of the ways God "connects" with us through our spirit.)

The second thought I would like to share is that you will likely not process these questions in a linear manner. You will likely answer the questions to varying degrees of certainty and possibly in varying order. For example, you may only answer Question #1 with 70% confidence and then move on to other questions. As you consider one of the later questions, you may find yourself returning to Question #1 again and processing it even more deeply. That is a standard feature of the learning process. We only learn in part and then need to return – often many times – to discover a deeper understanding of a truth we thought we had already learned!

> 1 Corinthians 13: [9] "For we know in part and we prophesy in part, [10] but when completeness comes, what is in part disappears. [11] When I was a child, I talked like a child, I thought like a child, I reasoned like a child. When I became a man, I put the ways of childhood behind me. [12] For now we see only a reflection as in a mirror; then we shall see face to face. Now I know in part; then I shall know fully, even as I am fully known."

If you are completely honest with yourself and continue to seek to understand what is true, you will eventually be able to answer all the questions with enough certainty to move forward confidently.

Finally, you may need to consult outside resources to find the information you need to answer some of the questions. For example, you may need to speak with a trusted friend or search for information from other sources. However, I would like to caution you to limit your "research" (at this time) to sources that communicate how they came to *accept* a particular truth. These sources will have completed the process of searching for acceptable answers to their questions. If you examine sources designed to *disprove* some point, you will likely be reading from someone who searched for a reason (excuse) not to believe or had failed to find acceptable answers on their own.

Remember, *you will __not__ find absolute proof for these questions.*

All you can do is consider evidence that is meaningful to you and then base your decision on faith – *determine what you believe is true. You must learn to trust the voice of your spirit.* It's not always easy, but it's part of the journey! Trust me, it will make more sense later. Hindsight is always 20/20!

Question #1: Is there a God?

There are only two acceptable answers to this question: "Yes" or "No". Either **God EXISTS**, or **God DOES NOT EXIST**. There are **NO OTHER OPTIONS**. The truthful answer, however, for most people is, "I don't know!" But we cannot move forward in life without making some significant decisions lacking absolute assurance! Like many critical decisions in life, this question requires us to live by faith!

It might be important to highlight what this question is *not* asking! This question does not ask you to decide who God is or why He might behave in specific ways. So, for now, suspend all your questions about the *nature* of God and any *resistance* you might have concerning the consequences of the decision you will make. Your inner questions, conflicts, and points of resistance are extremely important but must be addressed *later* in your journey. The question here is whether or not there is some outside, intelligent being who can *potentially* influence your life experiences in some way. The question is only about whether or not God exists!

As I mentioned in the Preface, when I seriously began pondering the question of God's existence back in the 1970s, I considered reasons both "for" and "against" His existence. However, for me, the bottom line came when I considered creation itself – everything that exists and its extraordinary "order" and complexity. Whether my perspective was looking at life through a microscope, a telescope, or my own eyes, I couldn't help but believe there must be a God of some kind.

Appendix A: "The God Thing"

Psalm 19: [1] The heavens declare the glory of God; the skies proclaim the work of his hands. [2] Day after day they pour forth speech; night after night they reveal knowledge. [3] They have no speech, they use no words; no sound is heard from them. [4] Yet their voice goes out into all the earth, their words to the ends of the world.

In comparison, randomness (e.g., "Big Bang Theory") seemed foolish. How could one even explain the *existence* of the "stuff" that could "explode" and then "randomly" become what we see and experience? And how can "simple" things become intricately complex without outside intervention? Indeed, there must be a "God" of some type. But then, when I considered the poverty, injustice, and cruelty that exist in the world, I wondered how a "good" God (what I had been taught to accept) could allow such things to exist.

Ultimately, I decided my problem wasn't that I didn't believe in God's existence. My problem was that I lacked an understanding of God adequate to answer those challenging questions about His nature. *So, I decided – by faith – that God is real, and that He created the "heavens and the earth" (Genesis 1:1).* I later added to this foundational belief that the God who created a reality with such incredible order and sophistication *must have also established principles or "truths" which govern every aspect of His creation.* That is, I came to believe God had also created a body of truth that, if understood and followed, would make the lives of the people He created optimally successful.

Somewhere during my journey to find the "right" answer to the question of God's existence, I also considered the consequences of responding "No" to this question. If there is NO GOD – no superior, "outside" authority – I am free to pursue absolutely anything I desire. But then, so are other people – even if it creates difficulty for others. If there is NO GOD, there are no absolutes in

264

life. Unless other people interfere, everyone can believe and do whatever they desire. Without God, humankind can create any governing structure they want. This means that whoever rules – whoever is most powerful – can make all the rules for everyone else.

From this perspective, not believing in God didn't seem to be the kind of foundation that could ever lead to a life of meaning, purpose, and fulfillment – at least not for everyone. I couldn't see any way to move forward without some foundational beliefs that would allow everyone to experience a meaningful and fulfilling life. The principle of "equality of opportunity" or "equal justice" seemed to be a principle of life that was "built-in" to my mind. I challenge you to consider this question: Do you believe some things are "good" and others are "bad"? If so, please recognize there can be no absolutes – no "good" or "bad" – without the existence of some entity with the authority to establish those standards. Since I believed that there was such a thing as "good" and "evil," my answer to Question #1 is a resounding "YES"! *I believe God is real and the Author and Creator of life!*

Reflection: Before reading any further, if you are ready to do so, you would be best served to answer this question right now. Do you believe there is a God? Do you believe that God is real? If you can answer "Yes" with a reasonable degree of confidence, then *allow that truth to soak in – there is a God who has the power to create everything that exists! And this same God has the power to influence your life profoundly!* You will be ready to proceed to the next question once you have allowed that truth to sink in.

However, if you are unsure – if you cannot say with a reasonable degree of assurance that you really believe God is real – then you should stop reading and begin the "journey" of answering this question before proceeding any further. Your process may look entirely different than mine (which took me several months to complete), but God will reveal Himself to you if you genuinely seek to discover the truth about His existence. *Coming to this conclusion and making that declaration is a <u>necessary</u> first step.*

It might be helpful for you to know that it took me about five years *after* answering Question #1 before I moved on to the next question. God needed to take me through a series of challenging circumstances before I realized I needed to give more thought to this "God Thing"! So, five years later, the next part of my journey began with the following realization: If God does exist, and He can create the heavens and the earth, then there indeed exists a "force" that can intervene in the circumstances of my life in significant ways. **I cannot be in *complete control* of my life.** And if that is true, it would benefit me to better understand, if possible, more about this "force." This realization motivated me to find out more about God. But where should I begin the search? If God is the source of life and truth, perhaps I need to go straight to Him for answers – if that is even possible. This led to the next set of questions.

Question #2: Has God revealed Himself in some way(s)?

This is another question that can only be answered "Yes" or "No". This question was already answered "Yes" (at least in part) through my process of answering the previous question. I felt that creation itself was, at least, in part, a "revelation" of who God is. That is, through His creation – the fantastic complexity of the "what" He chose to create, as well as all the intricate ways the physical components of creation synchronize and interact with one another – God "communicated" that He was powerful, planful, and creative. I'm sure you could think of other descriptors, but I quickly moved on to the next question.

However, before moving on to that question, let me point out that if your answer to Question #2 is "No," you are in the same position as if you had answered Question #1 with a "No" response.

If God does not reveal Himself, then we can never know anything about Him or whether He established any truths for us to live by. If you answer "No" to this question, live your life however you want and recognize everyone else has that same freedom.

Reflection: Before moving on, what do you believe? Has God revealed Himself in some way? Don't move on until you have honestly arrived at your own answer. What do you have *genuine faith to believe* about this question?

Question #3: Is God personal or impersonal? (That is, does God "personally" interact with people?)

Because of the way I posed this question, there are, again, only two possible answers: "personal" or "impersonal" (or "Yes" or "No" to personal interactions between God and people). Therefore, either God interacts with people personally (and, perhaps, individually), or He doesn't. As I reflected on this question, what struck me as most significant was the vast number of well-respected people throughout history who claimed to have been "following God" – and their commitment was so complete that many even sacrificed their lives – was adequate evidence for me to conclude God must personally interact with people in some way.

The "how" was an entirely different matter! (And that's why it's Question #4!) However, if your response is "impersonal," you're in the same place as if you had answered "No" to either Question #1 or #2. I suppose you could still search for truths about life, but you'd never know with any certainty if you were right or wrong. That leaves you in the same place as if you answered "No" to either of the previous questions. Just live your life any way you want and hope for the best! But also realize everyone else is free to do the same – essentially making everyone their own "god."

Appendix A: "The God Thing"

Reflection: Once again, before moving on, what do you believe? Is God personal or impersonal? Do you believe God personally interacts with His creation? Don't move on until you have honestly arrived at your own answer. What do you have *genuine faith to believe* about this question?

Question #4: How does God interact or "connect" with people? [NOTE: This is where "people of faith" begin to have serious disagreements.]

Unlike previous questions, this is an "open-ended" question – there are any number of responses one might give. I quickly constructed the following options based on my life experiences:

a) Through "holy books" or "holy writings" (e.g., Bible, Qur'an, The Book of Mormon, etc.)

b) Through an "intermediary" (e.g., prophet, priest, spiritual advisor, author, etc.)

c) One-to-one (i.e., the belief that God personally (and individually) "interacts" with people)

d) All the above!

I chose "d" – eventually! As I considered this question, I first had to acknowledge my belief that I had been exposed to many "sources" of what I would label "wisdom" – ideas that resonated in my mind and heart as being "true" about life. Whether it was through the words of a movie character, a song, a book, a poem, a billboard, or just a personal conversation or a life experience, there were many instances when I just *"felt"* I had been exposed to a valuable "truth" about life. Since God is the source of truth –

because He crafted every aspect of creation and the principles and truths that govern all creation – these experiences could reasonably be considered God "personally" revealing truth to me. (I would now characterize these experiences as God "speaking" to me through my spirit.) However, I was also exposed to circumstances where sources claimed to be speaking "truth" that seemed clearly "false" to me. Because so many "competing voices" claimed to be revealing the "truth," I had to consider whether there was a *reliable and objective source of truth.*

I first considered the "holy books" category, which I had been exposed to or heard about. Due to my Catholic upbringing, the Bible was the first book I considered. Coincidentally, as I worked through this question, a friend gave me a copy of Phillips' Translation of the New Testament. As I read through the first chapter (the Book of Matthew), it seemed as if many of the "difficulties" I had with previous religious experiences and questions were being "answered" by the text I was reading!

For example, one of my early problems with Catholicism was the "truth" I was taught about sin and Confession. I recall being taught that one must complete the "sacrament" of Confession to receive forgiveness for one's sins. Also, if a person commits a "mortal" sin (like murder) – and does not complete Confession before their death – they will go to Hell. I remember asking, "If my mother (who was really a "saint"!) had somehow totally lost control and committed a "mortal sin" and was then hit by a car and killed as she was running to church to complete Confession, would she go to Hell?" The answer I received was "Yes!" That just seemed stupid, even to a young kid! I remember thinking if God was really that petty – that one must enter a" booth" to confess one's sin and be absolved by a priest – He wasn't worth loving or following!

But reading through passages about sin, grace, and forgiveness in the Bible completely dispelled that notion. (I even wondered whether those religious "leaders" I had encountered had ever read the Bible!) At any rate, the more I read the Bible, the more I was convinced about its validity as a source of objective truth. In fact, I have experienced many circumstances where I felt God was "speaking" to me – revealing truths about life – as I read through the Bible.

Because I had found what I believed to be a valid source of truth, from that point on, I invested a great deal of time reading the Bible and listening to Christian teachings of biblical truths wherever and whenever I could. However, a few questions continued to concern me for probably several years: 1) How can I know if the Bible is totally reliable? 2) Are there any other sources of reliable truth? 3) How can I know that my "interpretation" of what I read in (or hear being taught from) the Bible is accurate?

I don't recall ever directly addressing any of these questions in a systematic and focused way. Still, because they were always in the back of my mind, I would take note whenever I was exposed to information relevant to that quest for a deeper understanding of sources of truth. Among the many things I discovered "along the way" concerning the Bible's reliability was how it came into existence.

While whole books have been written about the reliability and validity of the Bible, the long history of how the Bible came into being convinced me of both those concerns. The versions of the Bible that Protestants follow (the Catholic Bible contains some additional writings) consist of 66 individual "holy writings" (called "Books") from about 40 different "authors" that have been selected (from literally hundreds – if not thousands – of ancient writings) as "divinely inspired," over a period of thousands of years, by groups of people who were genuinely seeking to know what was true. Additionally, the fact that the books of the Bible have with-stood the scrutiny of thousands of sincere truth-seeking scholars for hundreds of years adds to the strength of the proposition that the Bible is a divinely inspired document. But this conclusion – that *the Bible is the only fully reliable and objective source of truth* – is so central to making life decisions that you **must take the time to come to this conclusion on your own!**

This discussion is vitally important because, by nature, we are selfish and self-centered individuals who cannot entirely rely on our own motivations when evaluating whether a belief is true.

> **Jeremiah 17:** [9] The heart is deceitful above all things and beyond cure. Who can understand it? [10] "I the LORD search the heart and examine the mind, to reward each person according to their conduct, according to what their deeds deserve."

We each *need* an objective, authoritative source of truth upon which to base important decisions. But even believing the Bible is a reliable source of truth isn't enough. How can we know our interpretation of what we read is correct? The short answer is we can't! There is always the possibility that our selfish nature will cause us to gravitate toward accepting "interpretations" that direct us in ways we "prefer" rather than the "right" ways. To this day, I always question whether my interpretations of what I read or imagine are accurate. I'll address this question in greater detail in another chapter.

While I have never engaged in an in-depth study of other "holy writings," I've been exposed to many critiques of different religions (from what I perceive to be reliable sources) that disqualify the "holy writings" of other faiths as being authentic and fully reliable sources of truth. One example is Jesus's statement in the Book of John:

> **John 14:** [6] "I am the way and the truth and the life. No one comes to the Father except through me."

If you acknowledge the Bible as a reliable source of truth, then (according to Jesus) only following Him and His teachings can reliably connect us with God. To my knowledge, no other "holy writing" supports the claim of Jesus' authority. This truth alone disqualifies other "holy writings" as being fully reliable.

While some have written about what they consider inconsistencies in the Bible, I have always found explanations from credible sources that dispel those arguments. So, for me, the Bible is the document that I (and most Christians) use as the most reliable source of truth. Whenever I am confronted with an important decision about what I should think or do, I strive to ensure that my choices align with biblical truths as I understand them. Additionally, I continue to pursue growth in my understanding of biblical truths.

[**NOTE:** Accepting the Bible as **THE ONLY** fully reliable source of absolute truth is a huge deal. You may need to engage in a much deeper study of this question than I have presented to reach this conclusion. You must understand that it is YOUR journey to discover this truth. You must take whatever steps are necessary for you to be able (by faith) to accept the authenticity and inerrancy of the Bible. You must decide what you believe to be true about God and the Bible. I encourage you to find acceptable answers, by faith, to these foundational questions. Your future depends on it!]

My goal in this chapter is *not* to convince you that my answers are accurate. I have only tried to explain the process I followed to find meaningful answers to what I believe are the most fundamental questions in life. You must find your own answers to these and other critical questions. *You are responsible for your own life. You must decide what is right, what is true, and what is good. And you are responsible for directing your life accordingly.* Like untold millions of others, I have discovered that a life dedicated to the pursuit of truth – especially to knowing and following God –

results in an increasing sense of meaning, purpose, and fulfillment.

While there is no end to the pursuit of truth – and directing your life accordingly – there must be a beginning. There must be a time when you decide God is real, that He created the heavens and the earth (and the truths that guide it), and purpose to direct your life toward knowing and following Him. Are you ready to do that now? If so, the Bible teaches us that the starting place is to be "born again" (See John, Chapter 3). Being "born again" means that your spirit comes to life and becomes the dwelling place of the Holy Spirit, empowering you to communicate directly with God Himself (Ephesians 1:13). Being "born again" *happens* by expressing to God your belief that Jesus is the Son of God, that He sacrificed His life to pay the penalty for your rebellion (sins) for all time, and that you desire to know and follow Him. It doesn't matter what words you say or how you do it; only that you communicate honestly from the depths of your heart and soul.

This will become a "prayer" that you express multiple times. Our growth as "believers" is much like peeling an onion. Each time a deeper layer of truth is "exposed," we are challenged to surrender ourselves more deeply to following God. That brings us back to a new "confession of faith" like the "prayer" outlined above, but each time, it will come from a deeper level of honesty and surrender. If you cannot make a confession of faith right now, that's OK. God is happy to give you as much time as you need. The decision to follow God is always yours. However, speaking from personal experience, the sooner you can honestly confess your faith, the sooner you will experience a greater sense of meaning, purpose, and fulfillment. So, I encourage you to identify the questions that hold you back and to be intentional about finding satisfactory answers. I would hate for you to miss out on such an inspiring journey any longer than necessary!

Appendix B: Levels of Rationality

Levels of Rationality

I have discovered that my thinking fluctuates between four different levels of reasoning as I respond to life experiences. Understanding this stratification of thinking processes might help you process your thoughts and feelings more productively. In the following explanation, I will use various forms of the terms thinking, questioning, reasoning, and rationality interchangeably.

Level 1 thinking (questioning) occurs naturally throughout each day. "What should I wear?" "What's the weather going to be like?" "I wonder how bad traffic will be on my morning commute?" "What should I plan for dinner?" Thousands of these types of questions come to mind automatically as we plan and live out each day. However, Level 1 thinking can also be generated by our emotions. "I *hate* that she did that; how can I get even with her?" "I wonder why he's acting like *that*?" "What's *his* problem?" Our minds automatically respond to many life experiences by generating questions that guide our response (if any) to these occurrences. The "answers" that come to mind in response to the

275

questions our minds generate often dictate our actions. Depending on our level of emotional, intellectual, and spiritual maturity, a "filter" may kick in and cause us to wonder whether we should act on any given thought or "switch" our thinking to another (more "mature") level. That shift, if it occurs, moves us to Level 2 thinking.

Level 2 reasoning occurs when we "catch ourselves" motivated to respond to a situation in ways we suspect may not be the "right" thing. For example, we know from experience that when acted upon, strong feelings like anger, fear, frustration, or jealousy can direct us to take actions we will later regret. Based upon such experiences, people often pause when they begin to experience powerful negative emotions to consider whether a more reasonable course of action is warranted. One might label this a "moral filter" that prevents us from reacting immediately to our life experiences. For example, caught up in strong negative emotions, a mature person will initiate Level 2 thinking by asking a question like, "How *should* I respond?" Level 2 thinking, for the Christian, shifts us from living a self-directed life to striving for a more God-directed life.

As we mature in our walk with God, we progress more quickly from Level 1, *reacting* to life experiences, to Level 2, *reasoning*. The "answers" generated from our Level 2 reasoning are often based on "rules" we have been taught to follow. The more we read and understand the Bible and desire to follow God, the more our actions will "line up" with our understanding of biblical truths. And the longer we practice Level 2 thinking, the "better" we will get at living by biblical truths.

However, as we mature as Christians, we come to understand that God is more interested in our relationship with Him than in our behavior. The motivation to "know" God and relate to Him personally moves us to **Level 3** thinking. (Before we examine the next level of thinking, I want to point out that non-Christians and less mature Christians rarely advance beyond Level 2 thinking. They are "stuck" merely trying to align their behaviors to a set of "standards" they have chosen to accept as "true" or "right." And many of those "standards" are followed because they believe they will be "rewarded" in some way for doing so.)

As Christians become more aware of biblical truths – by reading Scripture, attending a biblically "healthy" church, interacting with mature Christians, and other biblically sound practices – they discover that God desires a personal relationship with them. This awareness prompts them to reach out to God personally and intentionally, searching for a deeper understanding of who He is and how they should plan and live their lives. The change from "rules-based" reasoning to a God-focused "relationship-based" reasoning initiates **Level 3** thinking. Non-Christians are incapable of engaging in Level 3 thinking due to their lack of a relationship with God, which is established when one is born again.

Level 3 Thinking involves a 4-step process as we attempt to interact with God on a personal level.

Step 1: "Switching" your focus from yourself to God and directly asking Him what He wants you to do.

Step 2: Pausing until some "answer" is received.

Step 3: Obeying (to the best of your ability) whatever you believe God is directing you to do.

Step 4: Returning to God (later) to "process" the experience and get directions for what you should do next.

Appendix B: Levels of Rationality

While this may appear to be a simple process, it can sometimes take many months to complete all four steps, particularly when addressing a complex issue or life experience. For example, before we are ready to receive God's "answer" regarding what He wants us to do in response to a conflict with someone (Step 2), we often need to seek His help in processing several powerful feelings "attached" to that conflict (often from past relational conflicts). It is frequently difficult for us to understand (discern) what God is directing us to do until we have appropriately dealt with these past issues. Only at this point can we receive God's direction calmly and humbly. Additionally, sometimes, we must ask a trusted friend for assistance or wait for God to "walk us" through additional life experiences before we can fully discern and accept His guidance. Obeying (Step 3) is also a step that can be very difficult – and we frequently fail – which brings us back to God (Step 1) to process the feelings generated by our failure to follow His previous directions fully!

However, as we become more spiritually mature, we begin to understand that this back-and-forth processing of our thoughts and feelings with God is an integral part of the way God brings about transformation in our lives. And all the time we spend seeking God's guidance and support and trying to follow His leadership in our lives, we are deepening our relationship with Him. One surprising outcome of these interactions with God (Level 3 thinking) is that we find greater meaning and purpose in our lives. We also find ourselves spending more and more time interacting with God and experiencing ever-deepening levels of joy as He changes how we think and, therefore, how we live. We also begin to find fulfillment as God guides our lives. But we can experience even greater levels of meaning, purpose, and fulfillment as we direct our thinking to **Level 4**.

As Christians increase their capacity to understand God's ways and seek to follow them, they acquire an ever-growing mountain of knowledge. However, large amounts of information can often create confusion and frustration if we cannot organize and synthesize the information we accumulate into a structured knowledge base. The Bible uses the term *wisdom* to denote the synthesis of knowledge into a usable framework for guiding decision-making. Scripture challenges us to connect with God to grow in understanding and wisdom.

> 1 **Kings 3:** [9] So give Your servant an understanding heart ... to discern between good and evil.

> **Proverbs 2:** [6] For the LORD gives wisdom; from His mouth come knowledge and understanding.

> **James 1:** [5] If any of you lacks wisdom, you should ask God, who gives generously to all without finding fault, and it will be given to you.

But the "full life" – the life Jesus came to enable us to experience – involves much more than merely "controlling" our responses to daily life experiences. In addition to finding meaning, purpose, and fulfillment in our daily activities and experiences, God desires that we experience those same blessings in a "global" way – that the entirety of our lives would be richly and "fully" rewarding!

> **Jeremiah 29:** [11] For I know the plans that I have for you,' declares the LORD, 'plans for welfare and not for calamity to give you a future and a hope.

> **Proverbs 10:** [22] It is the blessing of the LORD that makes rich, and He adds no sorrow to it.

Isaiah 35: [2] They will see the glory of the LORD, the majesty of our God. ... [7] The scorched land will become a pool and the thirsty ground springs of water ... [8] A highway will be there, a roadway, and it will be called the Highway of Holiness. The unclean will not travel on it, but it will be for him who walks that way, and fools will not wander on it. [9] No lion will be there, nor will any vicious beast go up on it; These will not be found there. But the redeemed will walk there, [10] And the ransomed of the LORD will return and come with joyful shouting to Zion, with everlasting joy upon their heads. They will find gladness and joy, and sorrow and sighing will flee away.

This last passage from the Book of Isaiah speaks to God's vision for the lives of "His people" – those who choose to know and follow Him. The "full life" Jesus spoke of in John 10:10 is lived on a "highway" – actually, a *"high way"* of living – a life with meaning, purpose, and fulfillment that increasingly unfolds as we seek to understand and live by God's ways. And God's "ways" include – and are built on – knowing, loving, and following Him on a deeply personal level. That approach to life results in maximum joy, peace, and gladness of heart.

I have spent the past 40+ years doing my best to know and follow God. As my knowledge of God and His ways increased (often through my own failures), I frequently felt frustrated by my inability to synthesize all the information into a coherent and understandable whole. However, despite my frustrations, I persevered despite being unable to accomplish that task. Over time, my life became increasingly God-centered and grew in meaning, purpose, and personal fulfillment. (In all honesty, I can still be a jerk sometimes; it just seems to happen less frequently!)

In the several months preceding my retirement from teaching and ministry, I wondered what my life might look like in this next chapter. As I attempted to "prepare" for retirement, I began reflecting on all God had helped me understand and how He supernaturally changed me over time. I started to see that all the knowledge He revealed and helped me process "fit" nicely into four categories. I also began to realize that as the amount of knowledge and understanding increased within and among these four categories, and I aligned my life accordingly, the overall levels of meaning, purpose, and fulfillment I experienced also increased! All the information about God and His ways fit nicely as "answers" to four specific questions. **Reflecting on these four questions is what I label <u>Level 4 Thinking</u>**. These are the four most important questions in life!

1. Who is God?
2. How Has God Designed Life to Be Lived?
3. Who Am I? (And Who Does God Want Me to Become?)
4. What is God Calling Me to Do?

You will find it beneficial each time you reflect on meaningful life experiences to "sort" your "learnings" into one or more of these Essential Questions. As the contents of these "containers" increase with the answers God provides, you will experience an ever-increasing sense of meaning, purpose, and fulfillment. Periodically setting aside times of solitude and silence and allowing God to "walk you through" significant life experiences is an extremely effective way of finding answers to the four Essential Questions.

Appendix C: "What I Believe"

1. I believe God is real, and He created the heavens and the earth.

2. I believe God is personal – He desires to interact with every part of His creation.

3. I believe God has revealed Himself through Scripture (in the original languages). (I believe God reveals Himself in other ways – for example, through nature and other people – but those other sources are less trustworthy and dependable.)

4. I believe God desires a personal relationship with every person. Through regular, repeated, ever-deepening personal interactions with Him, we learn how to live and become empowered to do so.

5. I believe one initiates a relationship with God by a) believing Jesus is the Son of God and He died to pay the penalty for all sin, for all time; b) acknowledging you have personally and willfully sinned against God; c) asking Jesus to forgive you for your sins;

and, d) asking Jesus to come into your life and transform you so that you are empowered to follow Him fully. (The result of this "interaction" with God results in what is called "salvation" and can never be "un-done" or "lost.")

6. I believe that we will very often act independently – or even in defiance – of God and need, each time, to re-confess our sin and ask for forgiveness.

7. I believe God has created every person with a unique set of characteristics. Through our personal relationship with Him, we discover who we are, who we are called to become, and what He has called us to do. (It is also through our relationship with God that we become empowered to do what He has called us to do.)

8. I believe God places a "dream" in every person's heart that they have value and deserve to be treated with dignity and respect. Furthermore, this God-implanted dream encourages people to believe their lives should be meaningful, purposeful, and fulfilling. (Regrettably, most people pursue this dream in their own power and rely on their own wisdom and understanding. People respond in various ways when they realize their efforts are not producing all they have hoped for. Turning to God is the only healthy way to respond to this realization.)

9. I believe God designed life to be lived in "partnership" with Him – that is, there is a "God part" and a "my part" in all my endeavors. God's part is to provide the direction and resources for living, and my part is to do my best to understand and surrender to His leadership.

10. I believe we probably never fully understand nor fully obey all

that God desires of us, but His grace is always sufficient and greater than our ignorance or failure.

11. I believe God also designed life to be lived in "partnership" with others, and through those "partnerships," He would further guide us and help us grow.

12. I believe that through some of these "partnerships," we would also collaborate to advance His Kingdom's purposes on earth.

13. I believe God has designed the Church as a primary vehicle through which He desires to advance His purposes on earth.

14. I believe God has ordained each local church with a unique set of objectives to pursue.

15. I believe God desires each person to be an active, supporting member of a local church.

[A football team is a good analogy here. Each team (church) is called to accomplish specific goals (a unique vision). The coaches (God and church leaders) train each individual, as well as smaller units (e.g., the worship team), to develop unique skill sets and then direct them on how they should execute each play (objective or goal) they have been assigned to accomplish. The quarterback (pastor – assisted by a board of elders) is the team's on-field leader.]

16. I believe God has ordained para-church organizations to extend, assist, and support the work of local churches.

17. I believe God has called all people to be engaged in some capacity to advance His purposes on earth, but no one should be

pressured to do so. Each person must respond to God's individual call to serve.

18. I believe it is the responsibility of each person to respond to God's "call" and allow God to help them establish their own beliefs.

19. I believe that the four most Essential Questions in life that cry out for answers are:

- Who is God?
- How has God Designed Life to be Lived?
- Who Am I? (And Who is God Asking Me to Become?")
- What is God Asking Me to Do?

20. I believe that as we allow God to guide us into discovering more profound and accurate answers to each of the Essential Questions, we are transformed by His grace and experience ever-increasing levels of meaning, purpose, and fulfillment.

Appendix D: "Who Am I?"- Art

Personality/Temperament Measures:

Myers-Briggs Type Indicator: INTJ – "Rational Mastermind"
DiSC Personality Profile: CD – "The Questioner"
StrengthsFinder Attributes: Strategic, Relator, Ideation, Learner, Achiever

General Description:

I have an insatiable drive to understand 'how things work,' but not limited to general functionality. I am also motivated to understand the intent of the 'designer' – the goals they hoped to accomplish, as well as the relative priority of each goal. Furthermore, if I think something has been designed (or is functioning) poorly, I strongly desire to 'fix' it. This aspect of my wiring tends to stir up discontent whenever I confront something that I believe needs to be "fixed." For instance, I once spent hours reorganizing my classroom because I felt the layout was inefficient. (My wife laughs whenever she hears me say, "Who designed this?" or "What were they thinking?" And that often happens several times a day!) If the 'problem' I see stems from what I perceive to be injustice, it generally causes me to become quite angry. I tend to think of that as 'righteous anger '.

My inclination is not only to scrutinize the functioning of individual components but also to evaluate the design of the system in which they operate. I am driven by a strong desire to witness the entire system operate consistently, efficiently, and with integrity. When I identify shortcomings, I undertake a quest to refine the system, aiming to enhance overall productivity and effectiveness. This process often leads me to delve into the underlying values and beliefs that underpin a system and to advocate for those in positions of authority to reconsider their beliefs, goals, and practices. This aspect of my nature has often sparked conflict in my youth, and continues to do so occasionally in adulthood!

Appendix E: Personal Life Calling, and Mission Statement

Overview

> **Ephesians 2:** [10] For we are God's handiwork, created in Christ Jesus to do good works, which God prepared in advance for us to do.

God has placed a dream in your heart that your life is meant to have meaning and purpose, and the result of your life's endeavors should produce a profound sense of personal fulfillment. That's not a selfish desire; God has placed that dream in your heart because that is His desire for your life. Jesus even stated that He came to earth to make it possible for you to achieve that dream.

> **John 10:** [10] "The thief comes only to steal and kill and destroy; I have come that [you] may have life, and have it to the full."

The only obstacles preventing you from experiencing the "full life" God has planned for you exist inside you. You will not fail to experience the full life because of prejudice, bigotry, hate, or any other stumbling blocks you might encounter in life. What *will* prevent you from experiencing the full life is the fear of failure, feelings of inadequacy, procrastination, laziness, lack of direction, or any other belief or character attribute that keeps you from moving forward in life. And all those internal issues can be overcome as you connect with God and follow His leadership. You have all the resources necessary for experiencing the "full life" present within you. However, you must remove the "lies" and personal shortcomings that prevent you from moving forward and replace them with the truths and character attributes that lead to success and fulfillment. This is the process of "renewing your mind," the Apostle Paul talked about in Romans, Chapter 12:

Romans 12: [1] "Therefore, I urge you, brothers and sisters, in view of God's mercy, to offer your bodies as a living sacrifice, holy and pleasing to God – this is your true and proper worship. [2] Do not conform to the pattern of this world, but be transformed by the renewing of your mind. Then you will be able to test and approve what God's will is – his good, pleasing and perfect will."

The process of "renewing your mind" includes removing false beliefs, clarifying beliefs that are only partially understood, and discovering (and clarifying) truths you have not yet learned. Jesus also stated that the renewal process – the discovery of "truth" – will "set us free," and those "truths" are learned as we purpose to know and follow Him.

John 8: [31] "If you hold to my teaching, you are really my disciples. [32] Then you will know the truth, and the truth will set you free."

We experience the "full life" that Jesus came to provide for us as we walk in relationship with Him and allow the Holy Spirit to renew our minds. The many falsehoods we embrace – about ourselves and life – prevent us from accomplishing all God desires. Only the voice and presence of God Himself can speak the words, deliver the healing, and provide the power, motivation, and resources each of us needs to overcome the obstacles within us and move forward into the truths that truly set us free.

While we must discover many truths, it's genuinely not *WHAT* you know but *WHO* you know that makes the difference. You can only discover those truths by walking closely with God. Only God can direct you in the ways that will accomplish all His good purposes in and through your life. You must discover the best ways to truly "encounter" Him and then build those ways into your daily life. Only in Him, with Him, and through Him will you discover and walk in His ways.

Acts 17: [28] 'For in him we live and move and have our being.'

[The following is a brief summary of my own personal calling.]

Personal Calling – Art

General Statement:

1. To love, worship, and serve God.

2. To be an instrument (by my words and deeds) through which people:

a) are challenged to believe God is real,
b) are challenged to consider the possibility that their

understanding of God and His ways might not be entirely accurate and,

c) become more aware of how God is at work in their lives.

3. To understand and live out God's unique purposes for my life in ways that advance His Kingdom purposes in the world.

Personal Mission Statement:

To help people better understand who God is and how they might be blocking what He wants to accomplish in and through their lives.

About the Author

Art Girard is a retired educator and pastor with over six decades of experience spread over two professional careers. He spent 41 years as a high school and college mathematics teacher and principal, inspiring students, teachers, and parents with clarity, patience, and a passion for learning. During the later part of his educational career, he served for 20 years as an associate pastor, preacher, teacher, and counselor, offering spiritual guidance, support, and encouragement to congregants.

Art is known for his unique blend of faith and wisdom, combining his deep knowledge of biblical principles with a heartfelt approach to helping others discover their unique identity and life purpose. His style is informative, inspirational, and comforting, bridging the analytical and the spiritual. This unique perspective enables readers to find meaning and fulfillment through an understanding of God and His design for living.

Throughout his career, Art has been celebrated for his ability to translate complex ideas into accessible and encouraging language, whether in the classroom, the pulpit, or through his writing. His work is a testament to his lifelong commitment to education, faith, and the well-being of others.

Now retired, Art dedicates his time to writing books that are not just informative but also inspiring and uplifting, drawing on his extensive experience as both a teacher and a pastor. His latest work, *Finding Meaning, Purpose, and Fulfillment: Making Sense of God, Life, and Success*, invites readers to explore the intersection of faith and practical living.

He lives with his wife, Crystal, who has been a constant source of support and encouragement throughout his journey. Art enjoys spending time with his daughters and grandchildren, reading, and involvement with his faith community and friends.

You may connect with him at art@artgirard.com if desired.

Website: artgirard.com